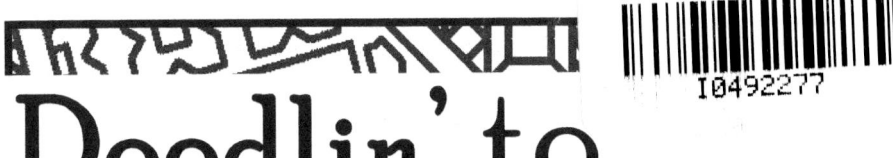

Doodlin' to

De-Stress

Patterns Volume 2

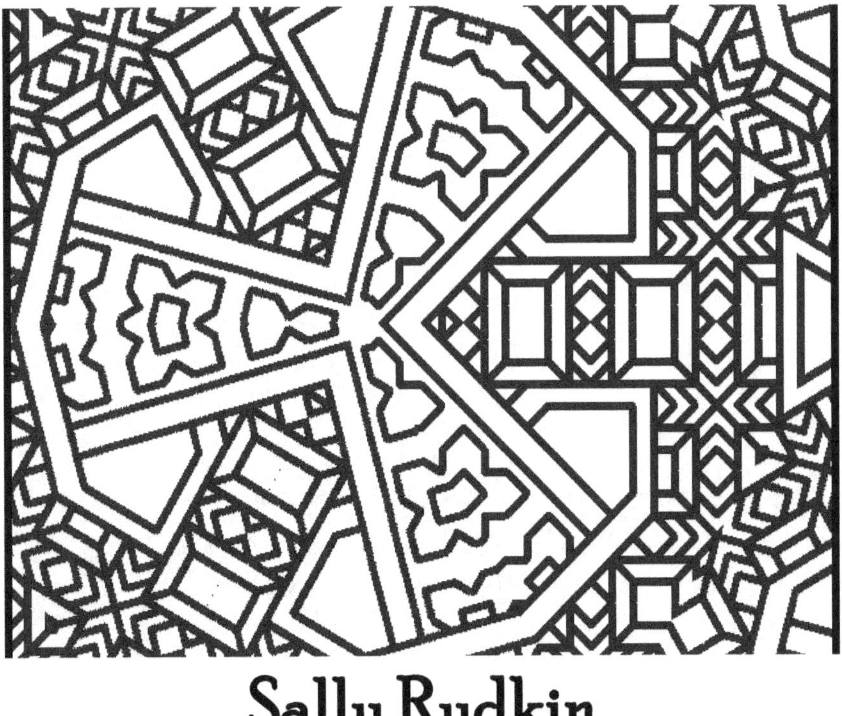

Sally Rudkin

Stitchin'spiration

STITCHIN'SPIRA-

POST OFFICE BOX 1571
MECHANICSVILLE, VA 23116 USA
(804) 368-7751
ADMIN@STITCHINSPIRATION.COM
WWW.STITCHINSPIRATION.COM
© 2020 DESIGNS BY SALLY RUDKIN ALL RIGHTS RESERVED.

DOODLIN' TO DE-STRESS!

Calm yourself as you color the patterns. From simple patterns, to intricate designs, this coloring book has what you need. Grab the book, and color to your heart's content.

Included are 50 designs to calm your nerves. And, each page includes the same design on the front AND the back of the page, so you choose. Have twice the designs to color – or choose to color each one time, and let the design bleed through. You decide!!!

ABOUT THE AUTHOR:

Stitchin'spiration is the home of creativity, playing in fabric, thread, and color, and is the home of Sally Rudkin. She's a designer of blackwork samplers of all kinds, along with some cross stitch and other sorts of needlework. These coloring books highlight her love of pattern and texture.

Keep an eye out for more, you just never know where Sally's creativity will take her!

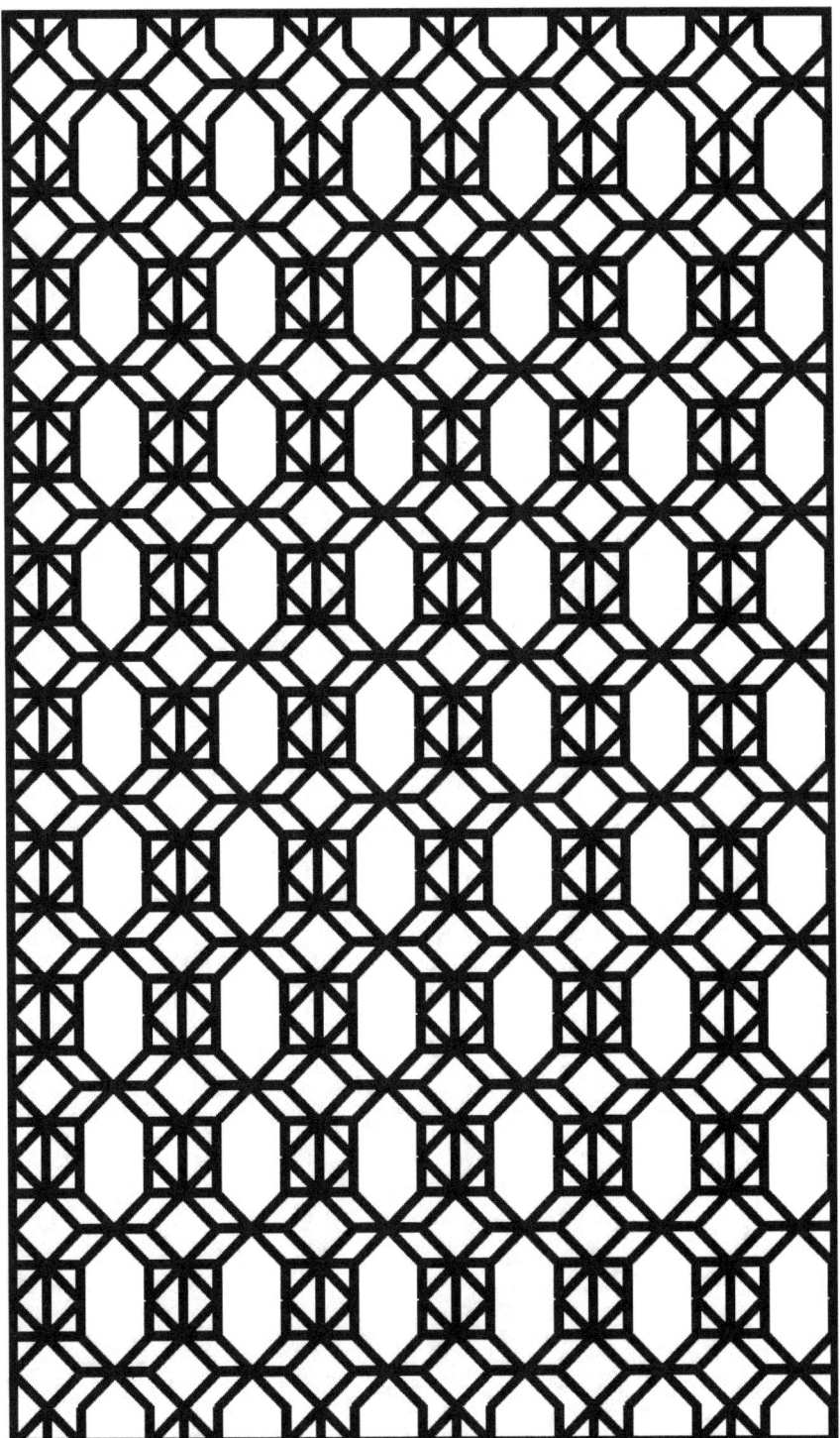

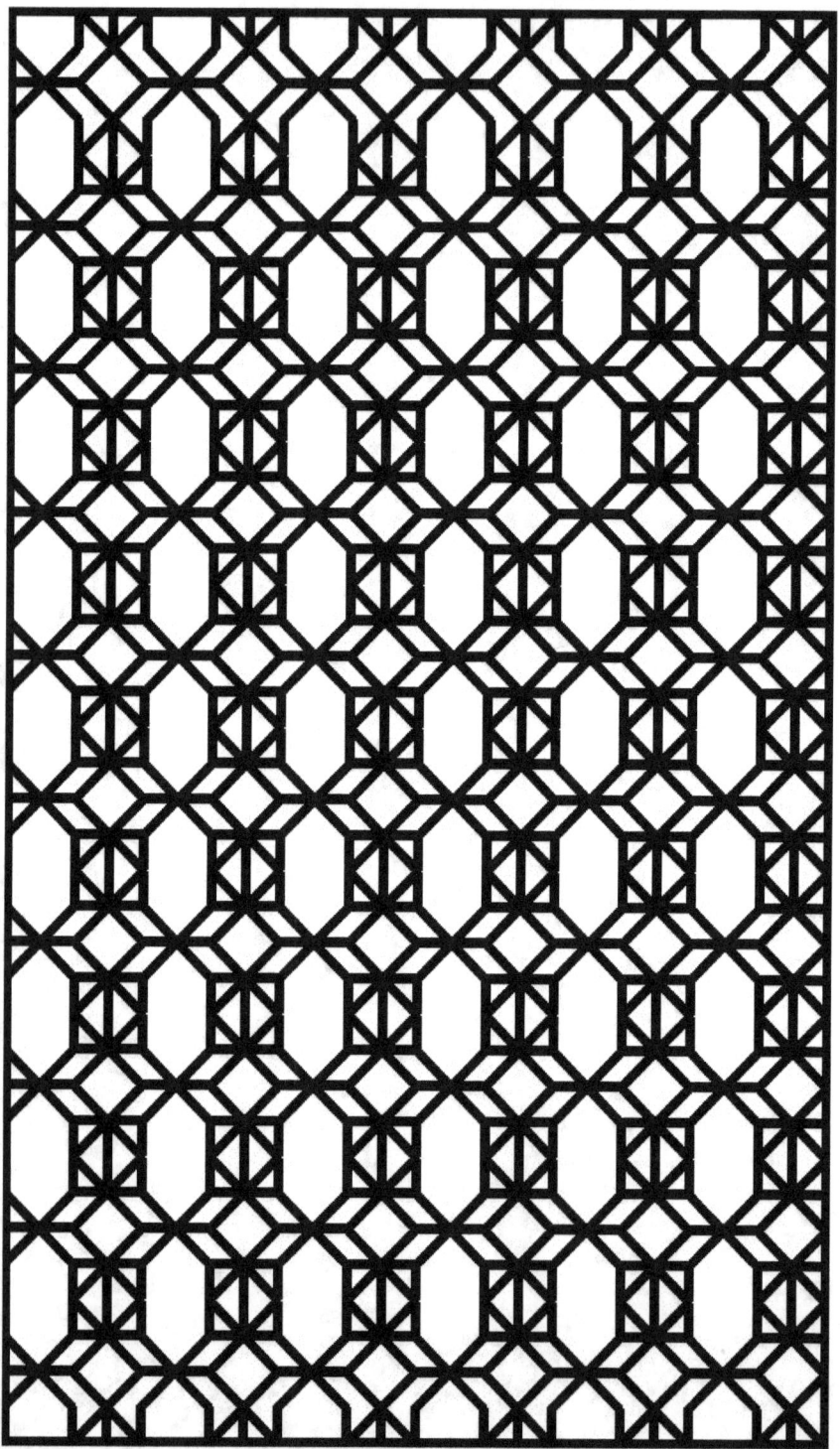

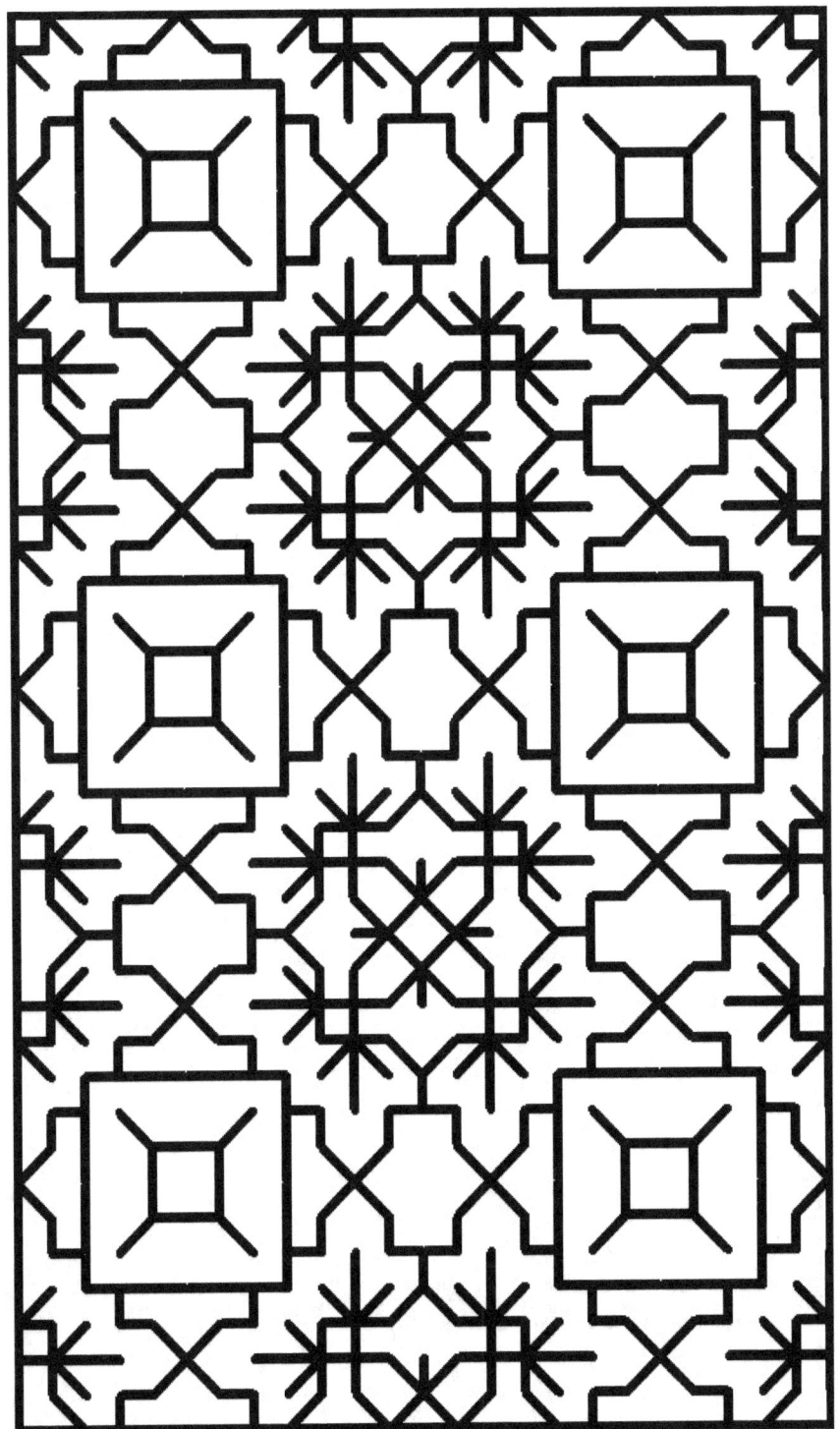

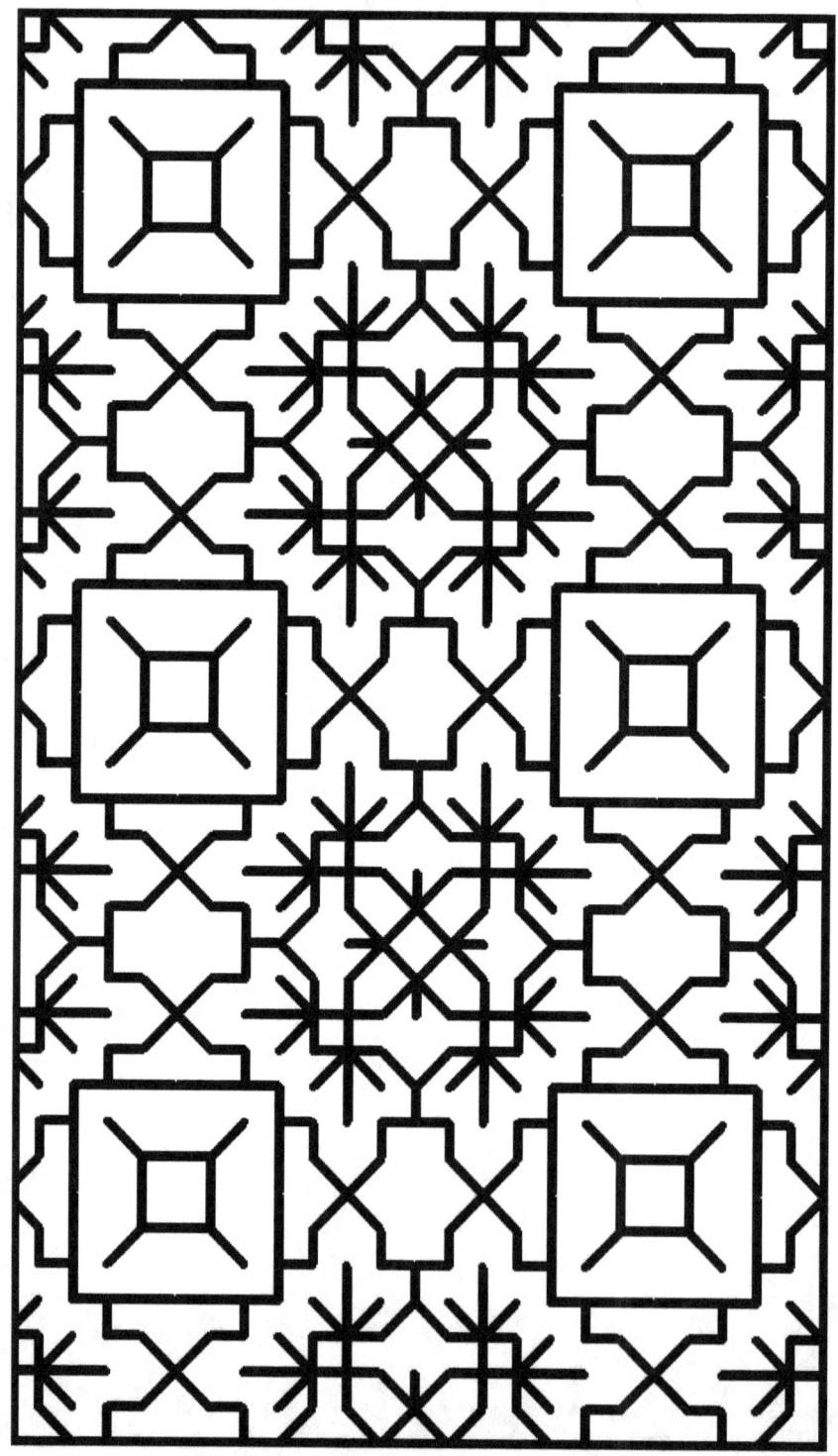

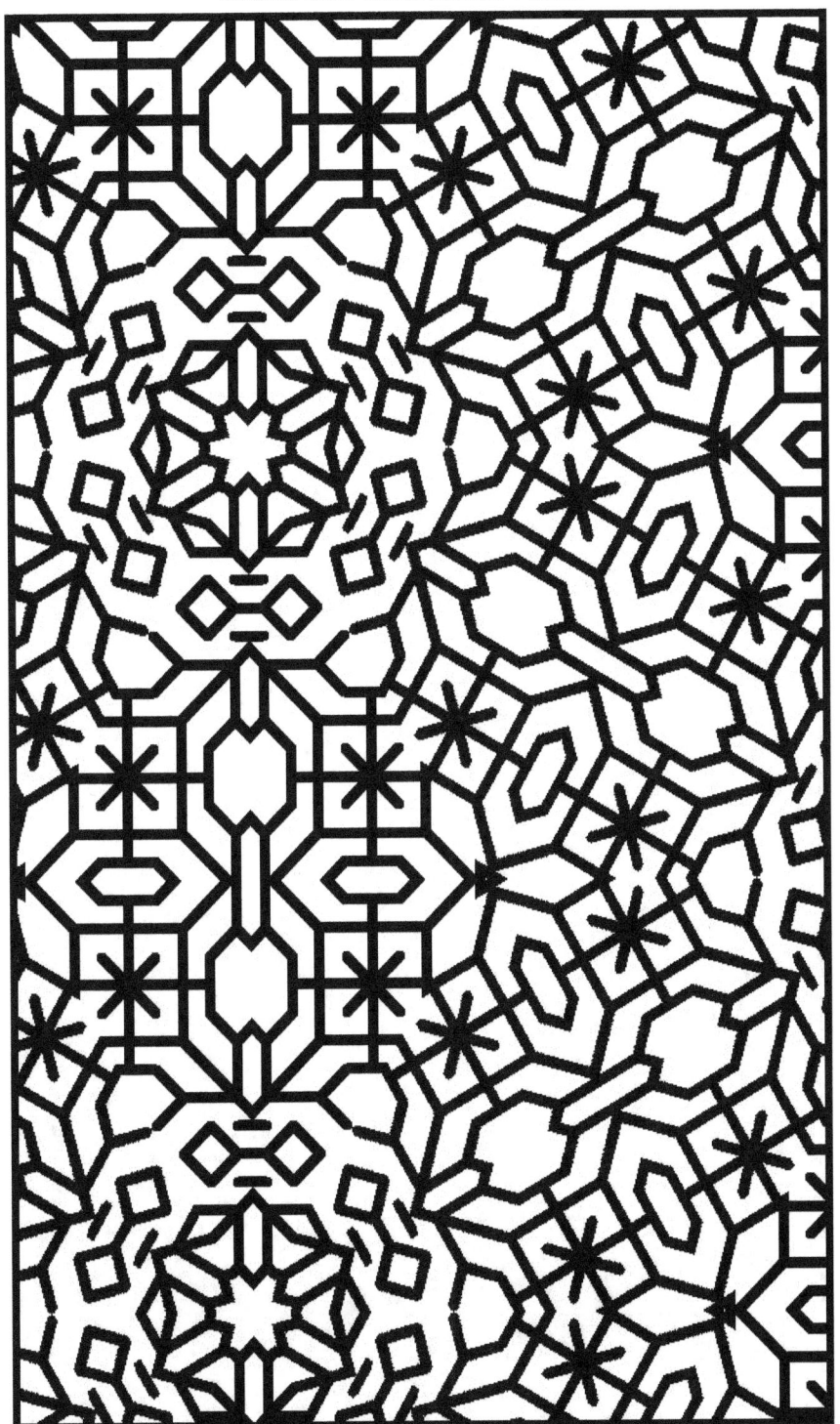

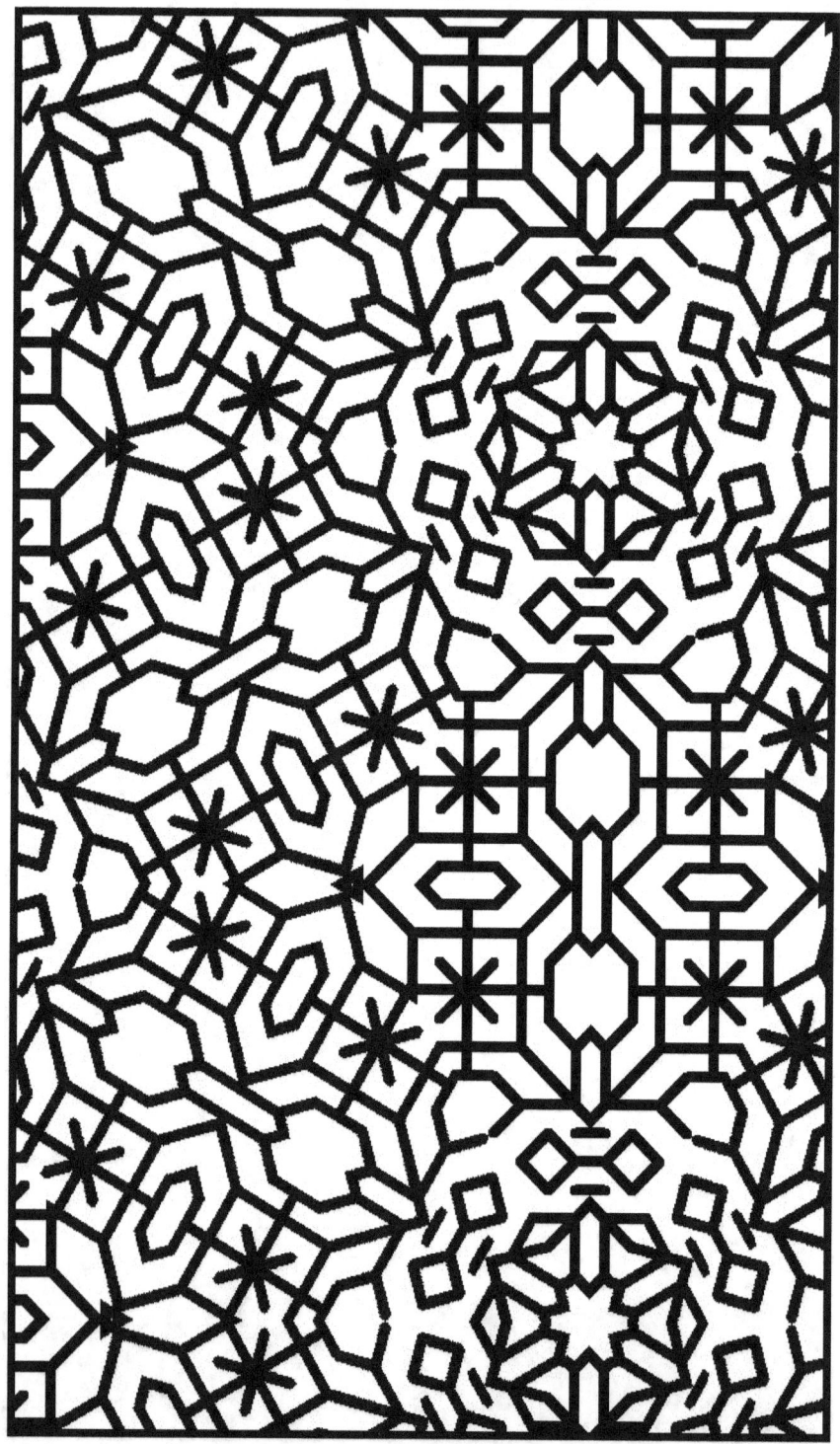

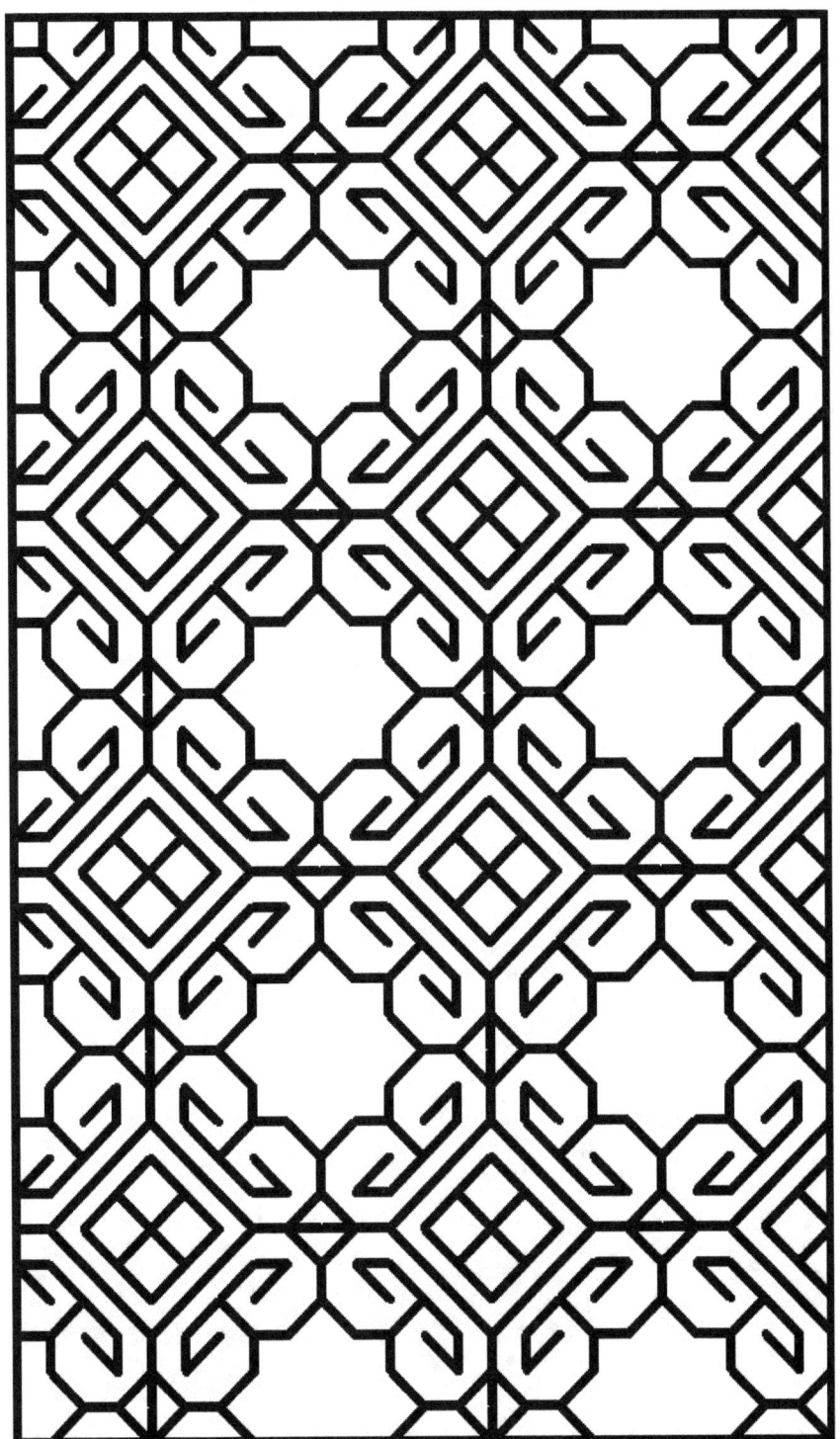

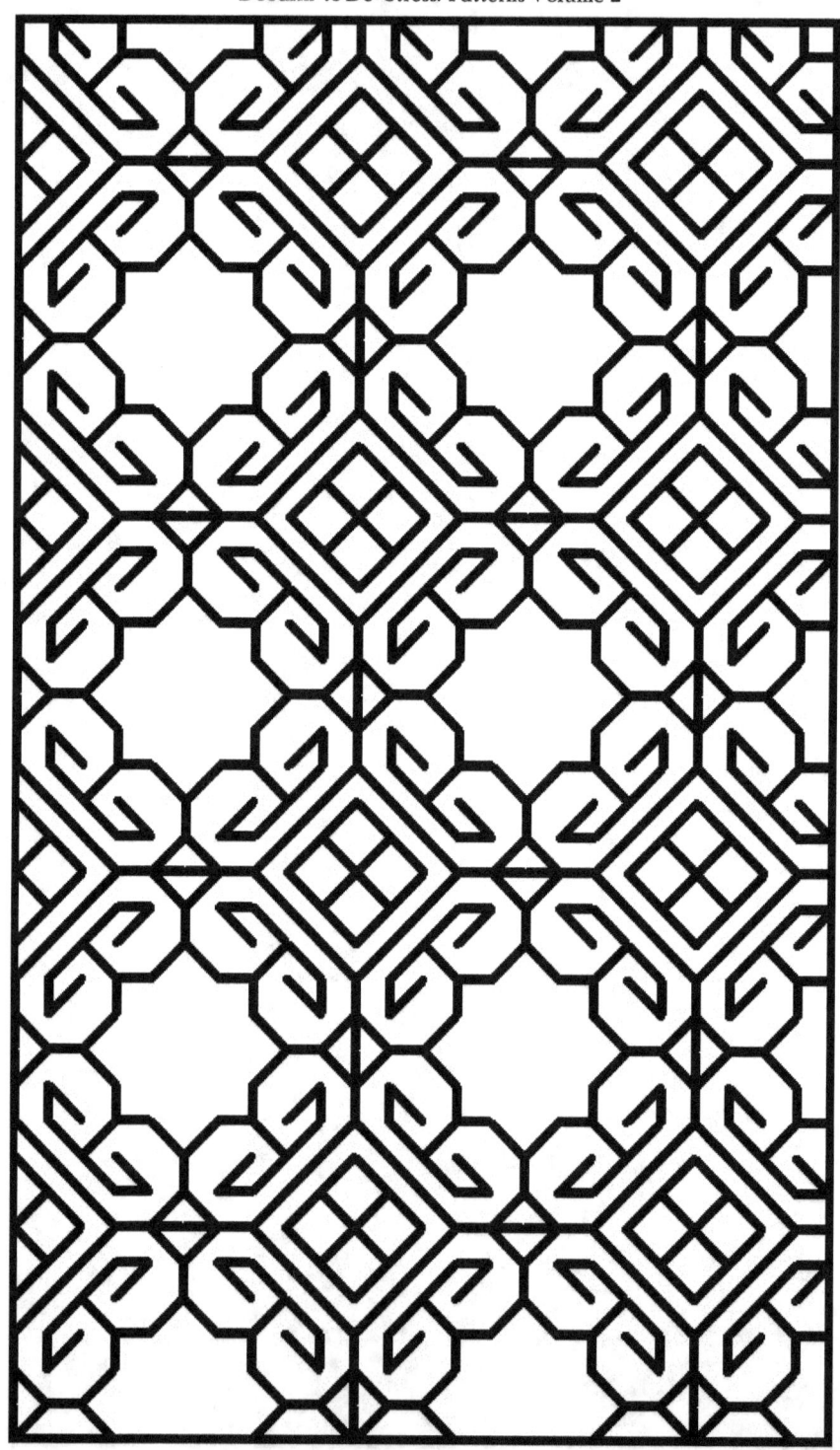

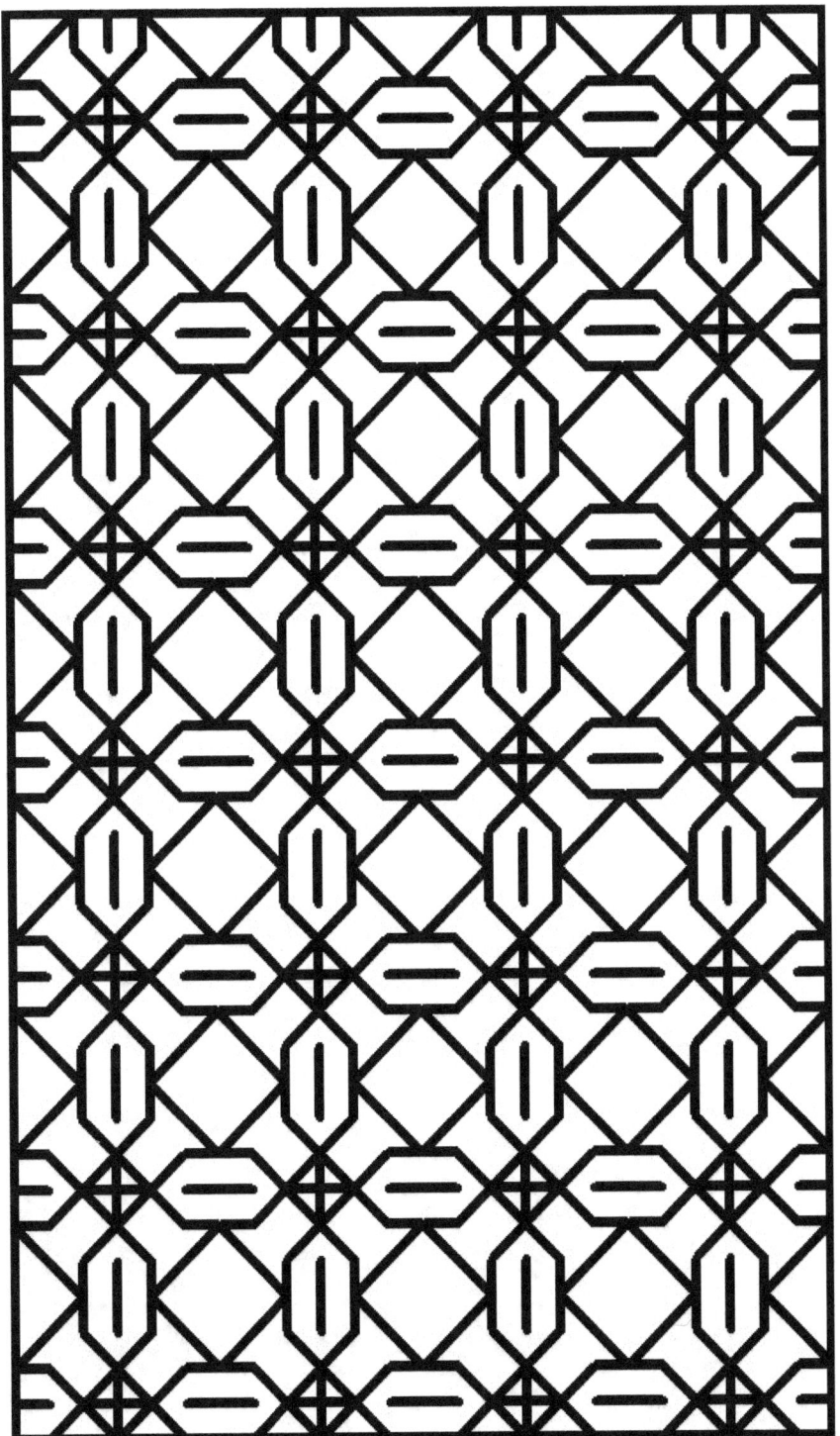

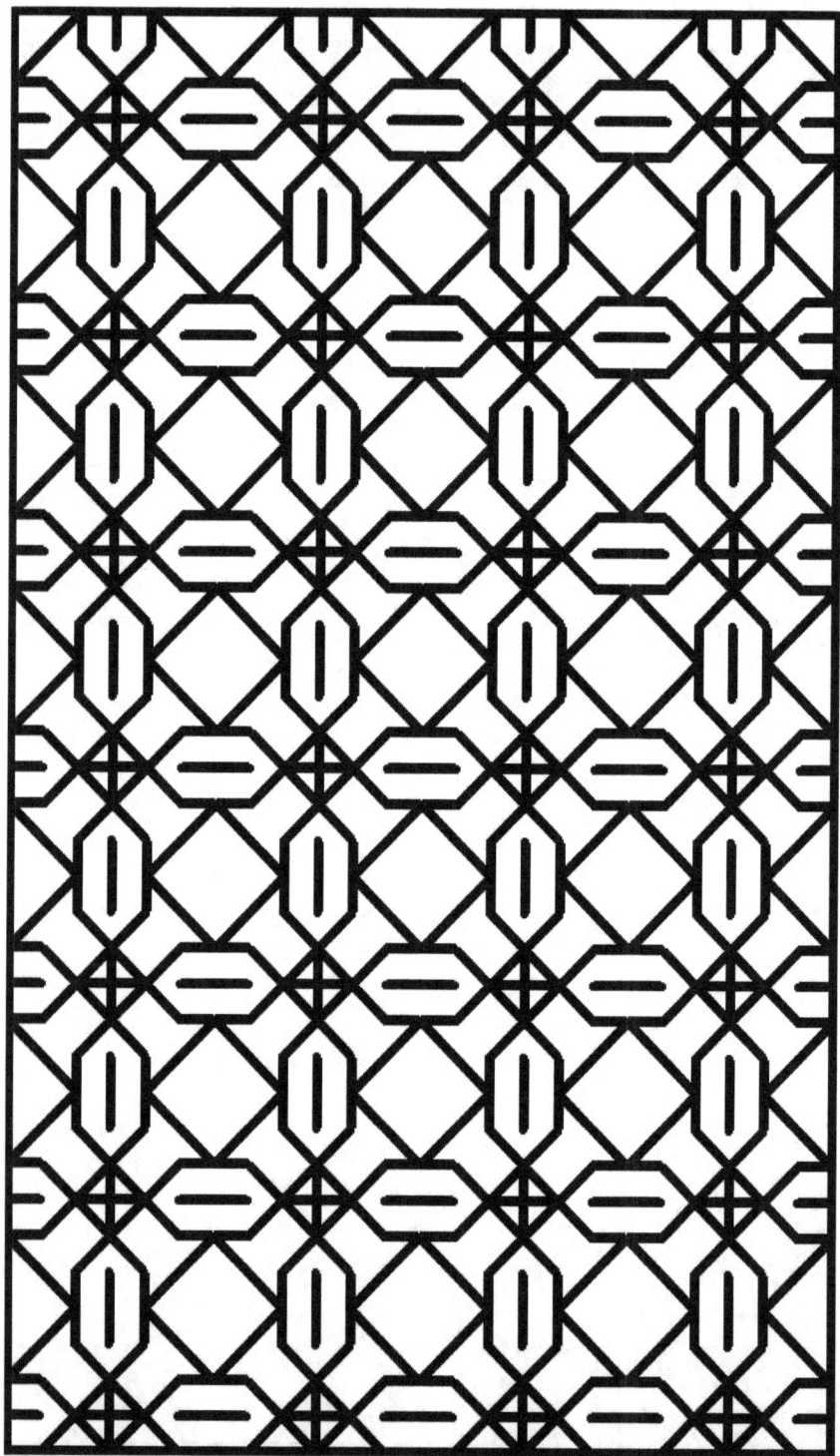

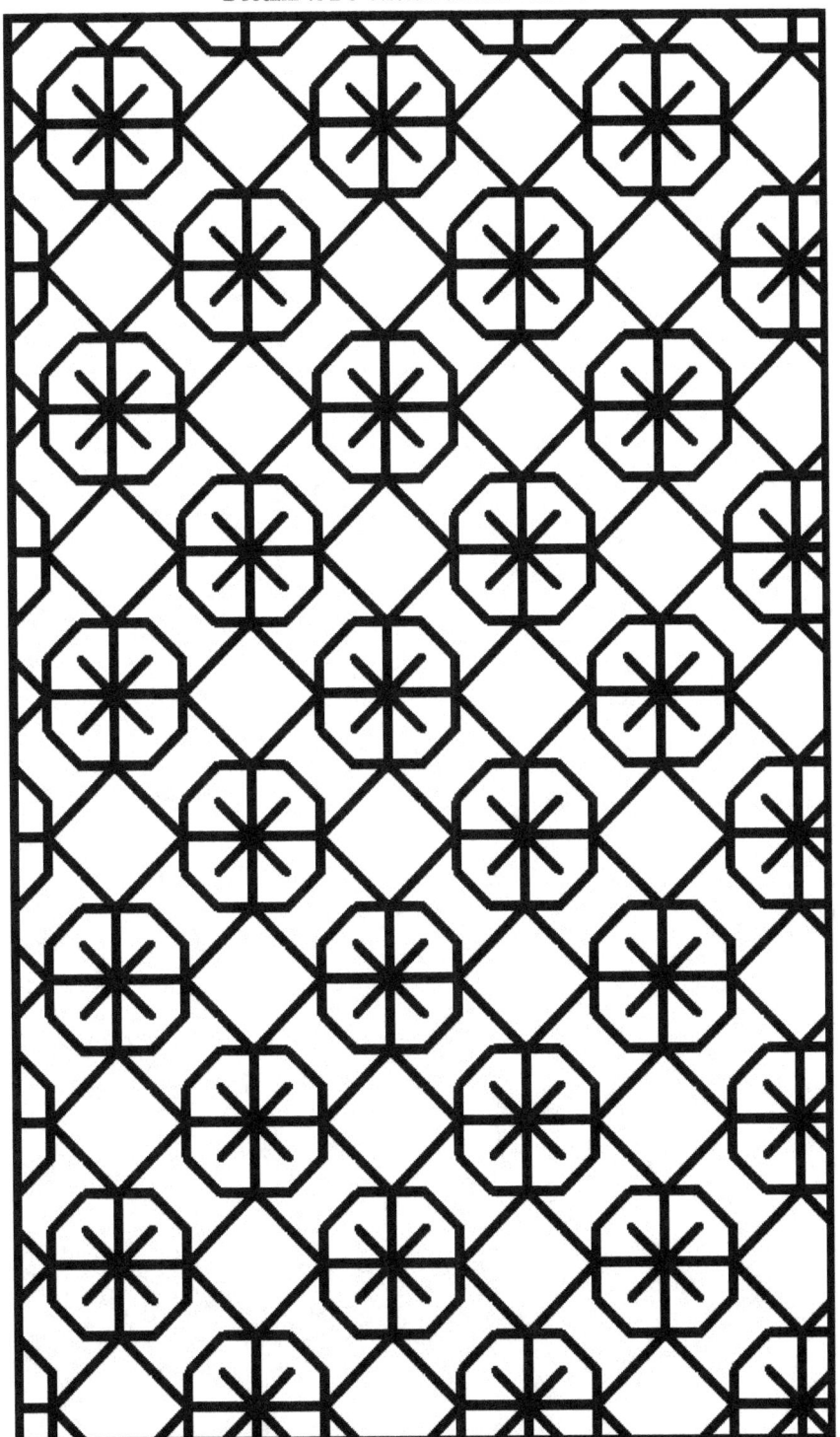

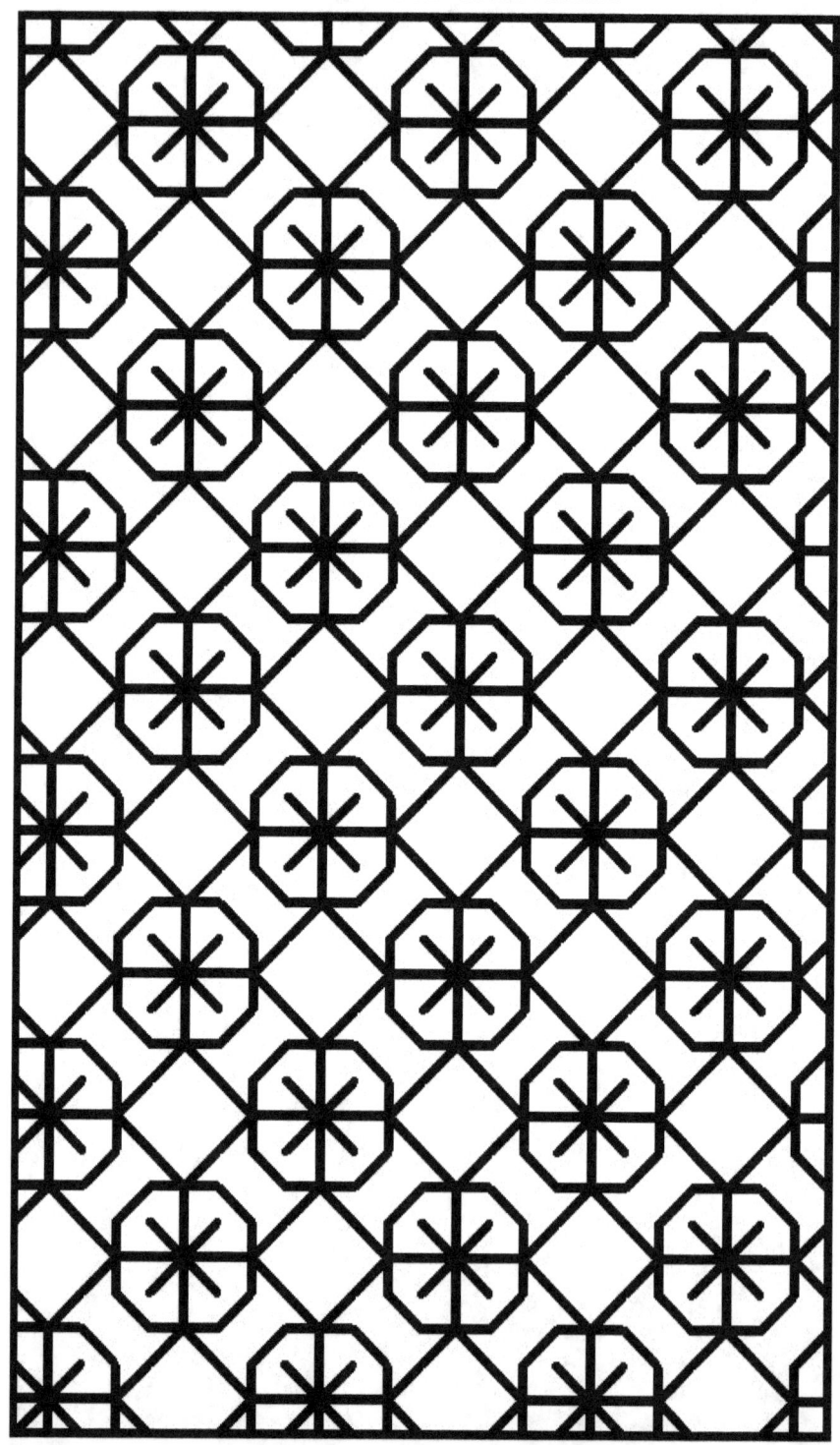

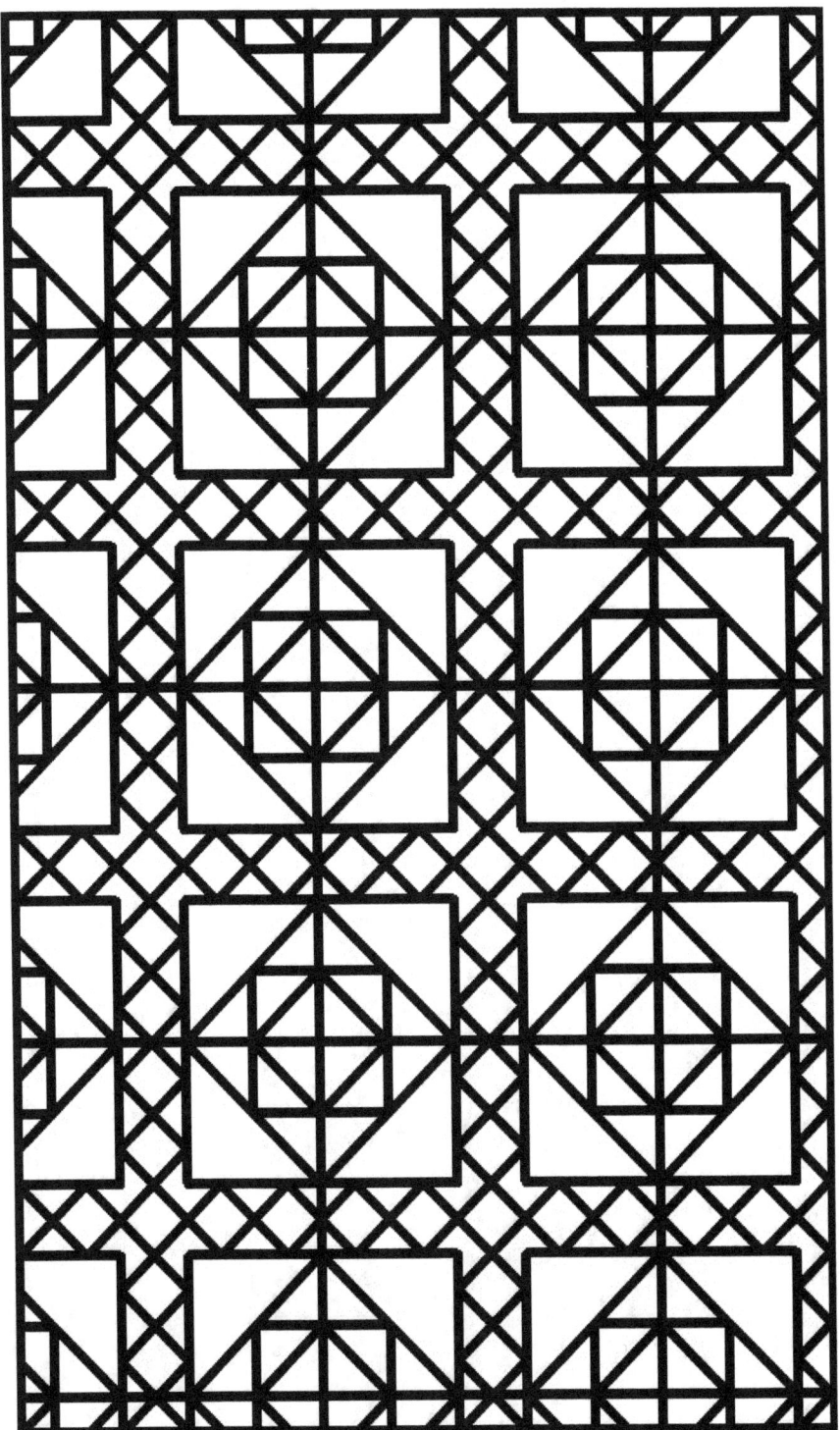

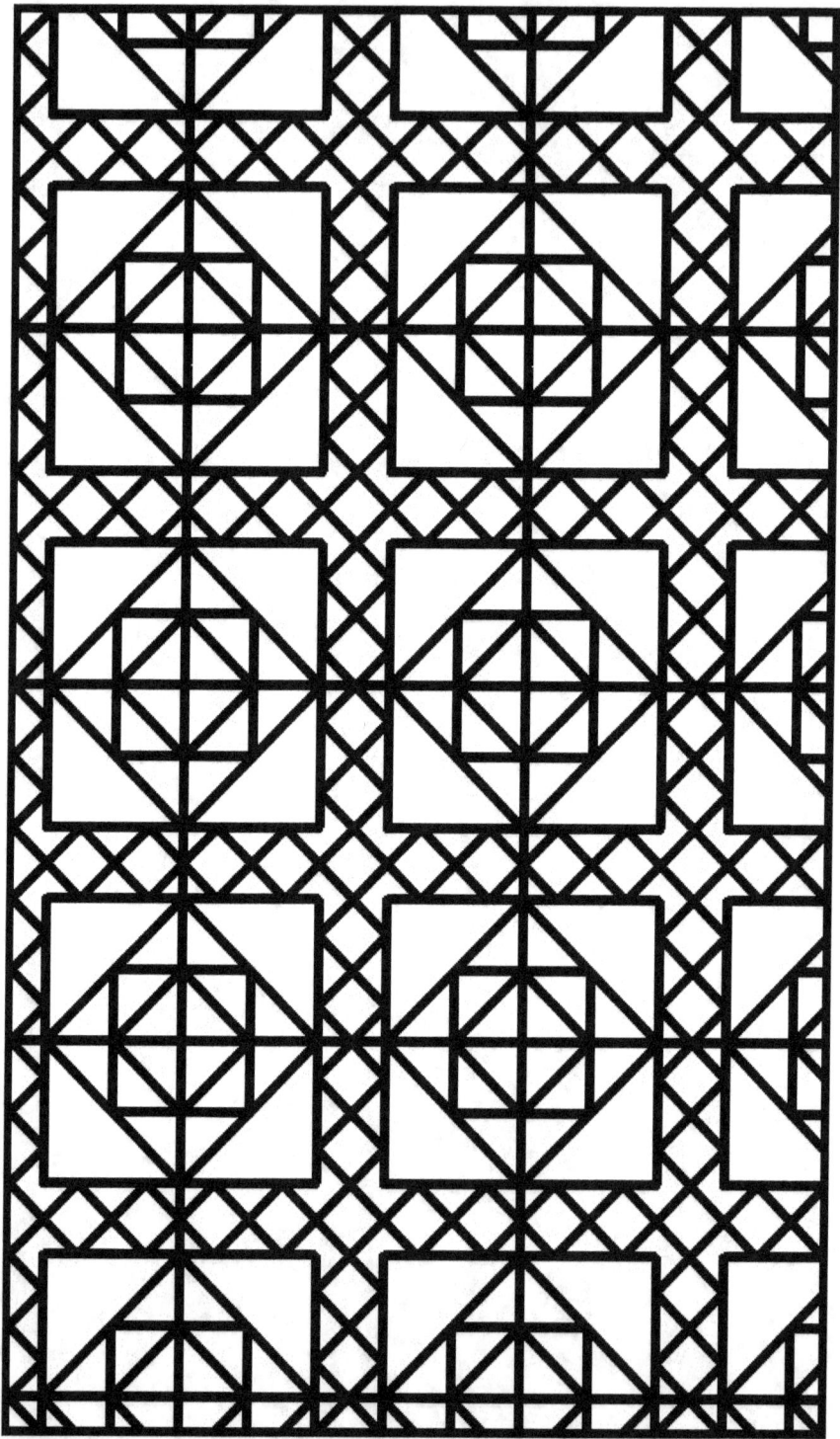

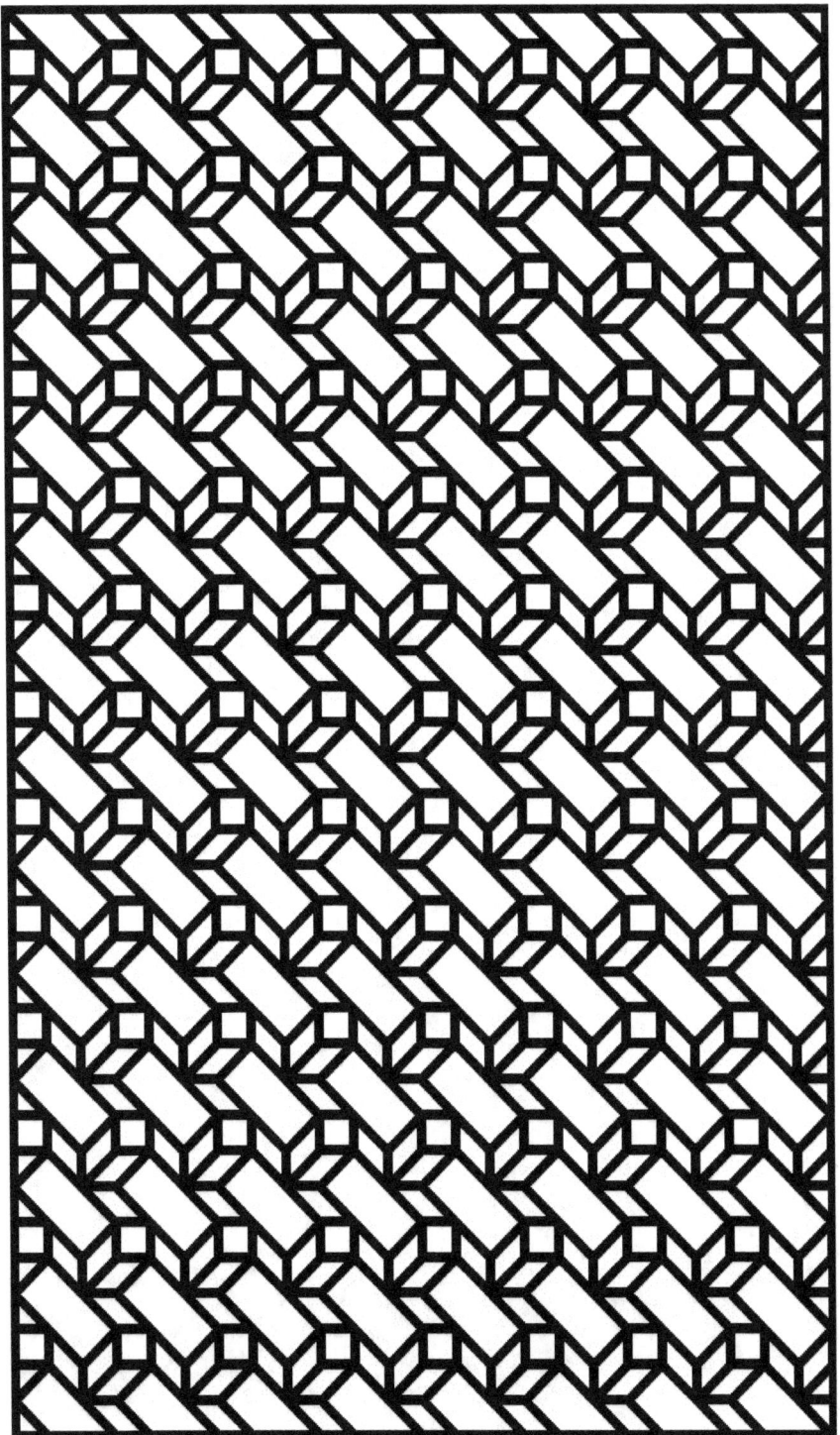

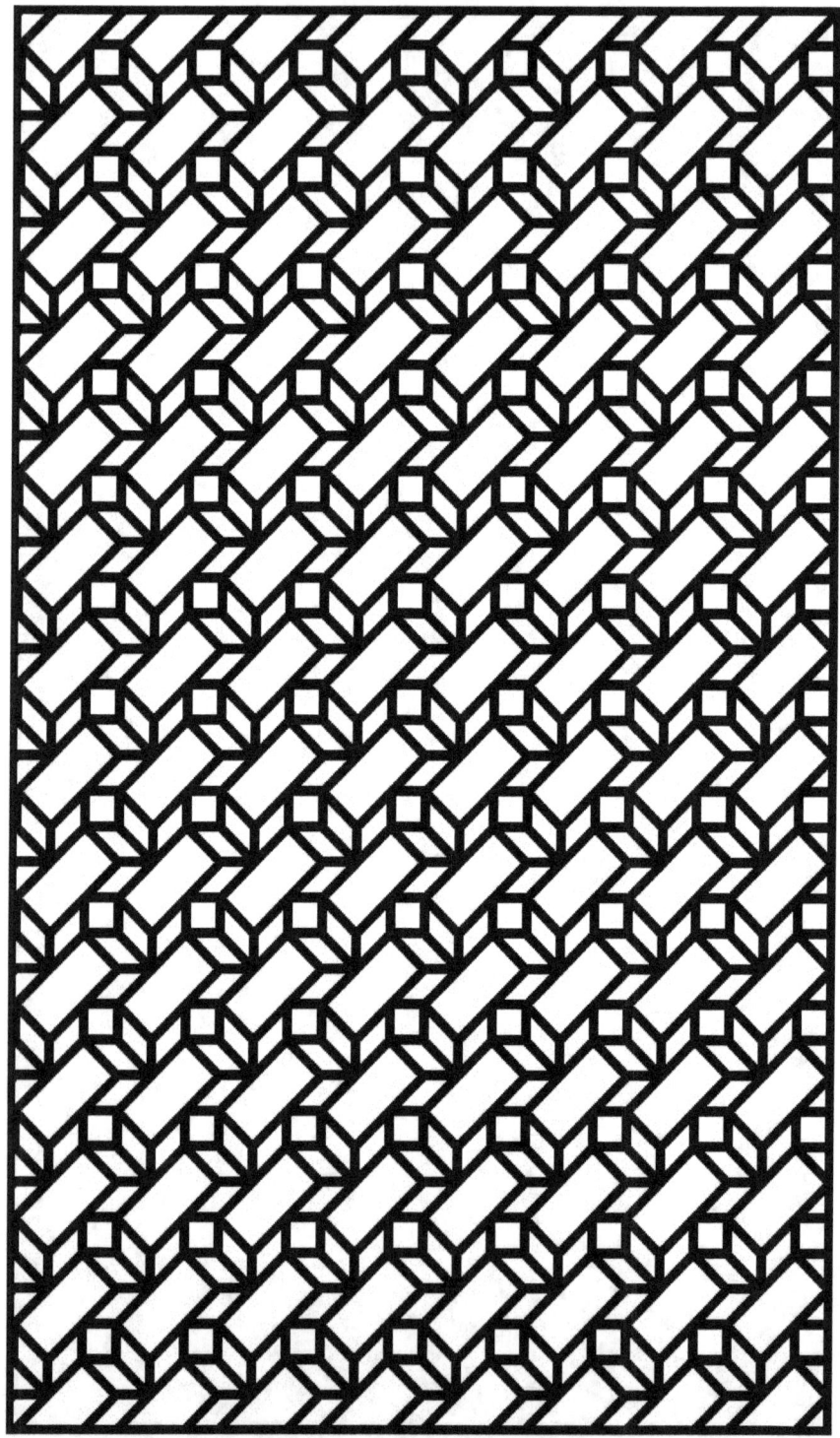

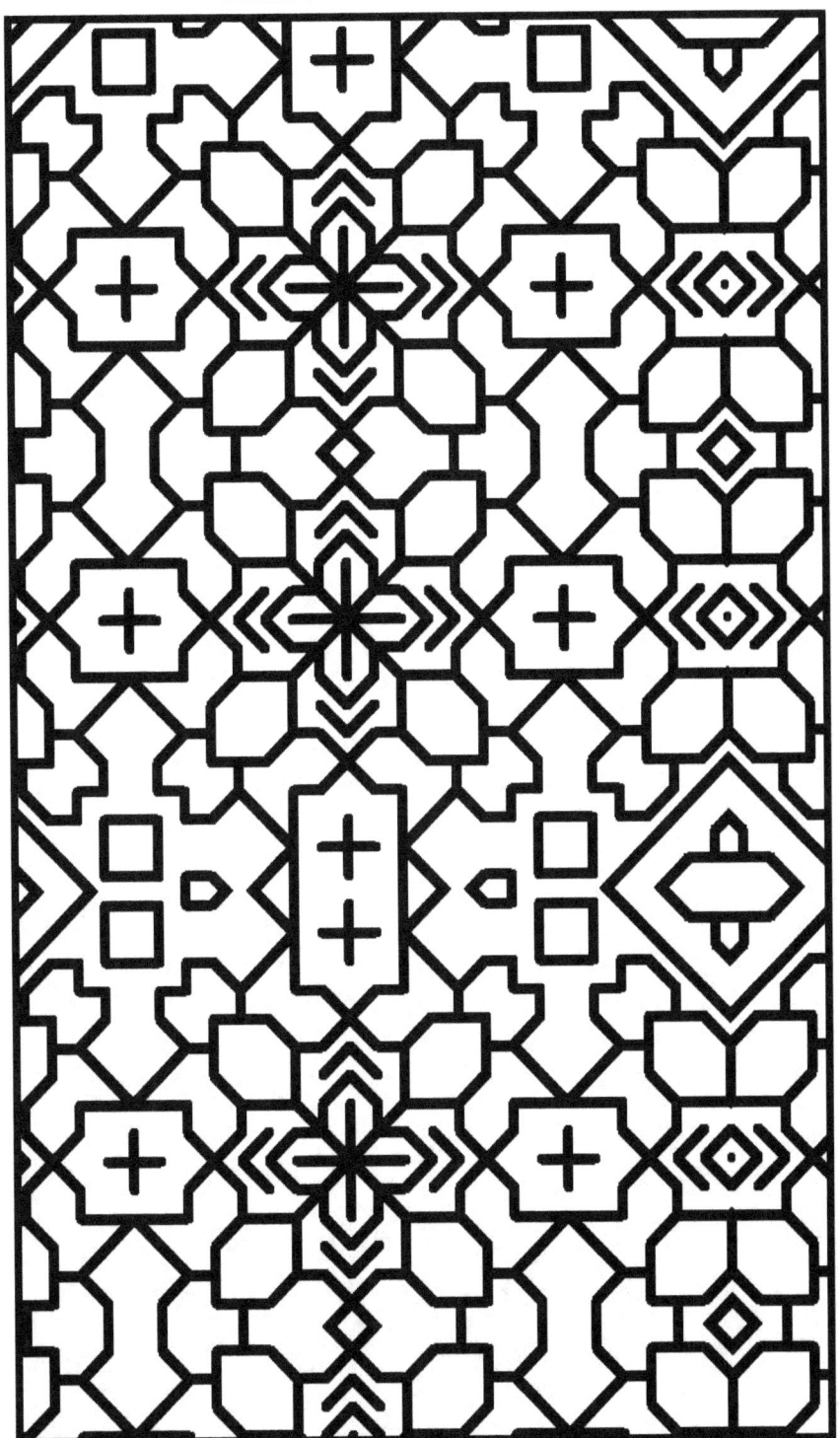

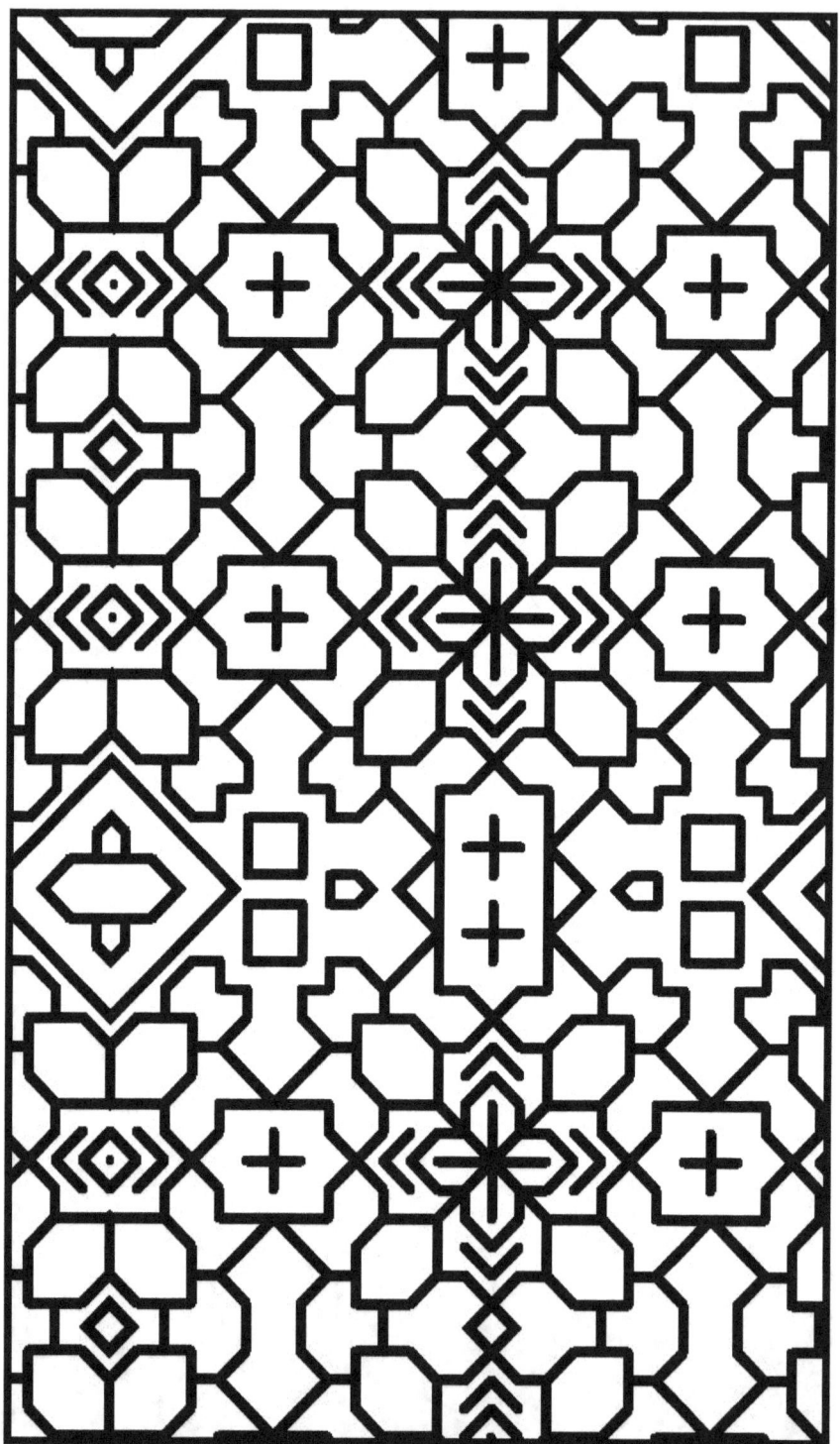

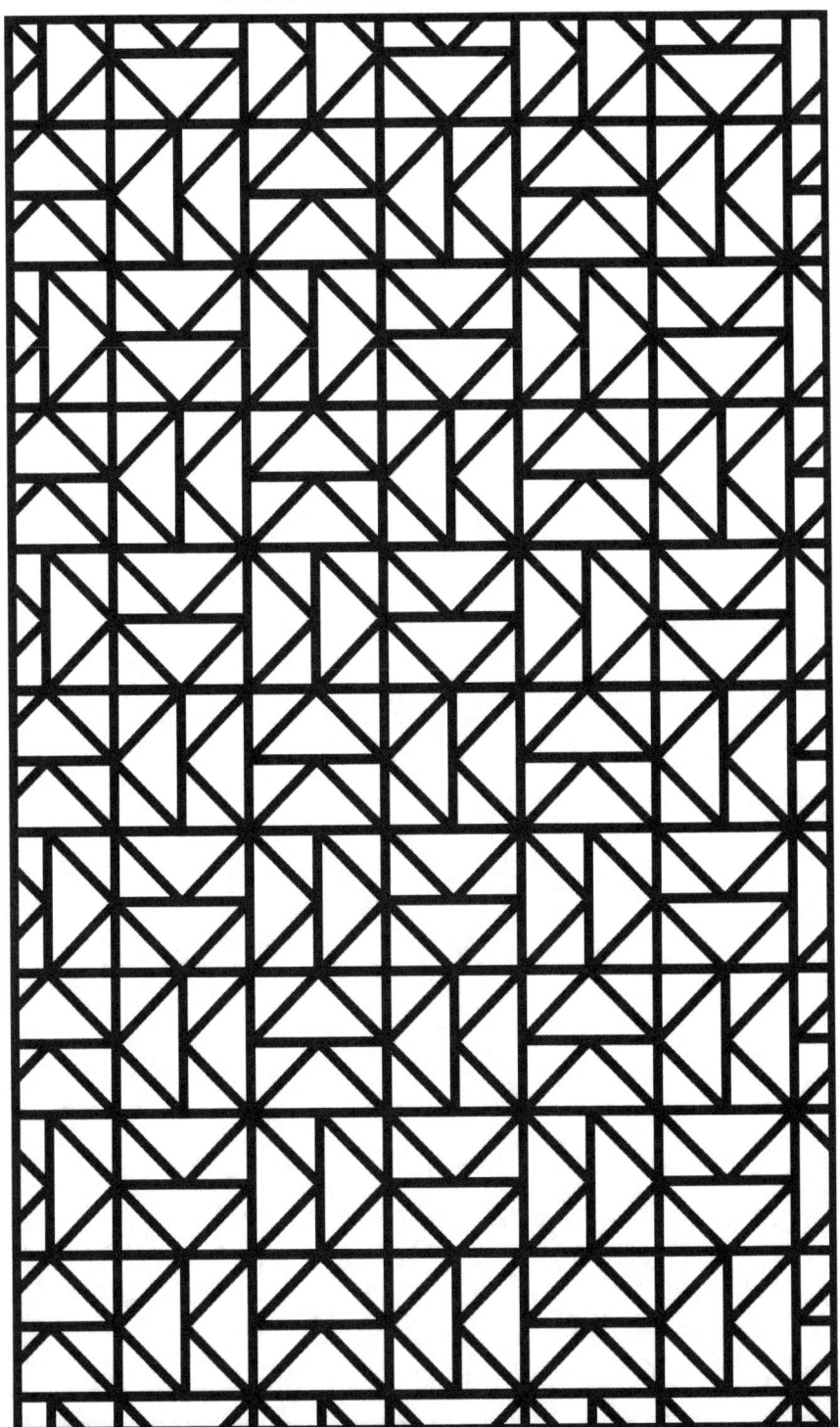

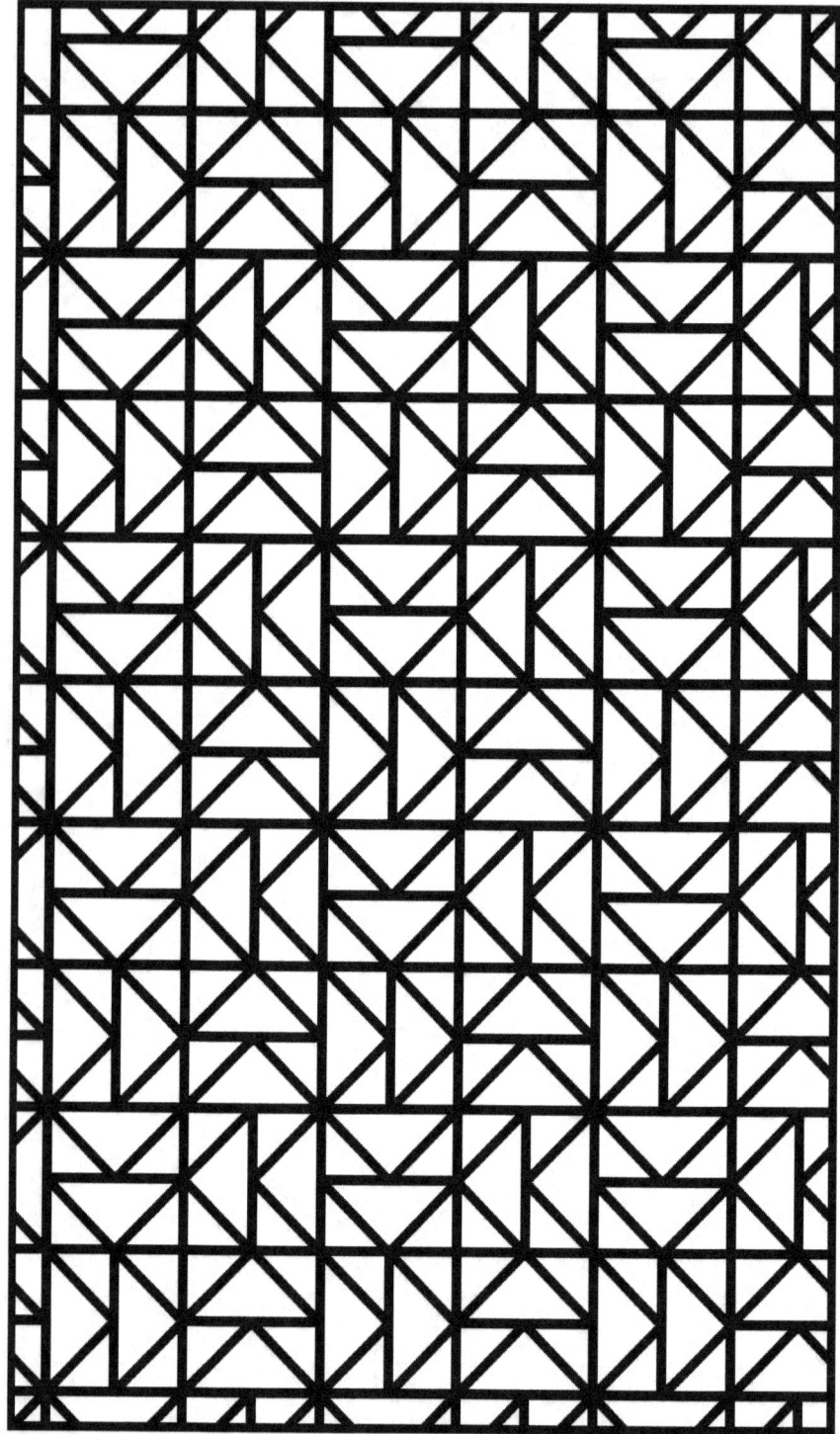

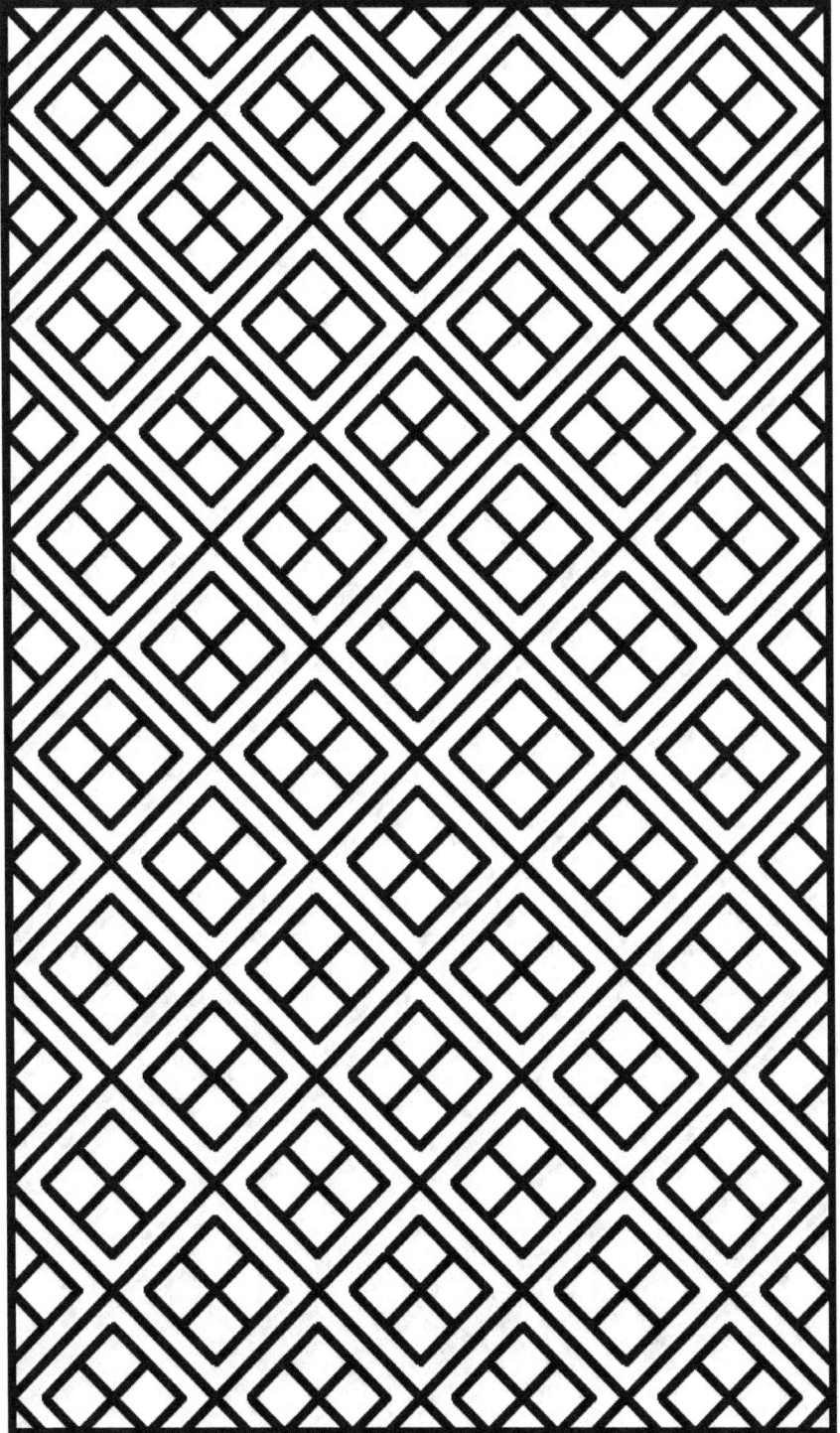

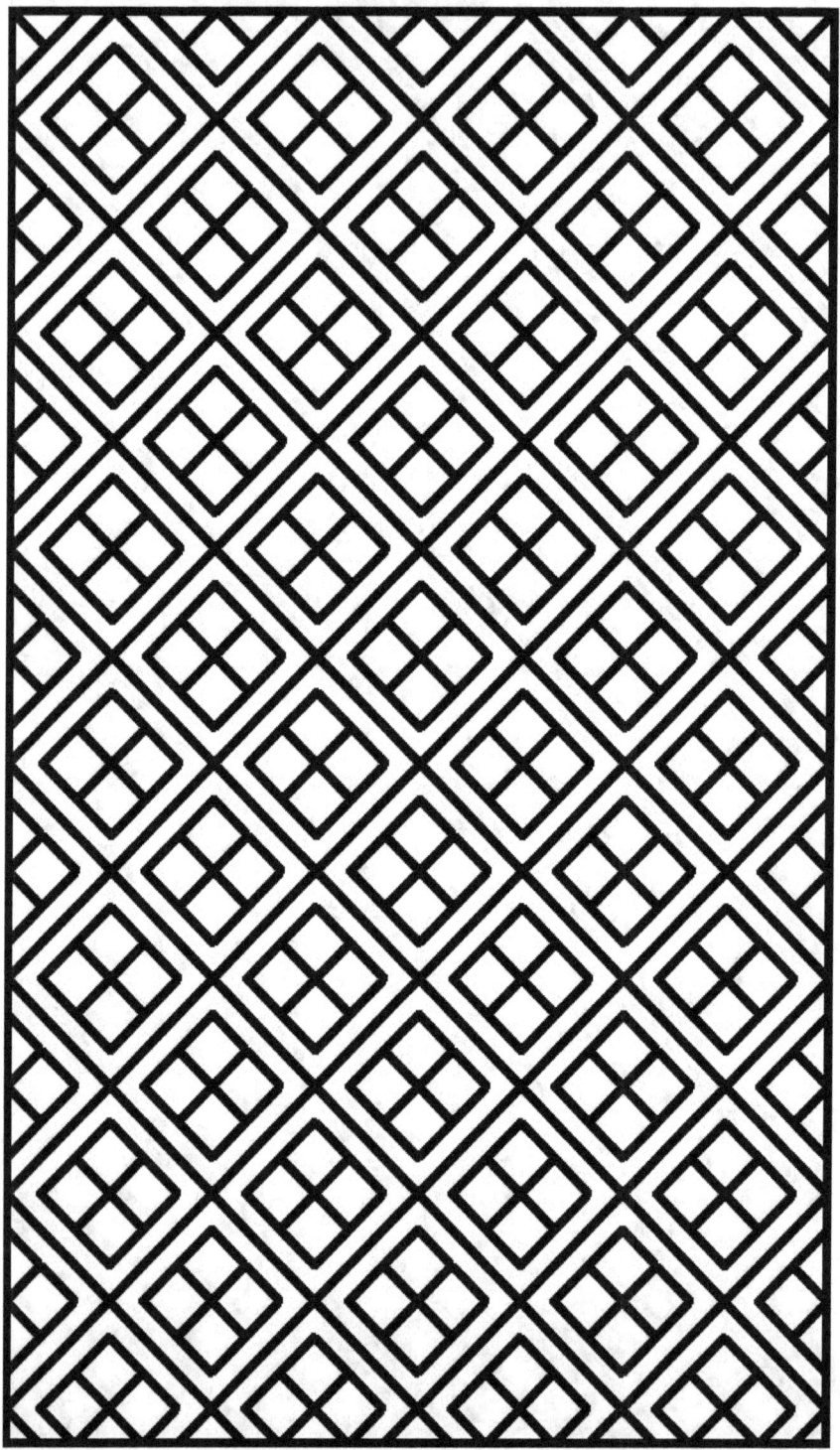

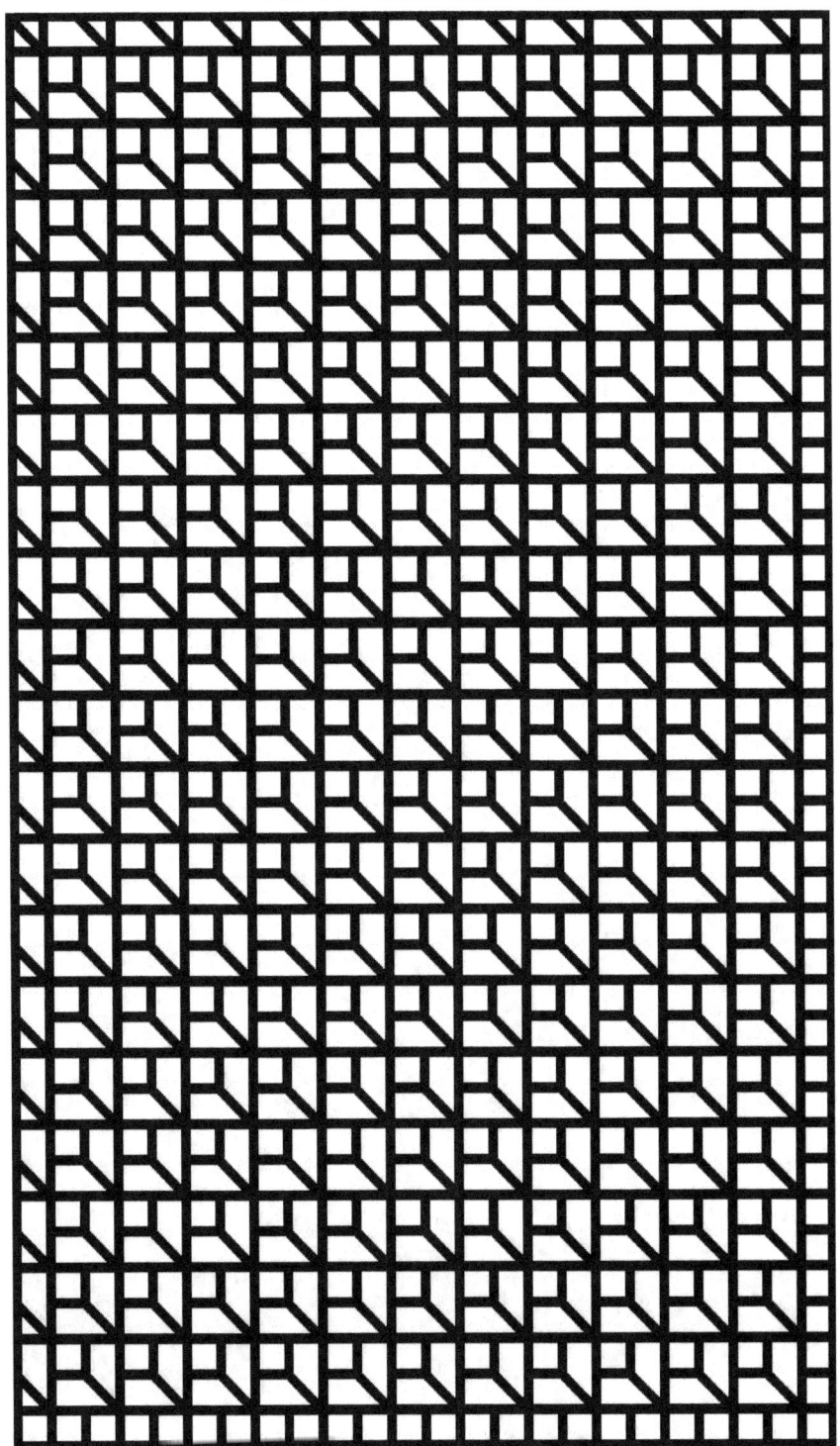

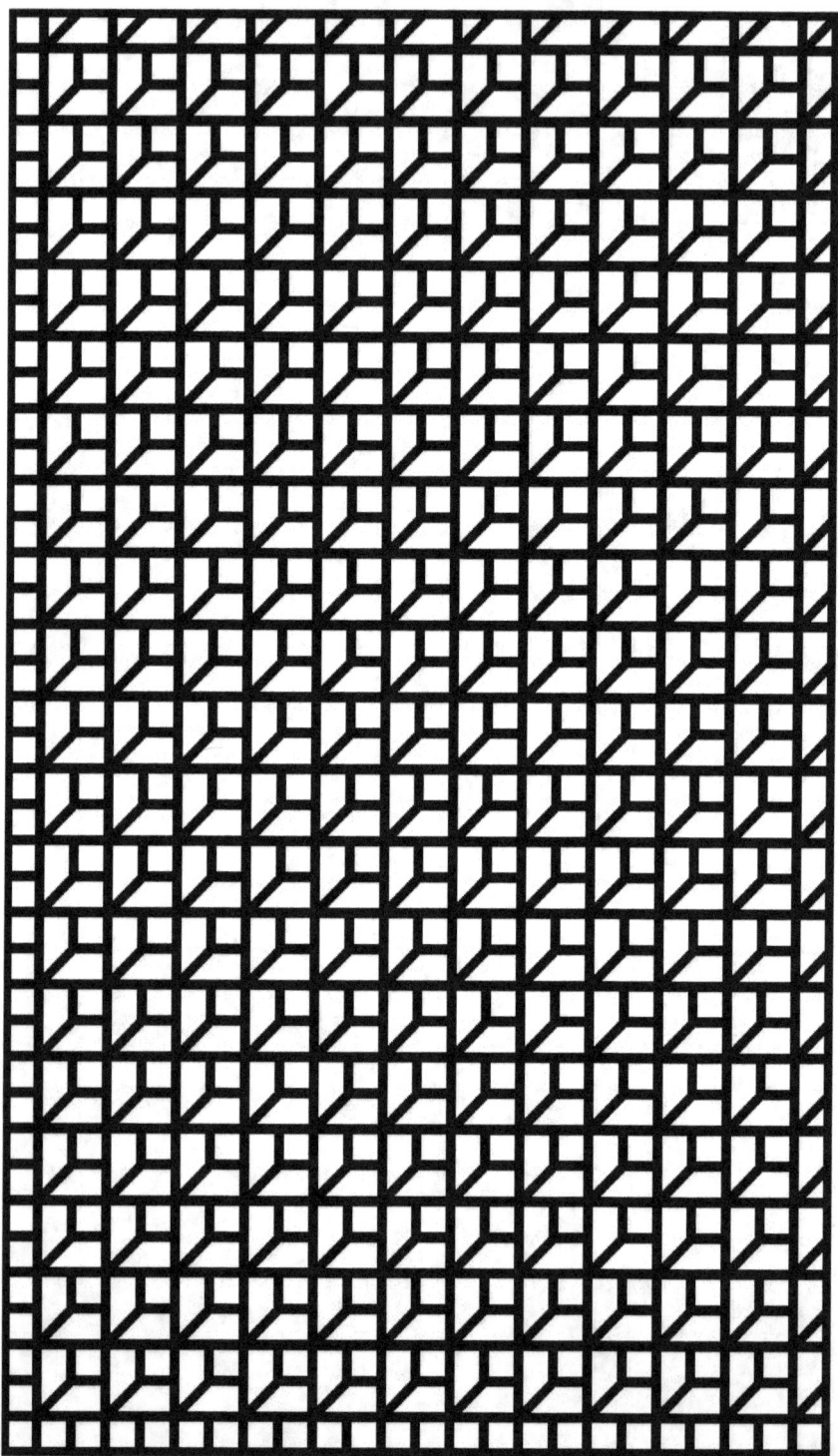

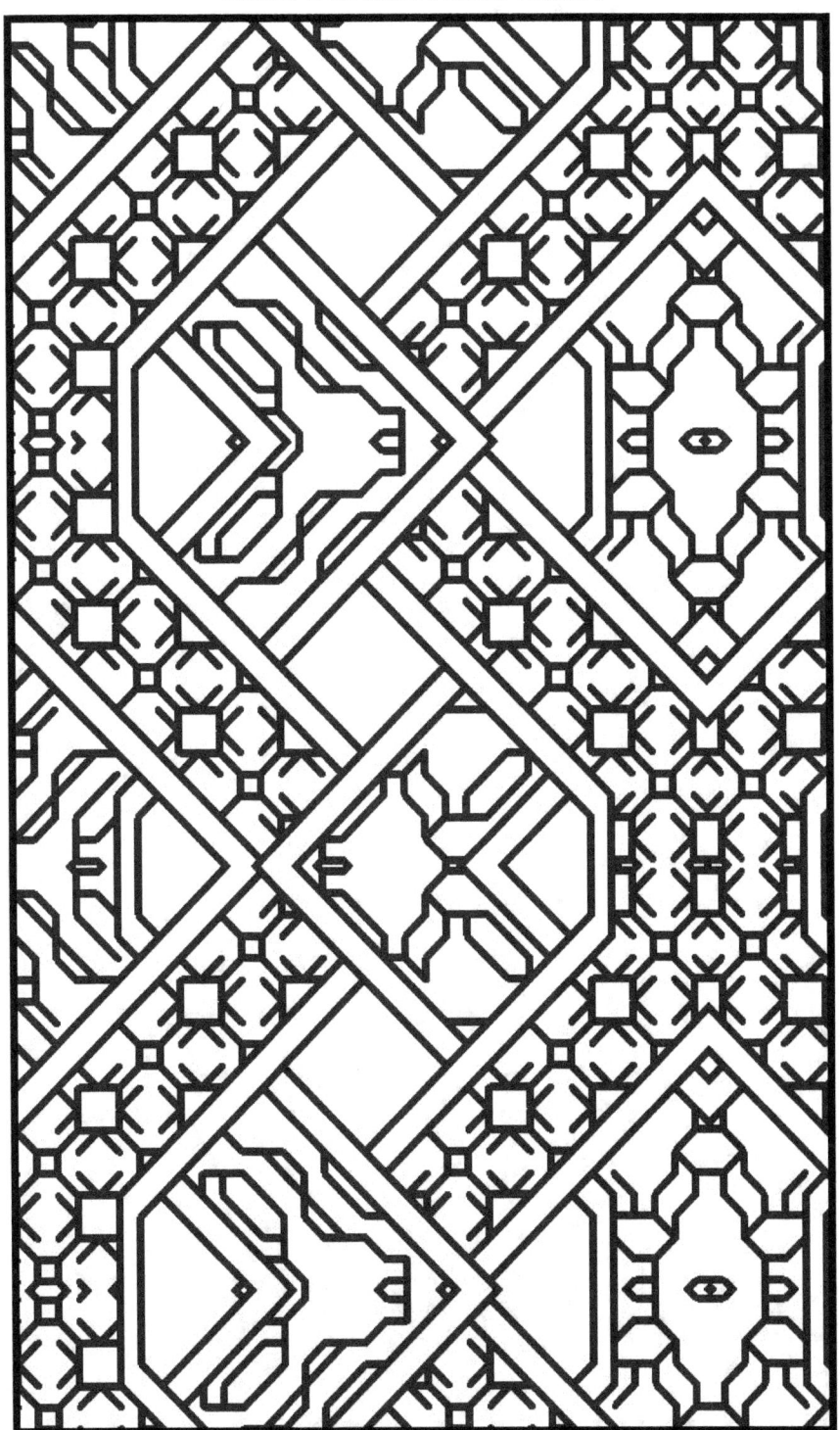

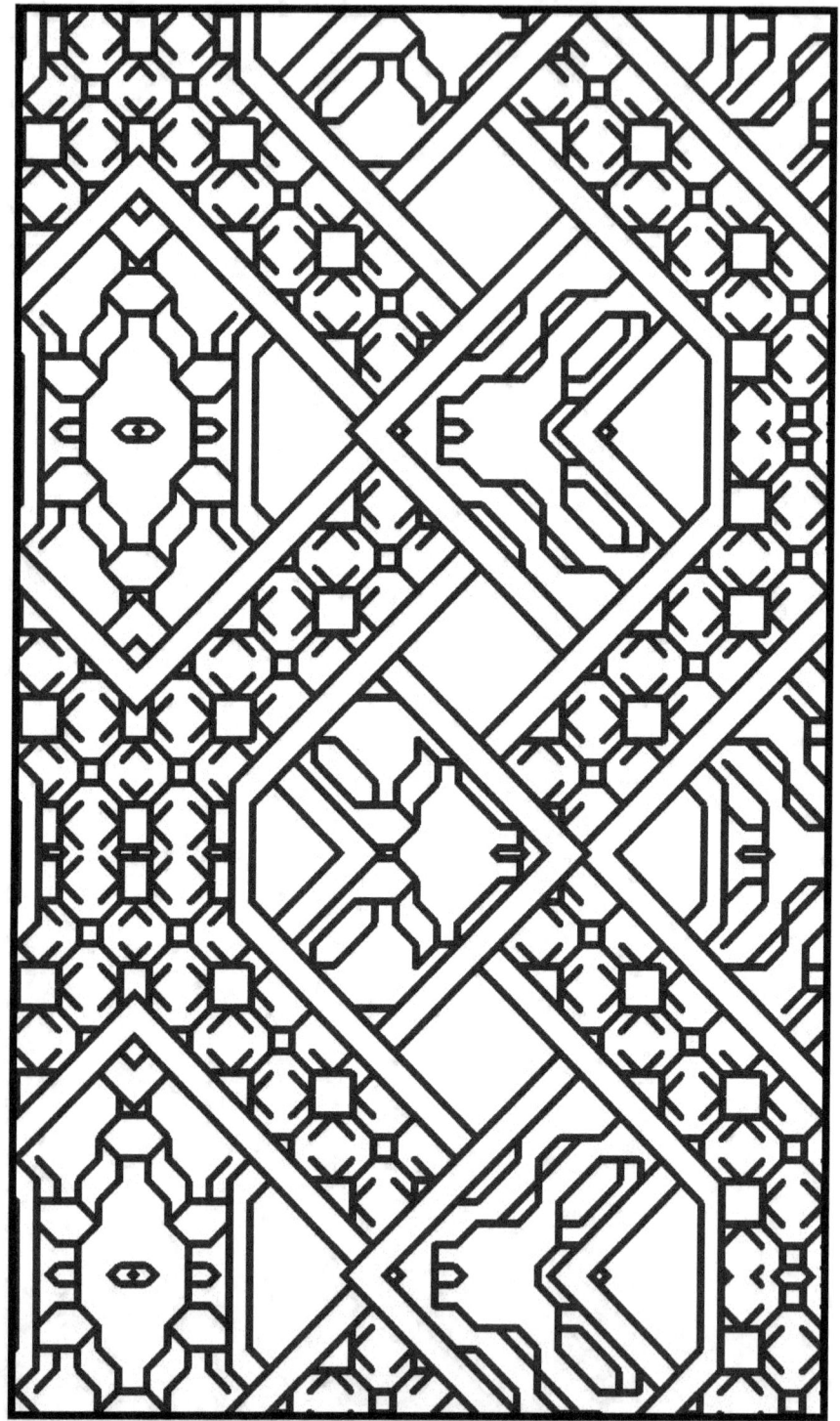

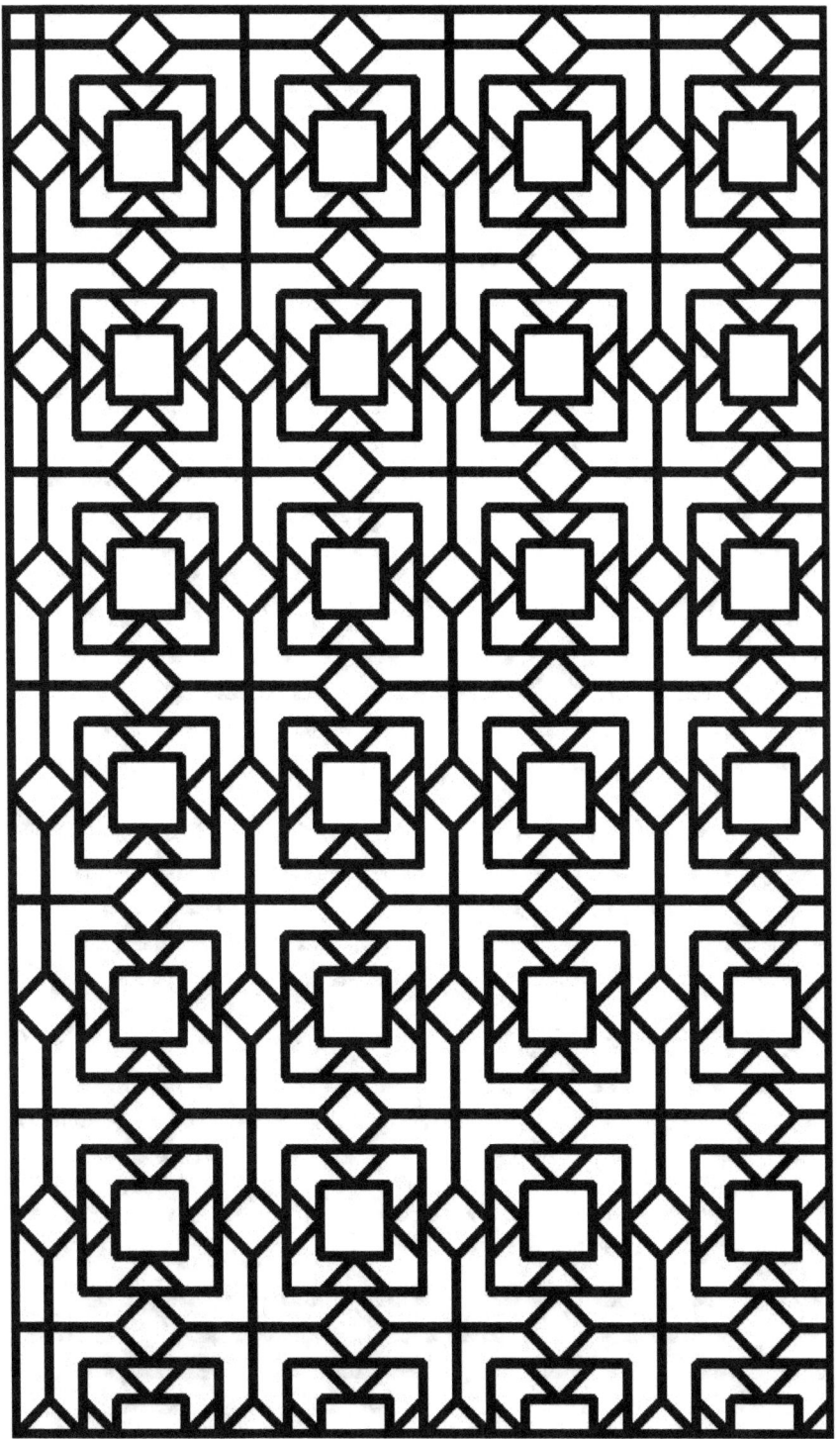

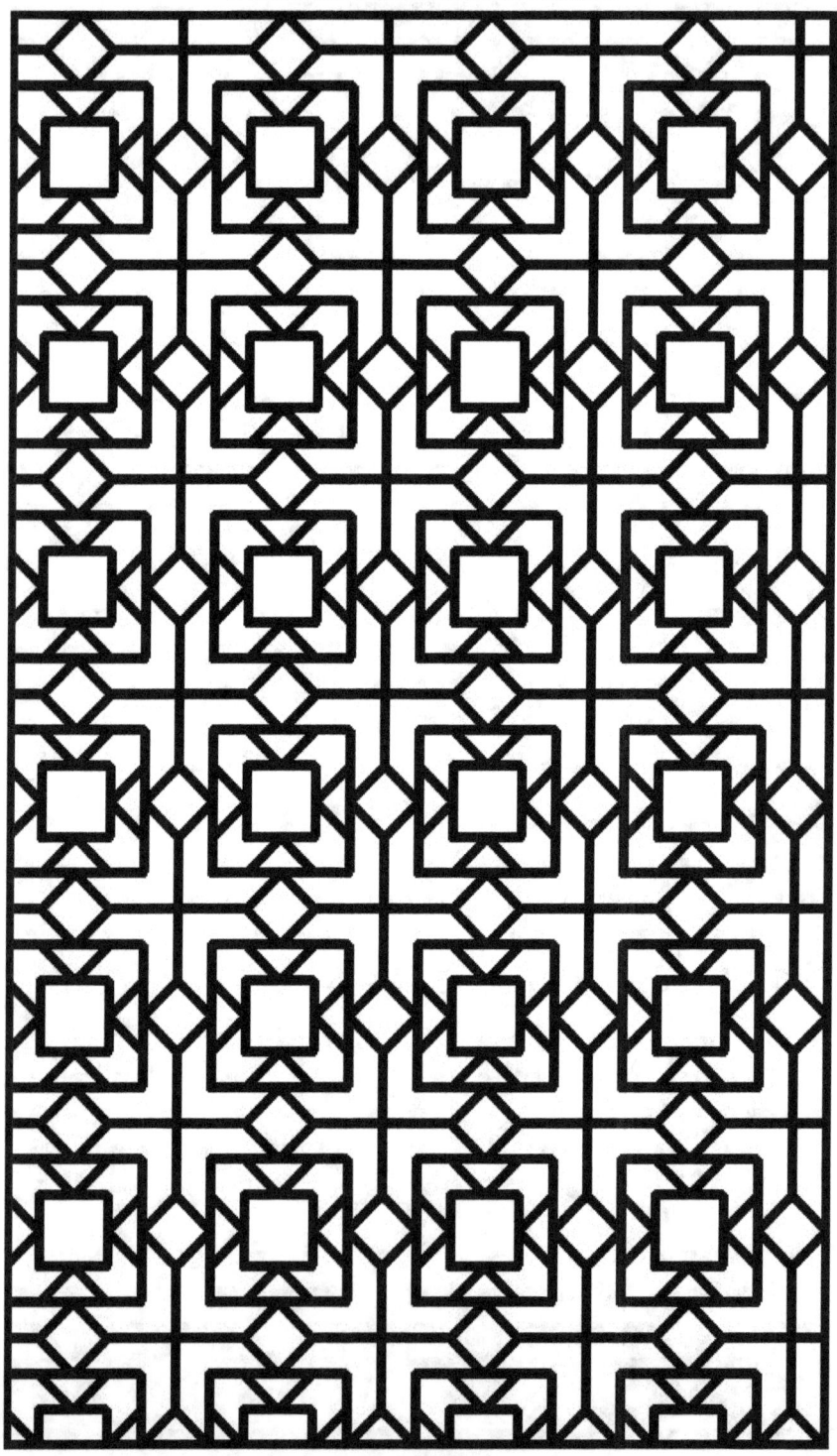

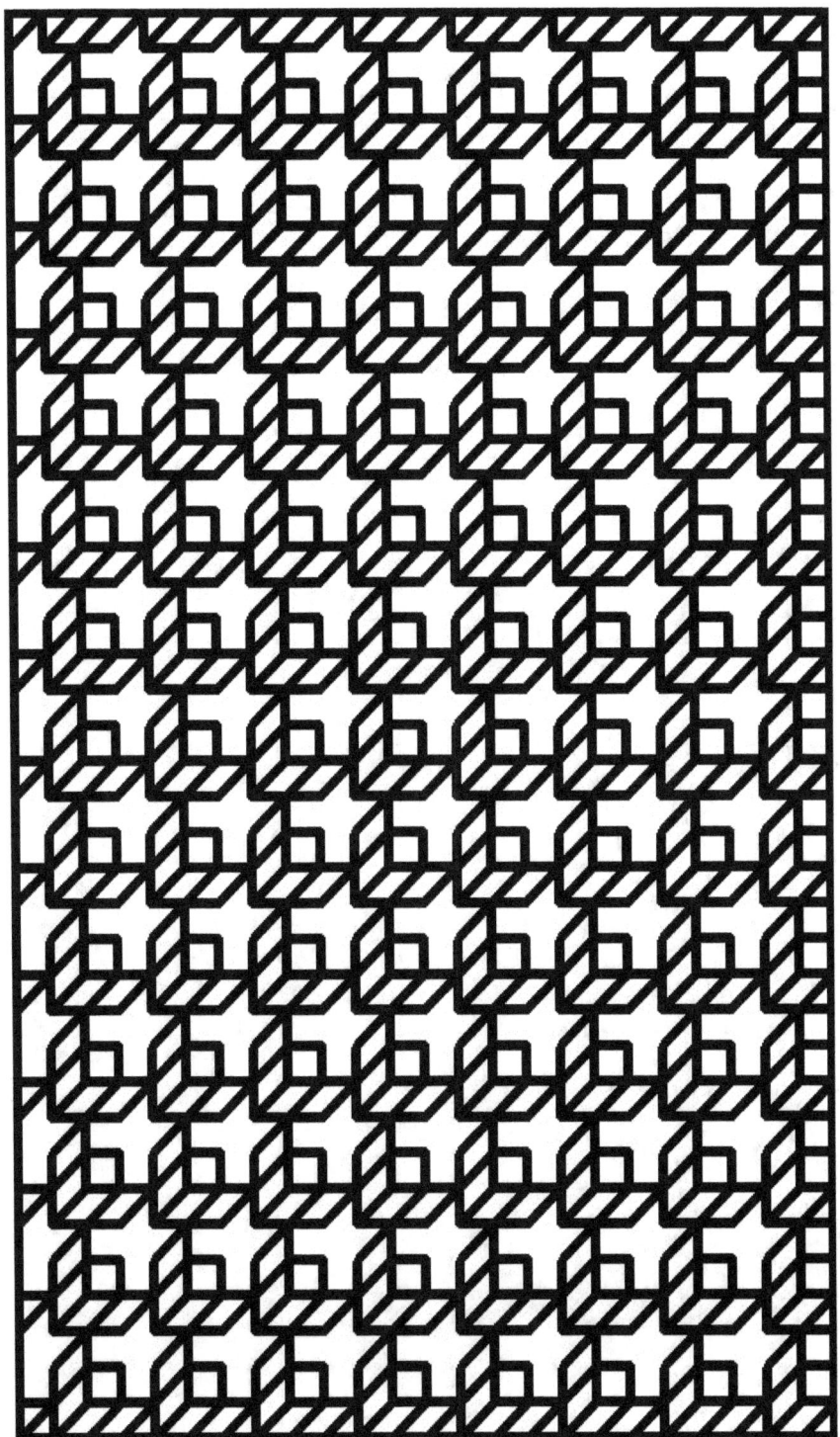

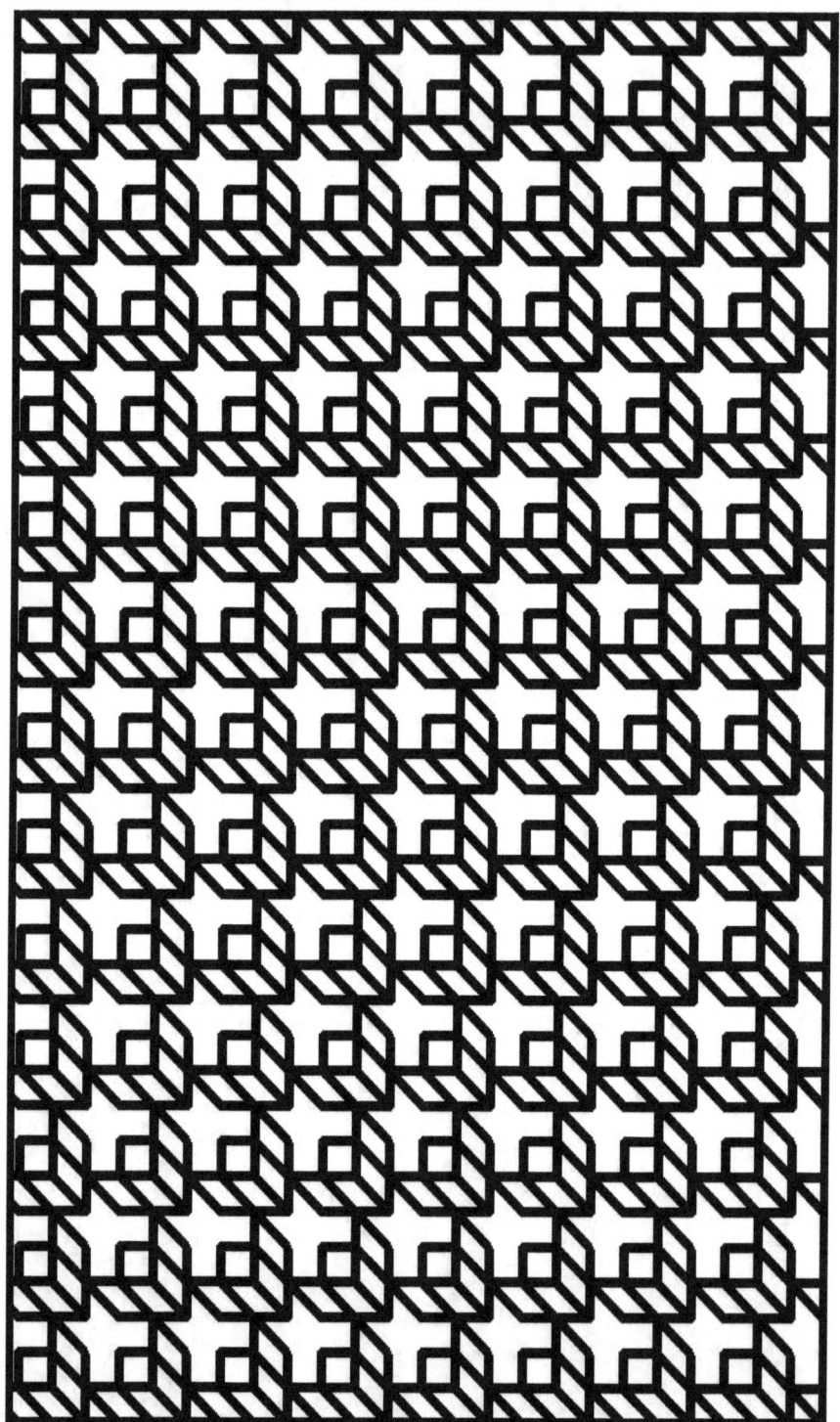

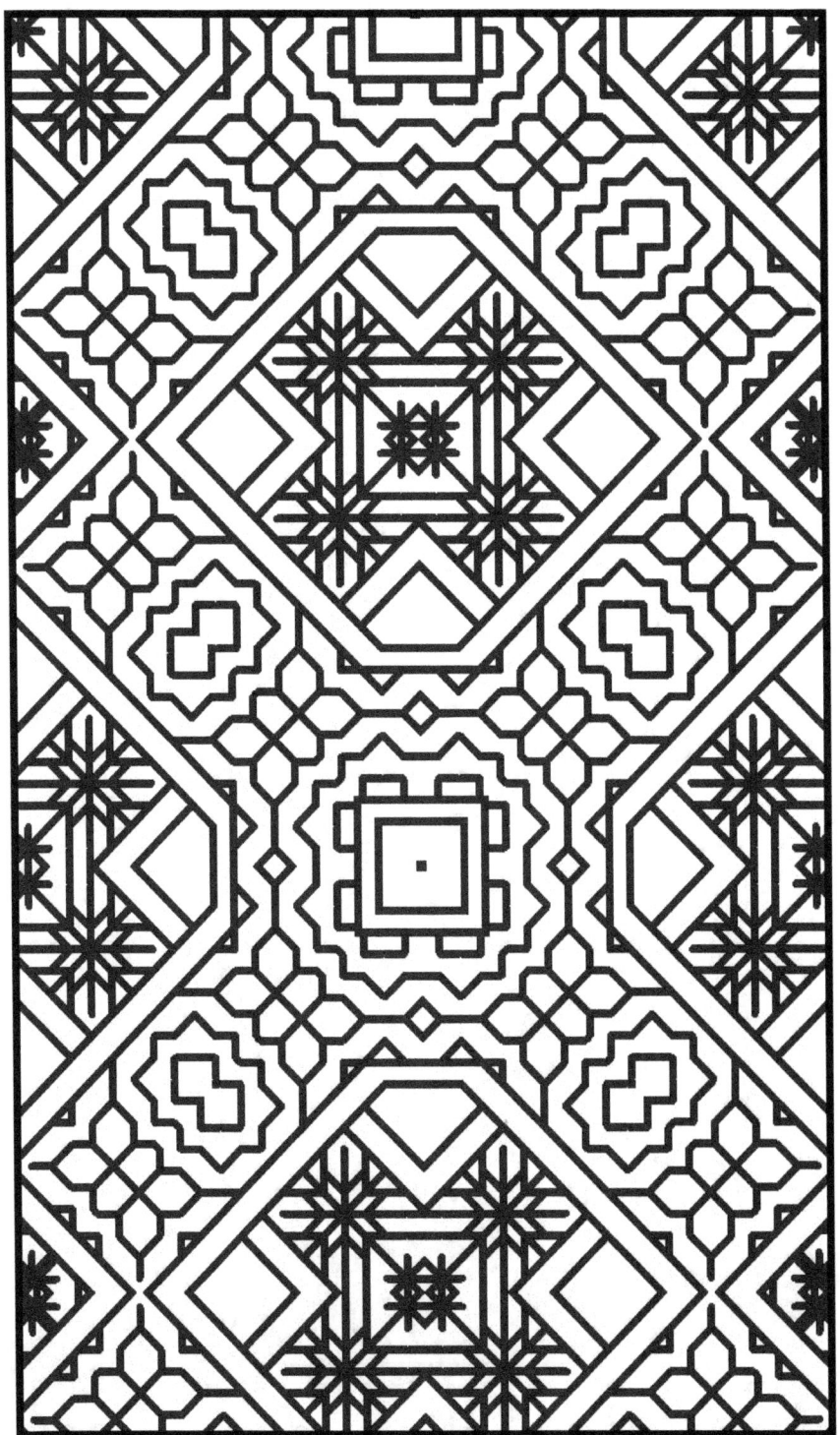

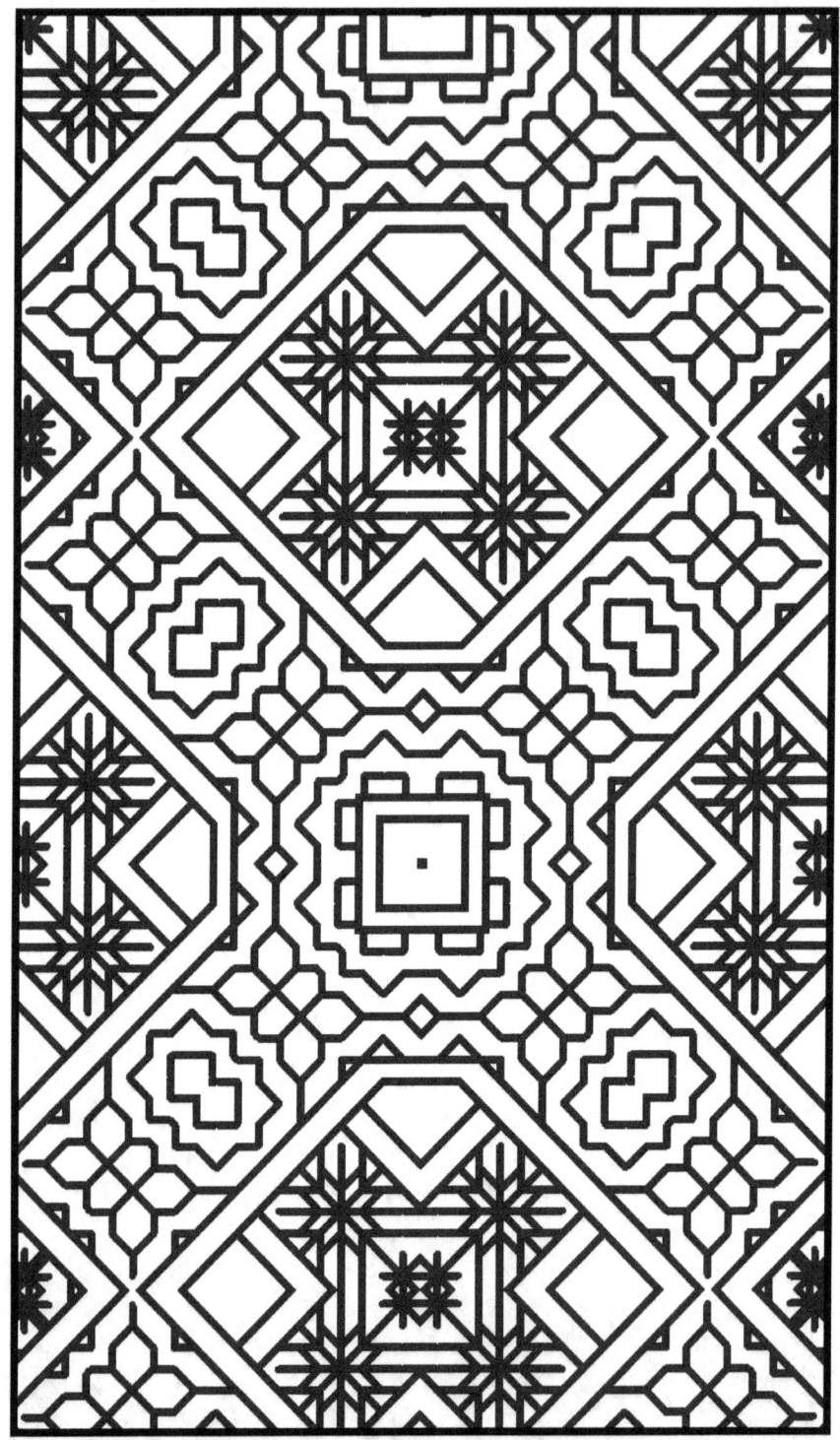

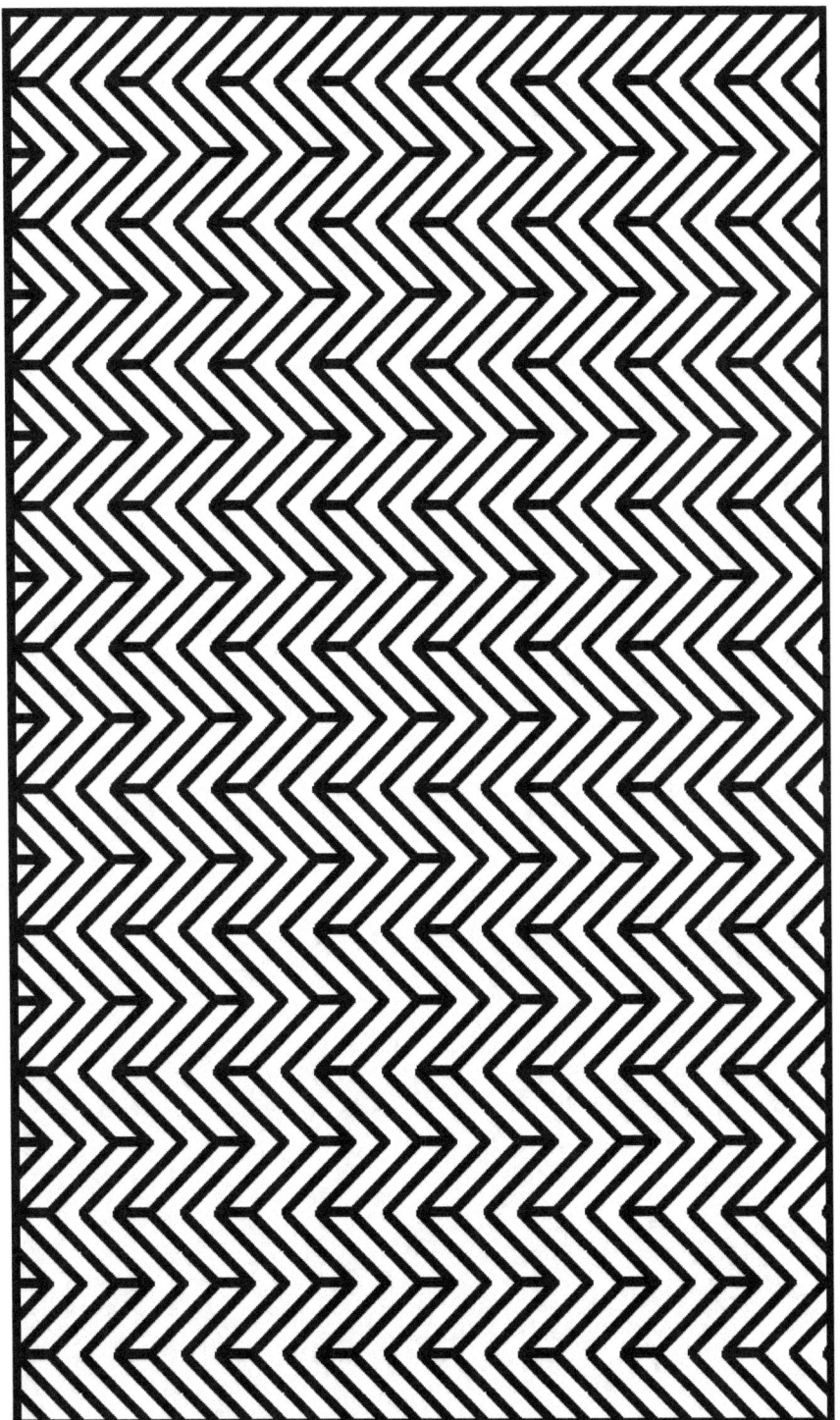

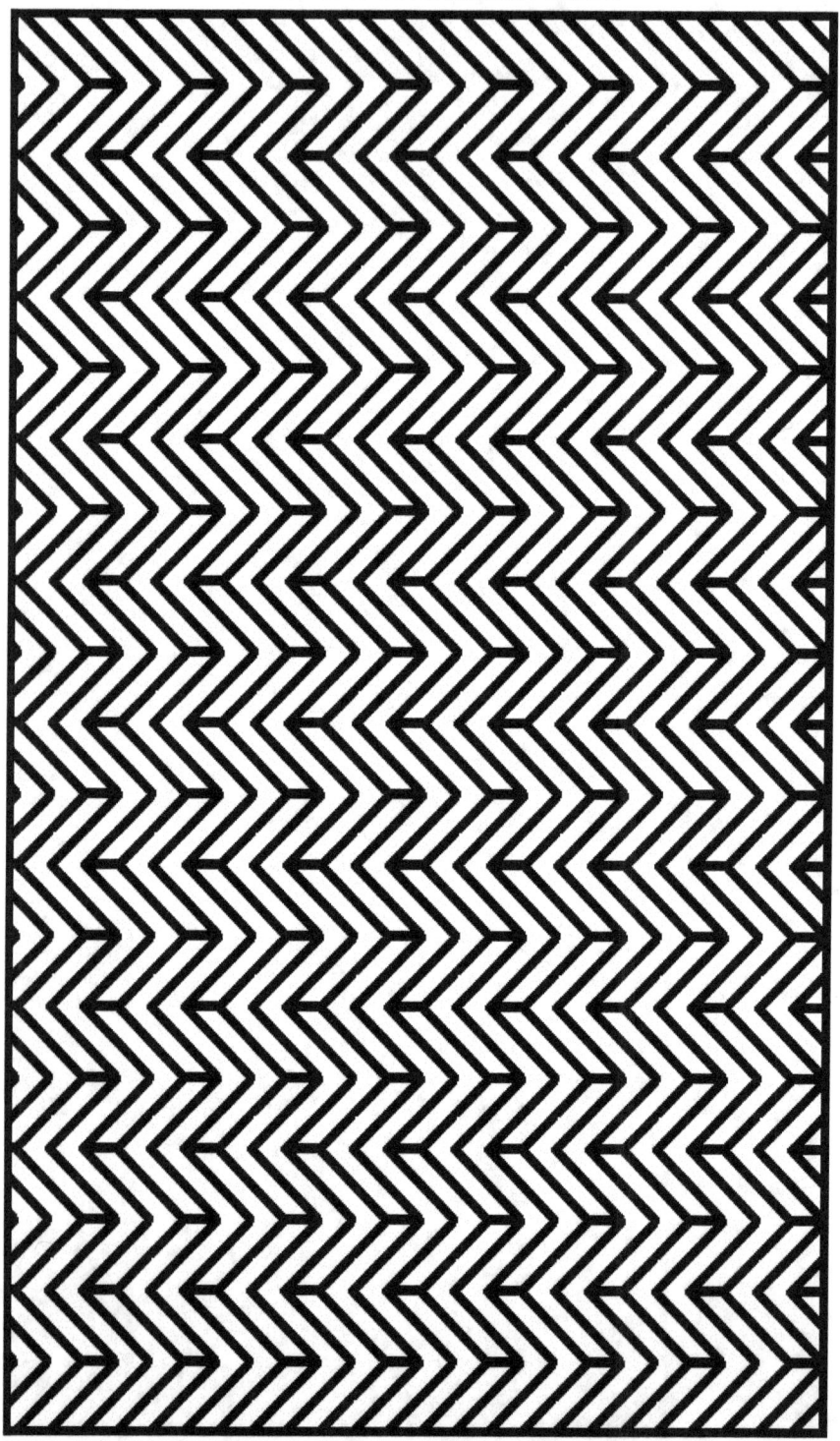

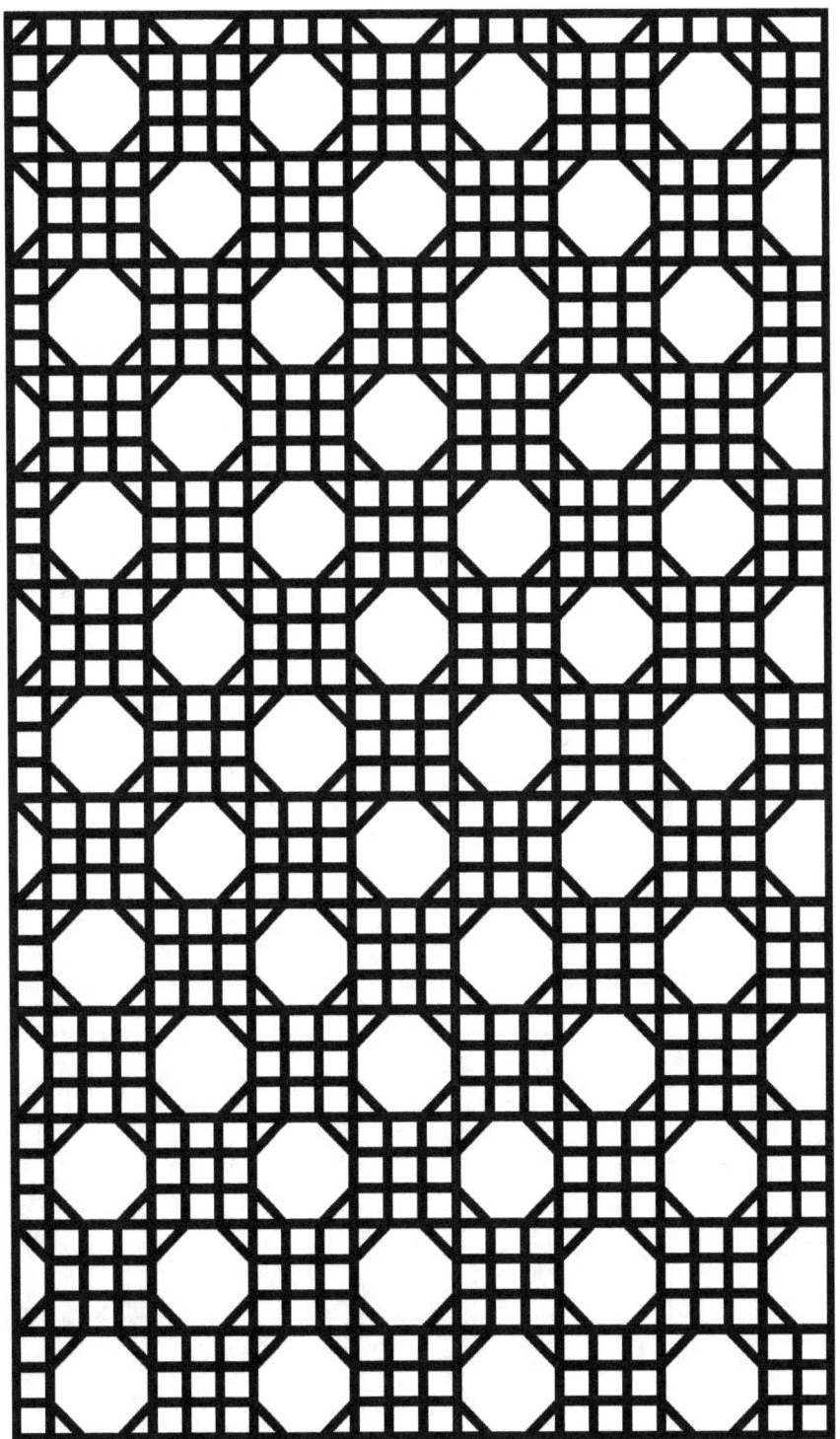

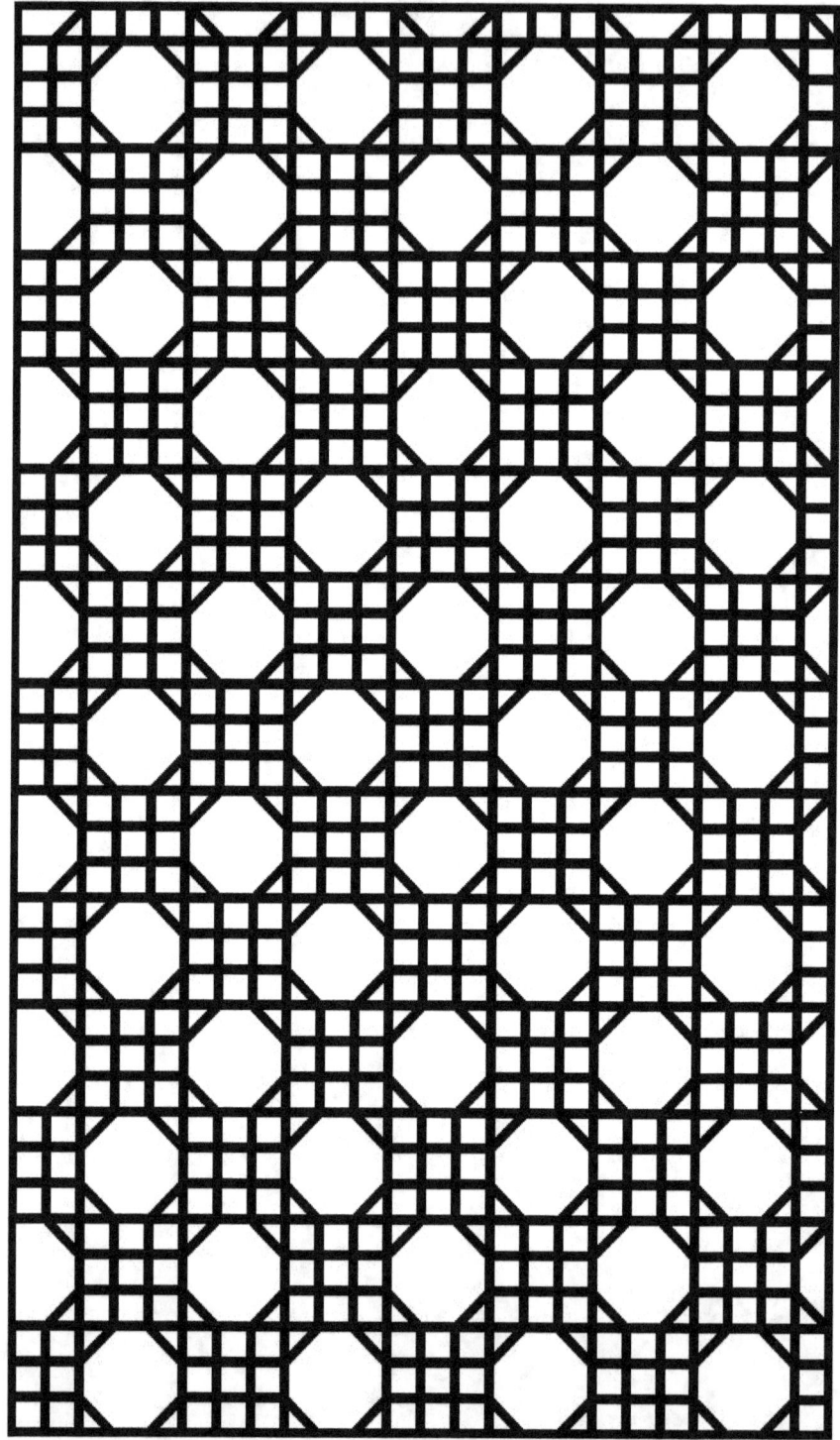

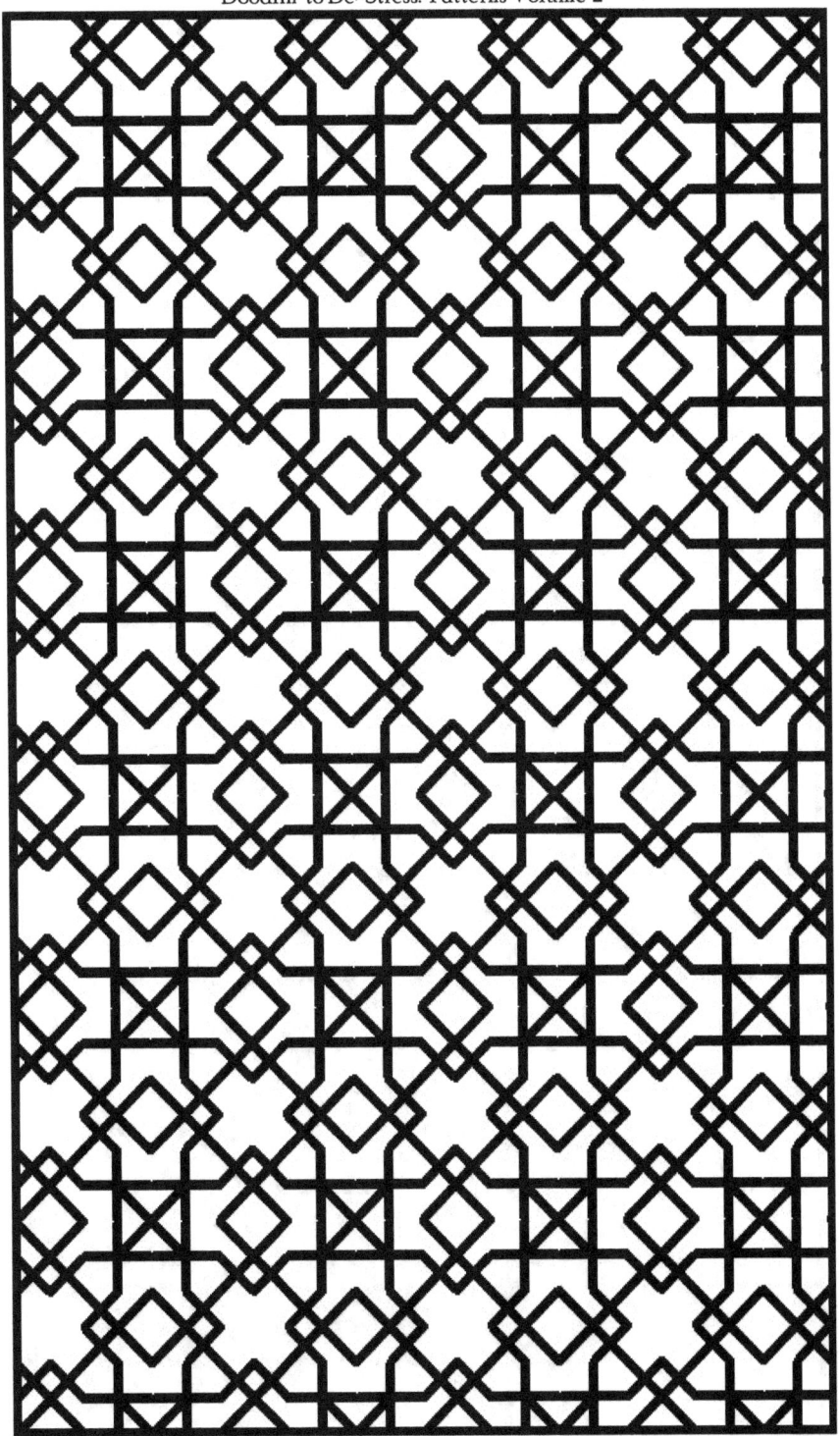

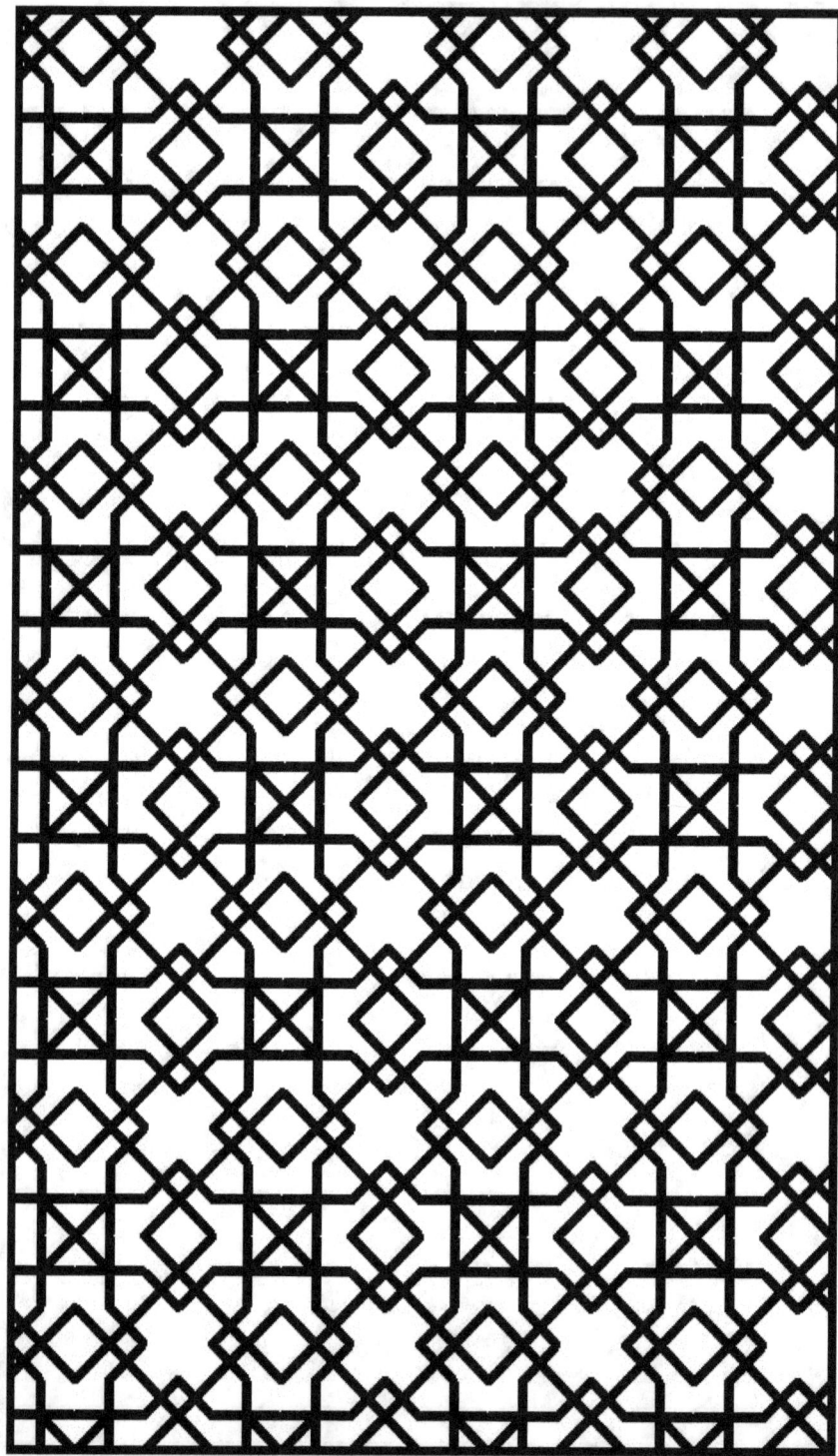

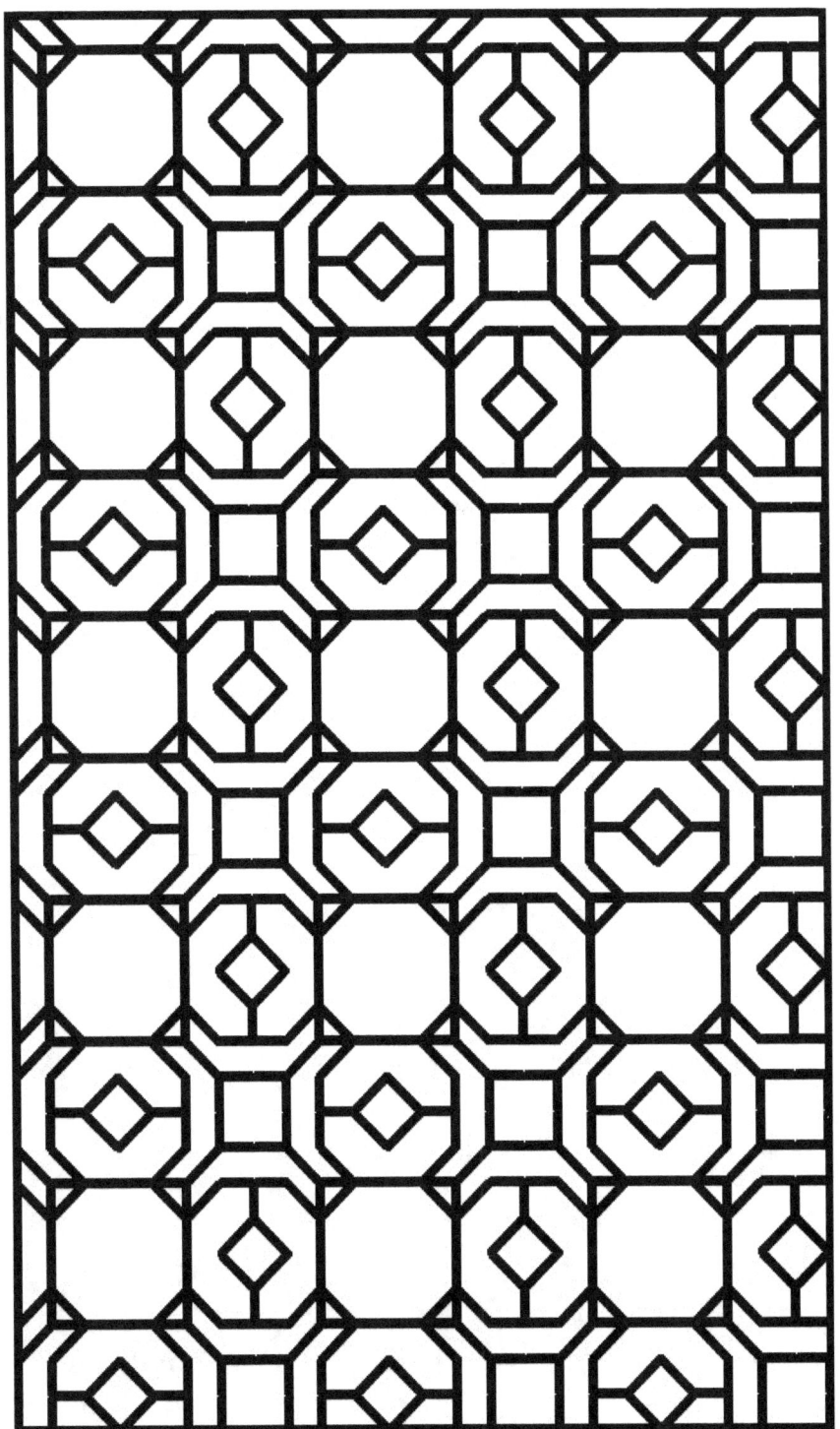

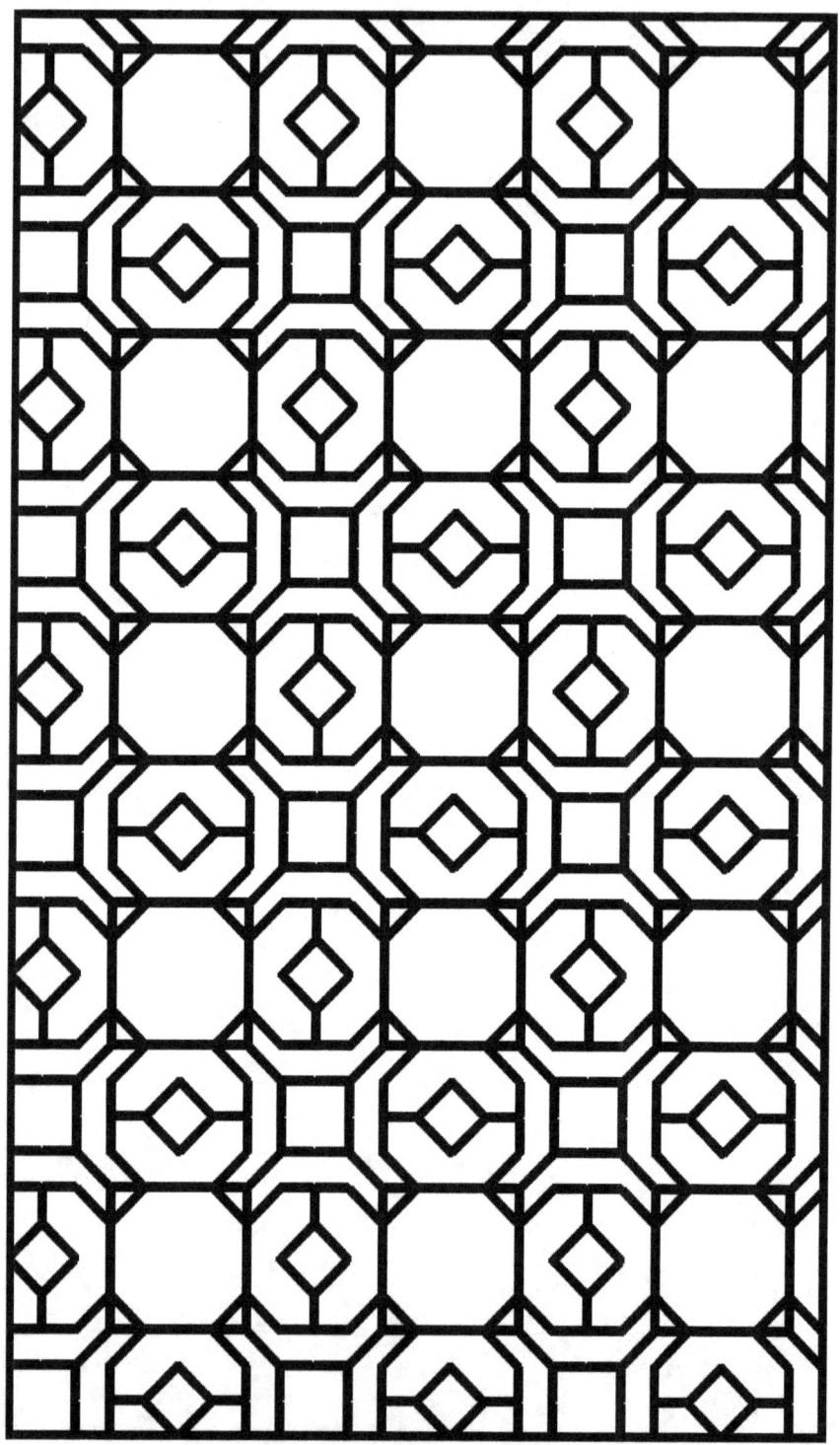

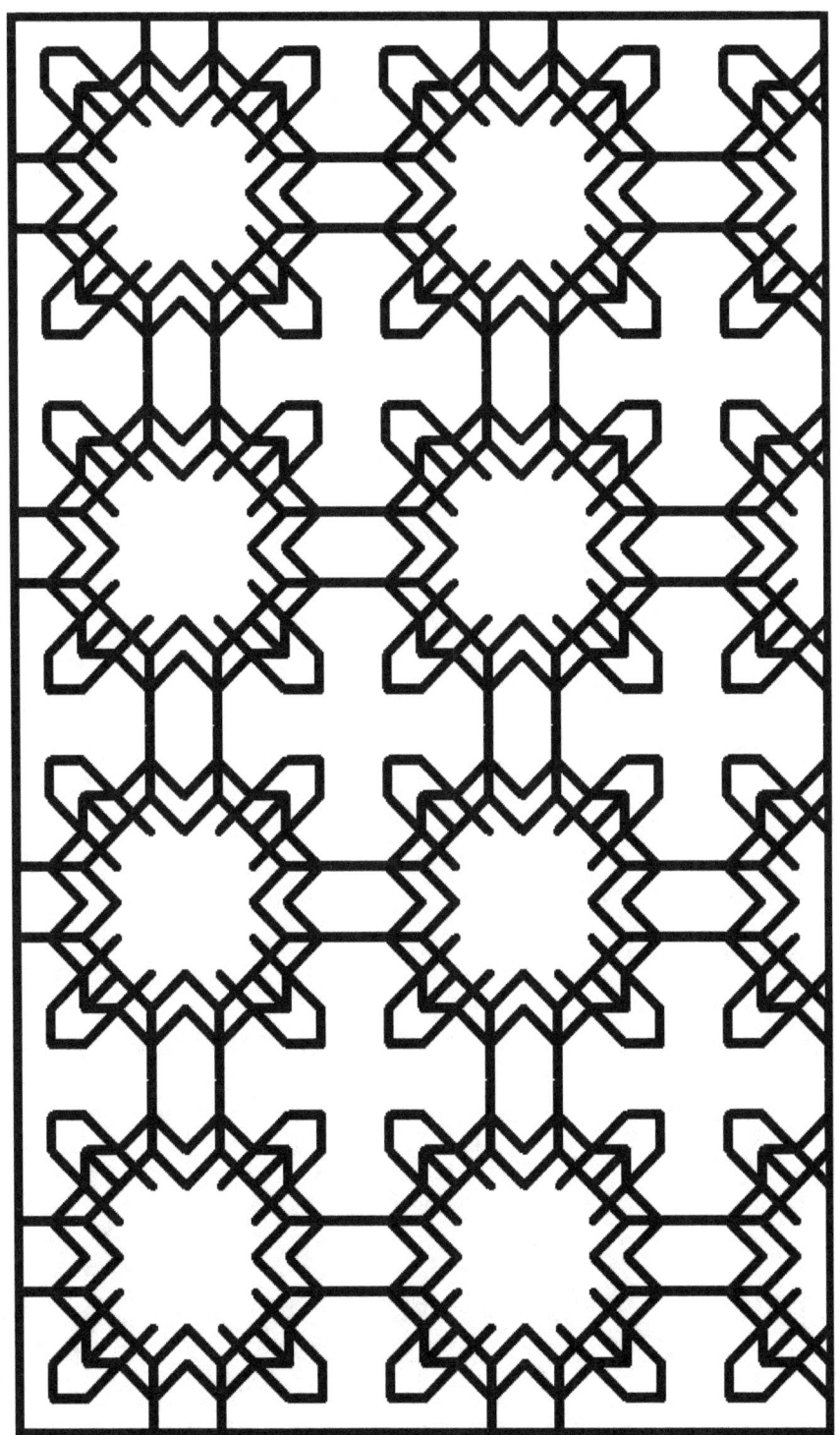

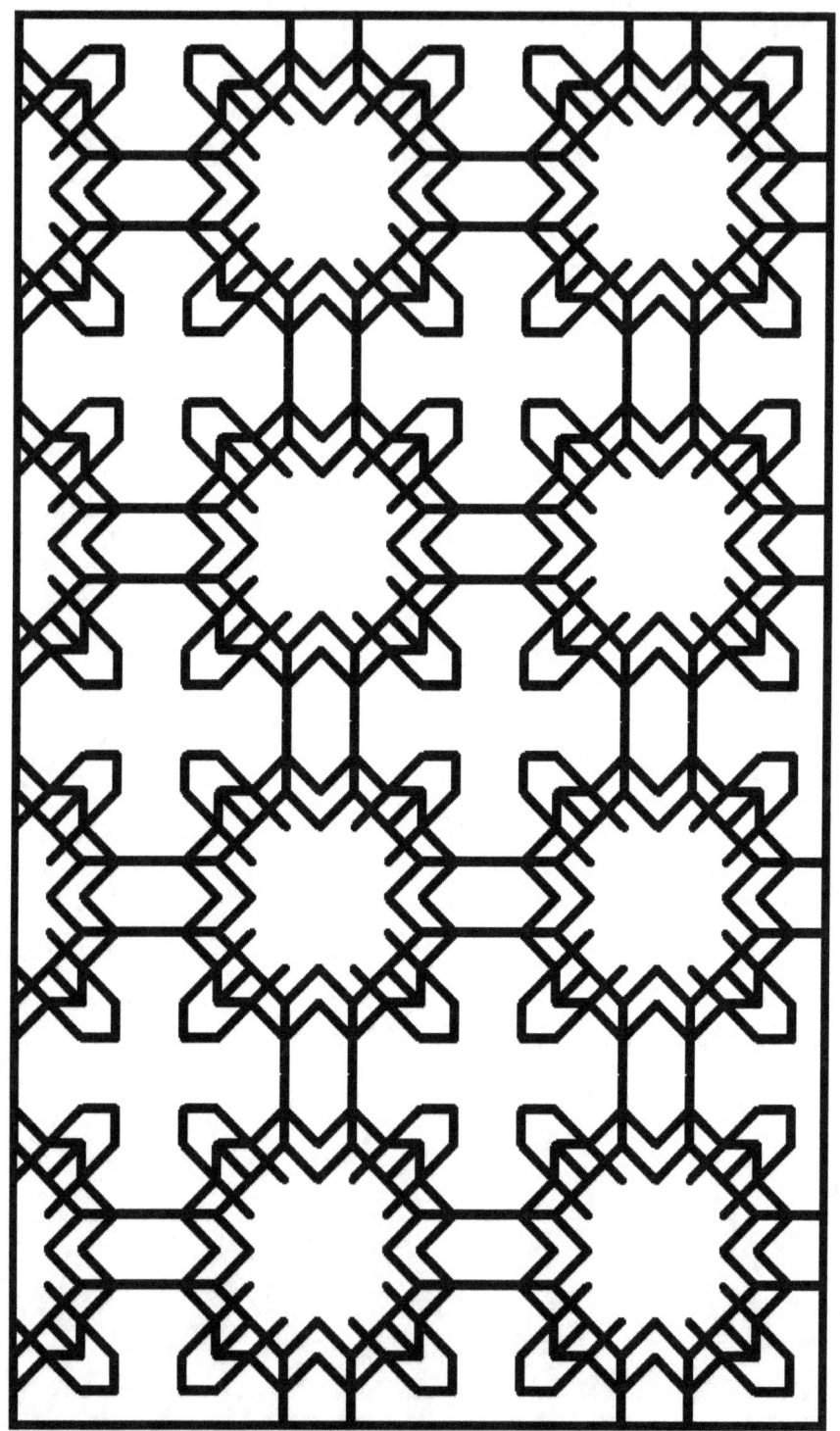

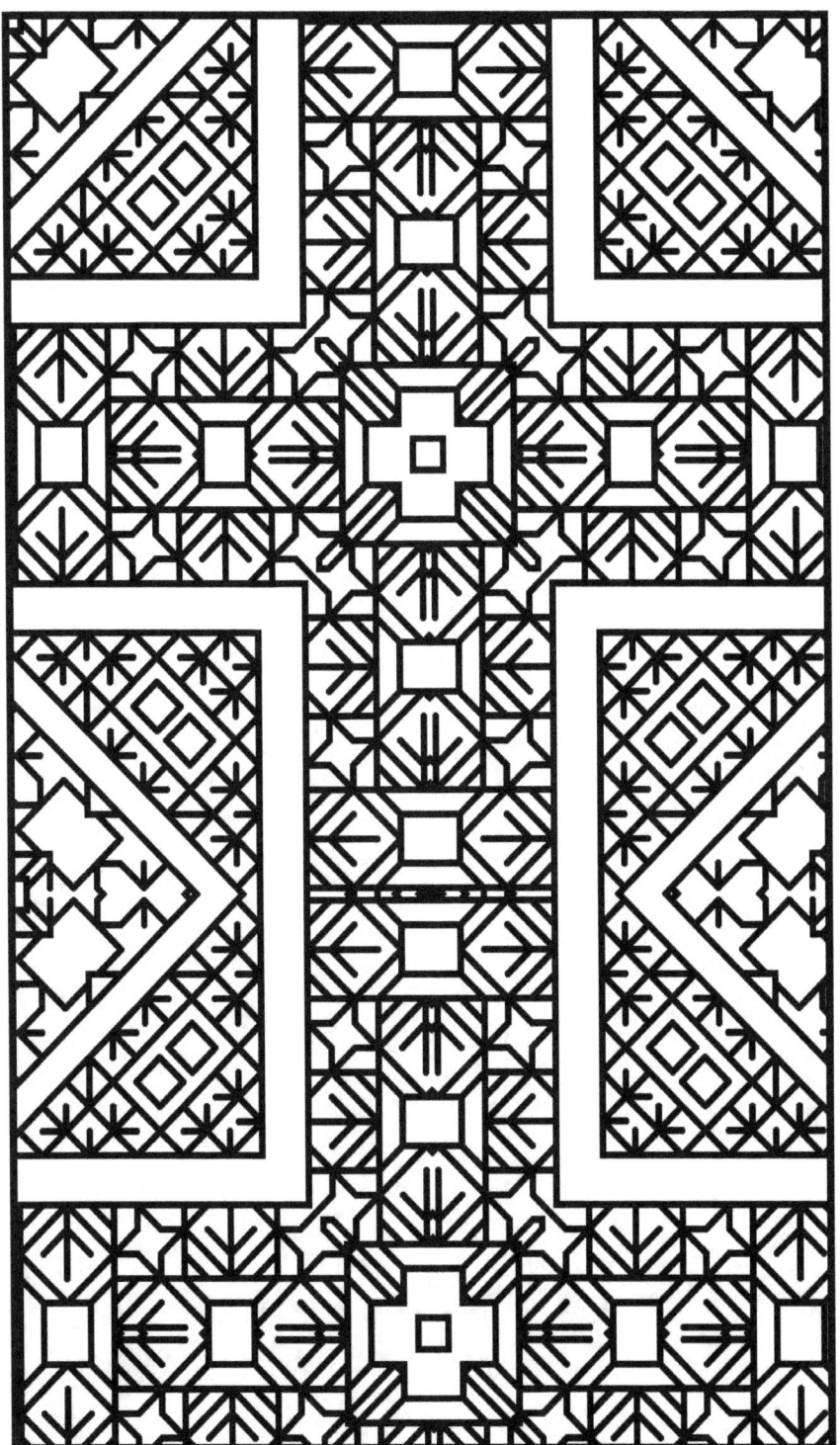

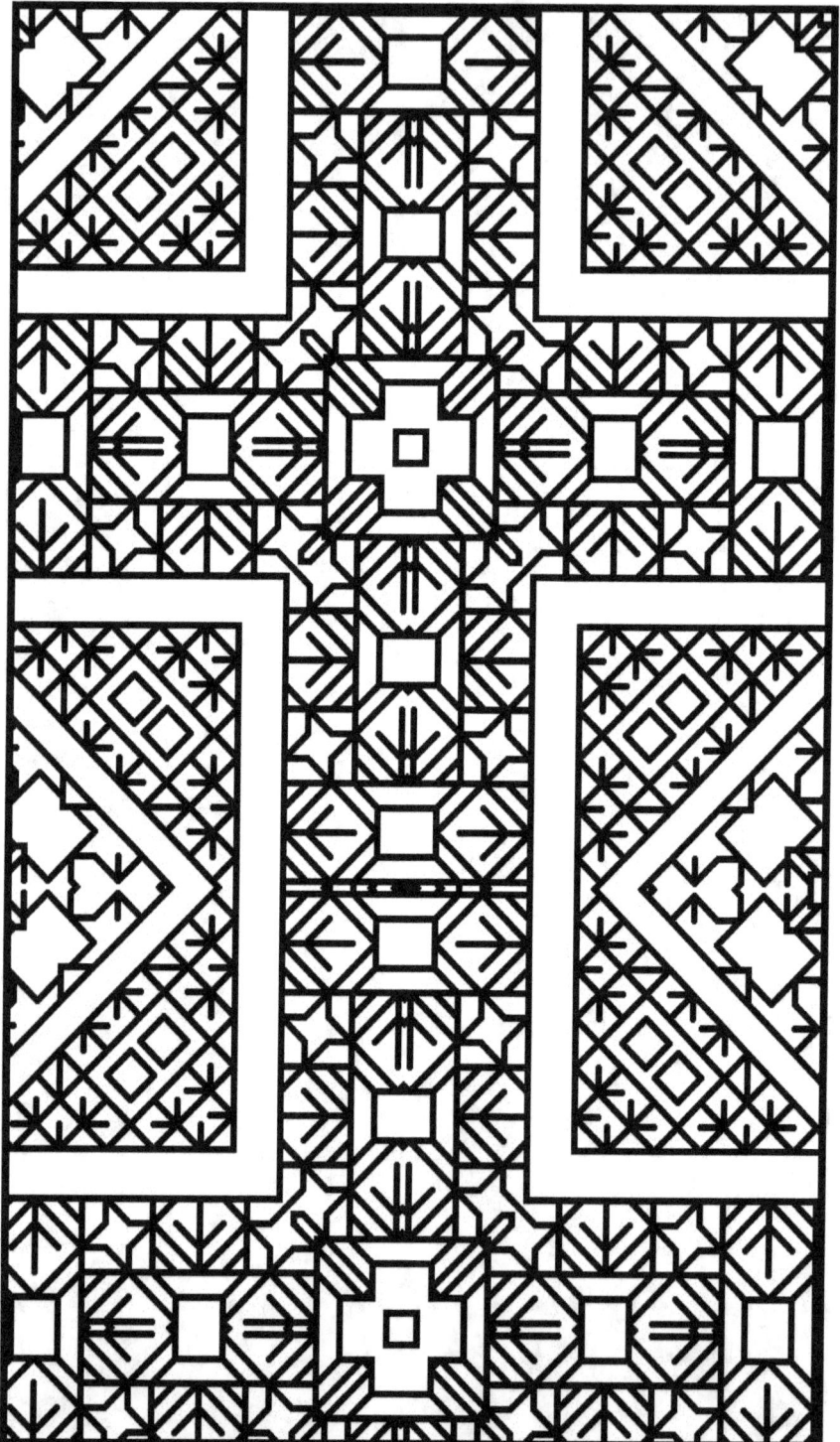

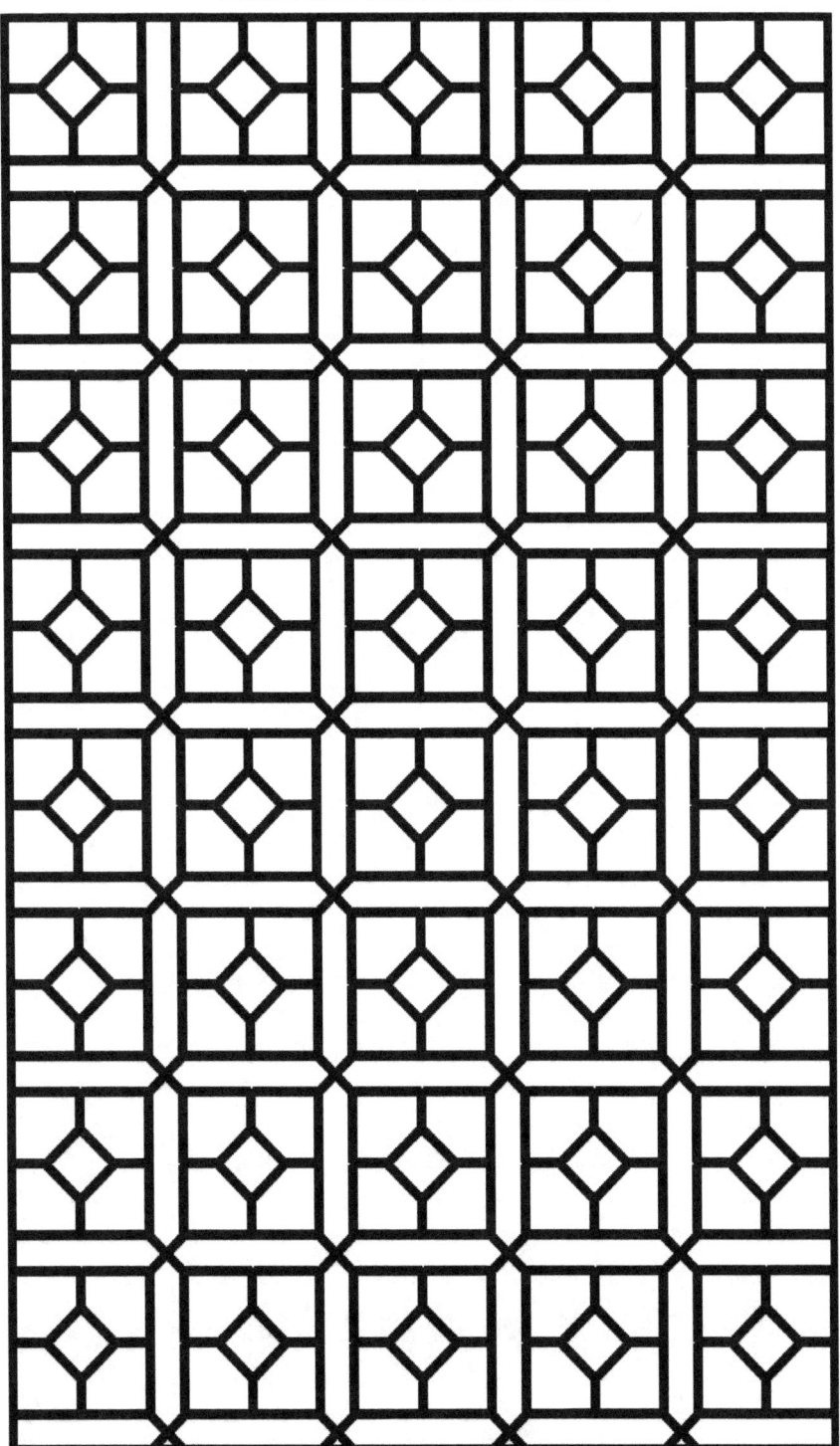

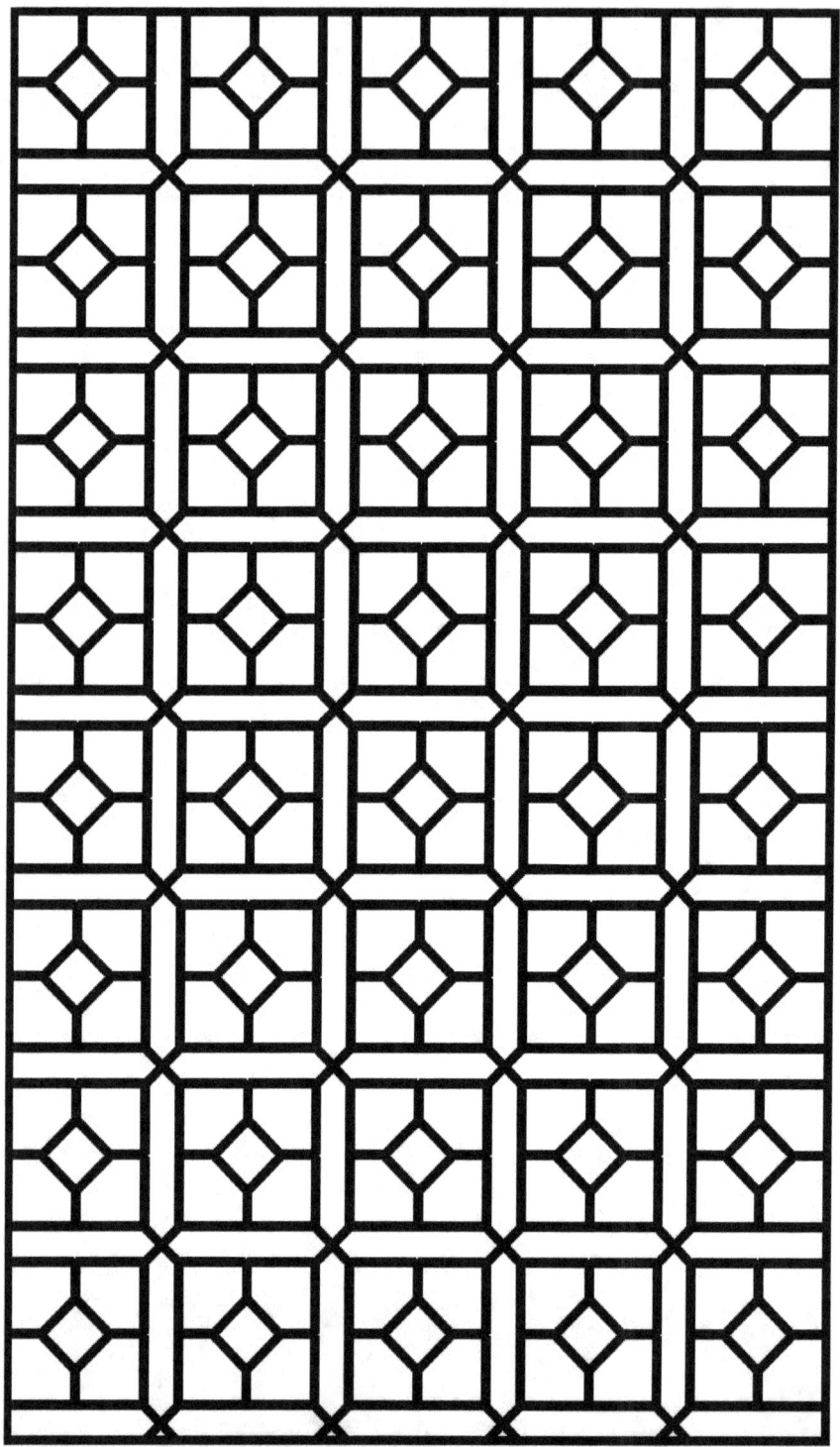

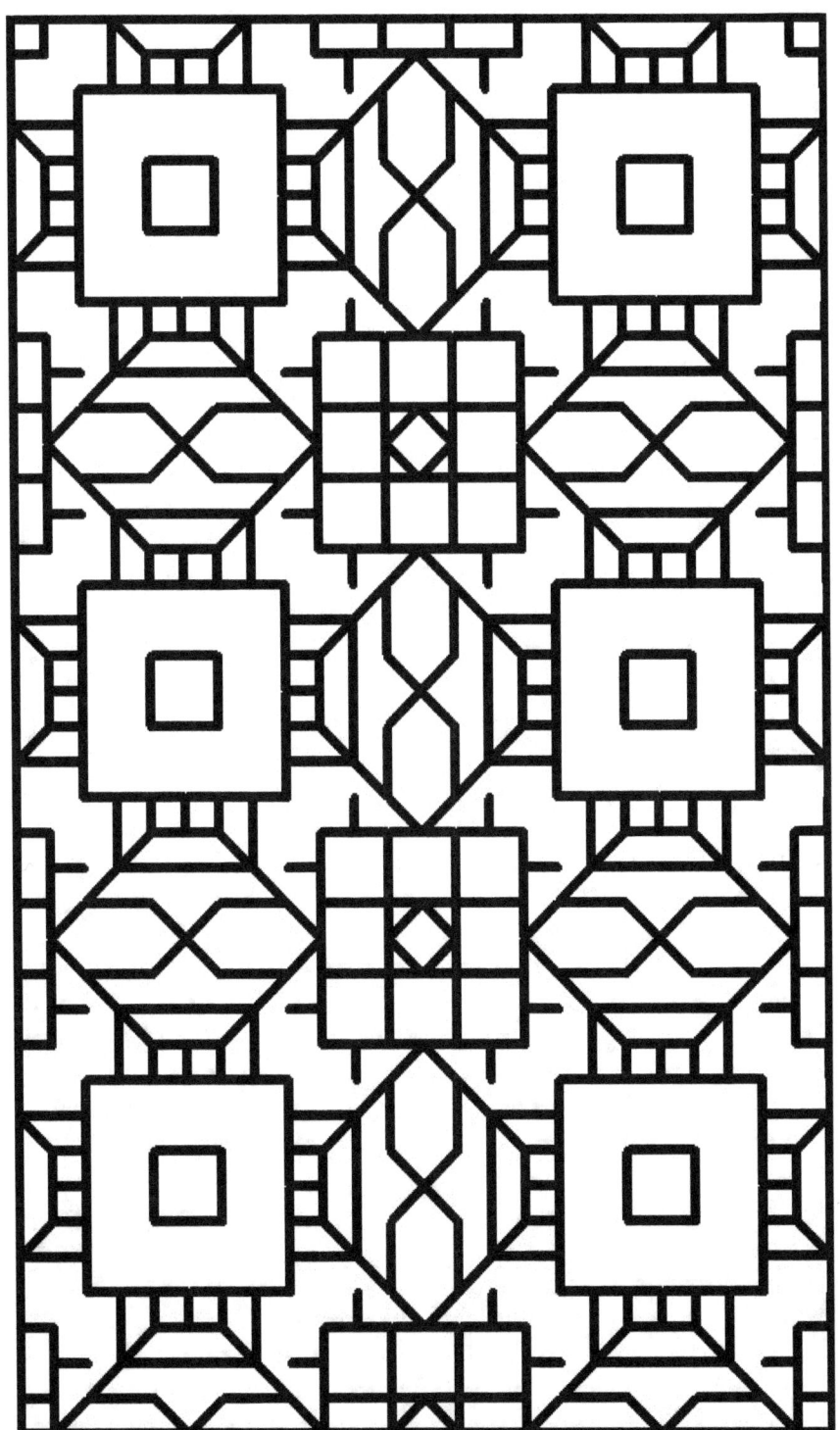

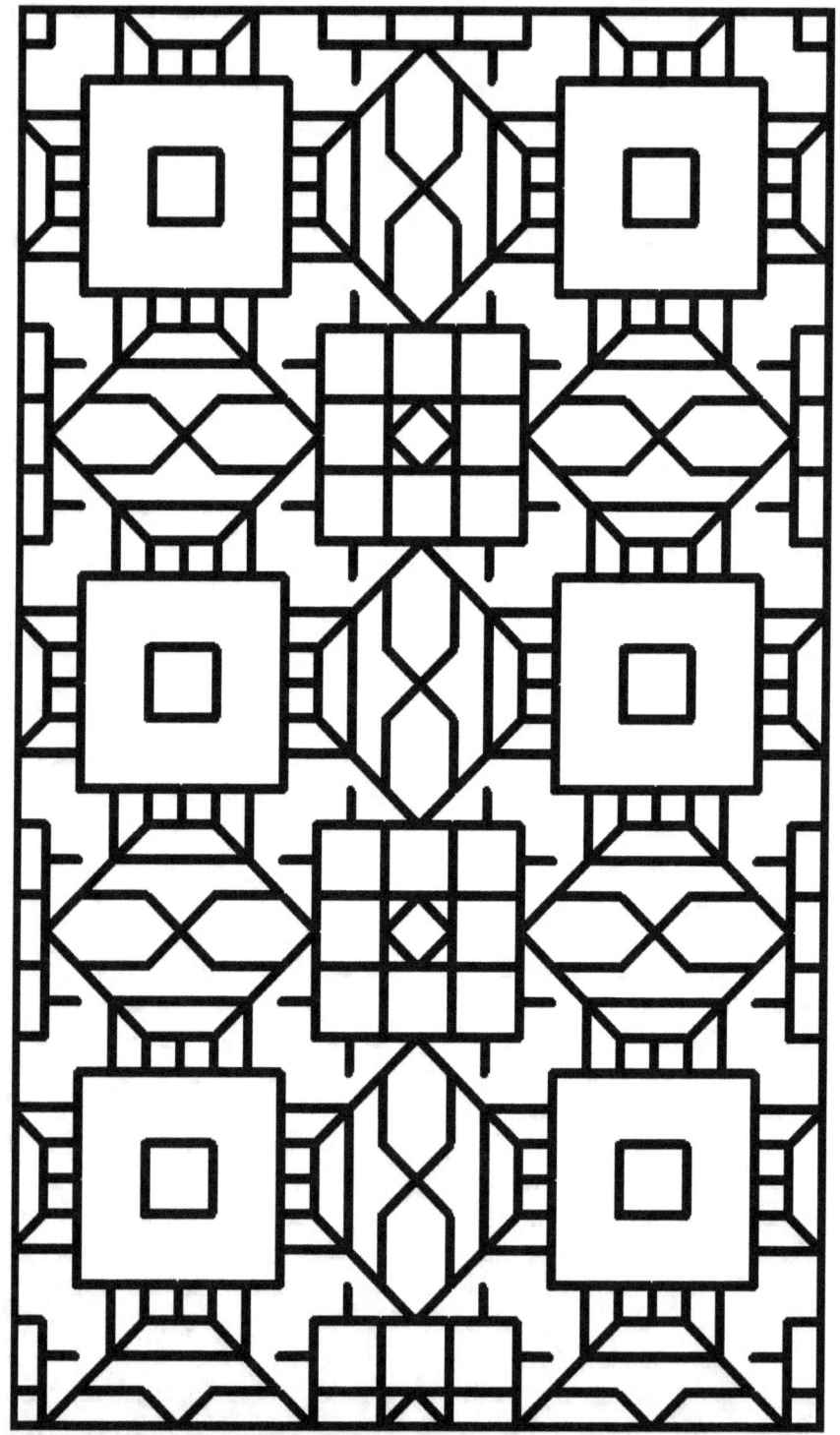

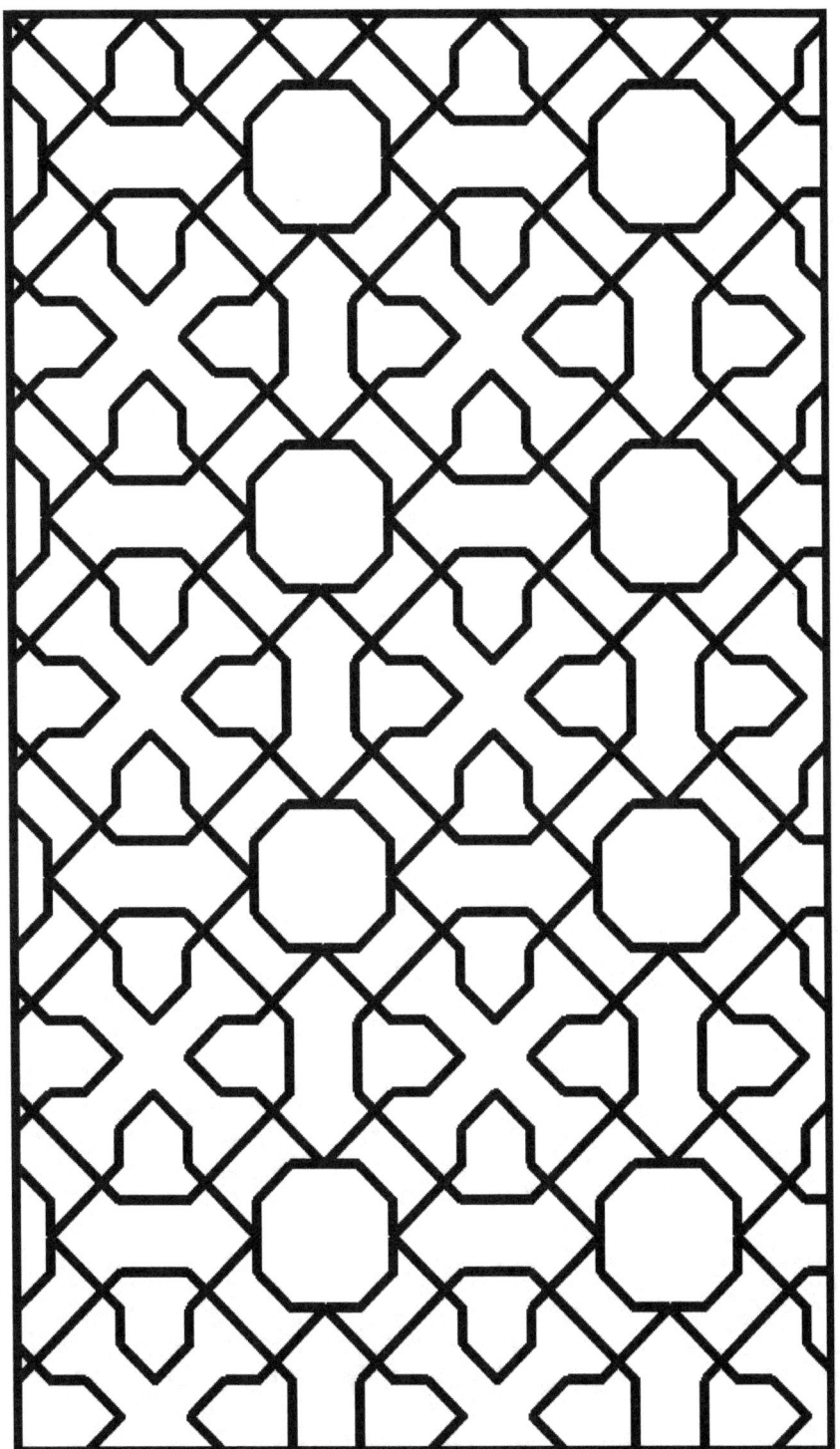

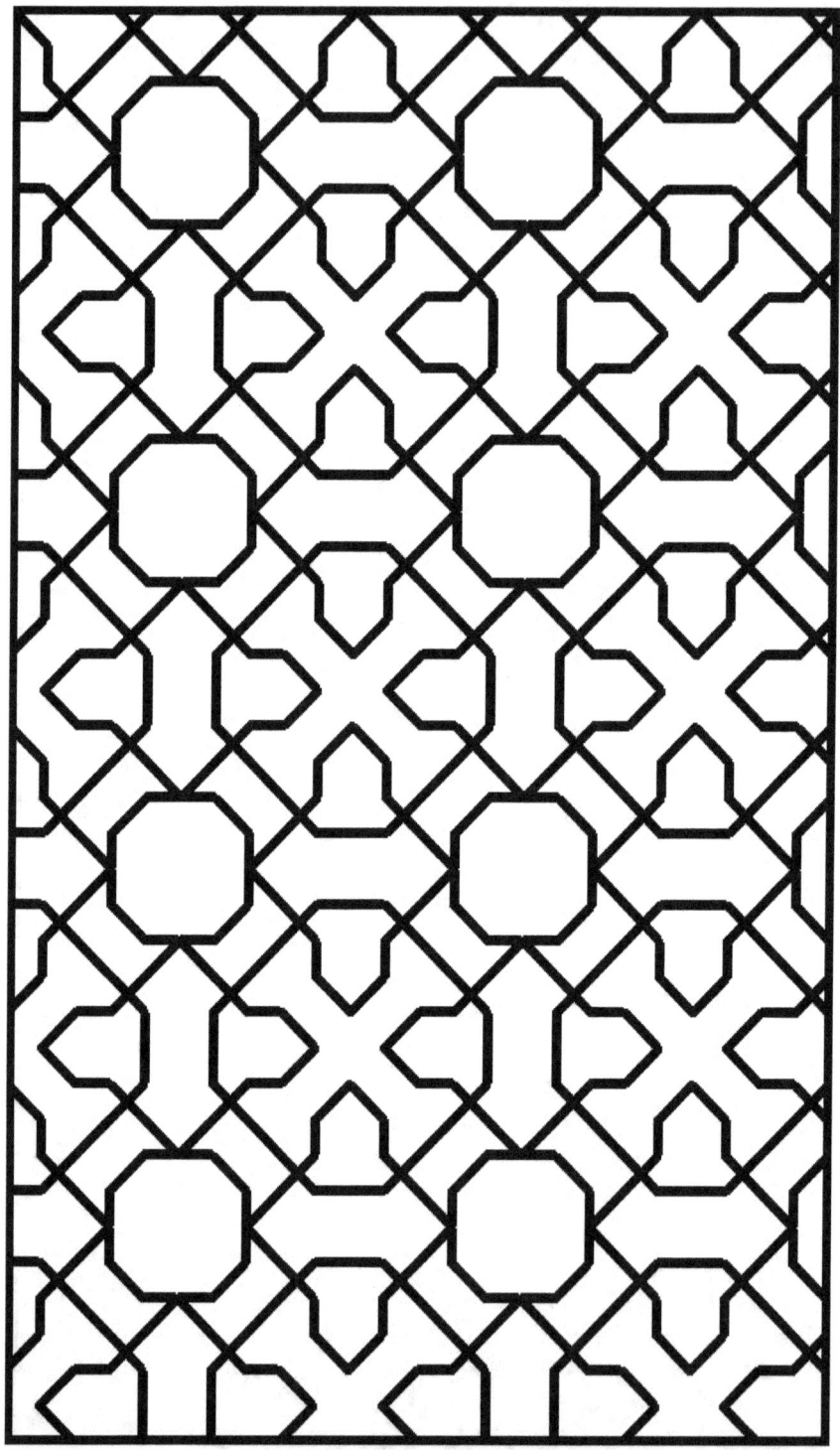

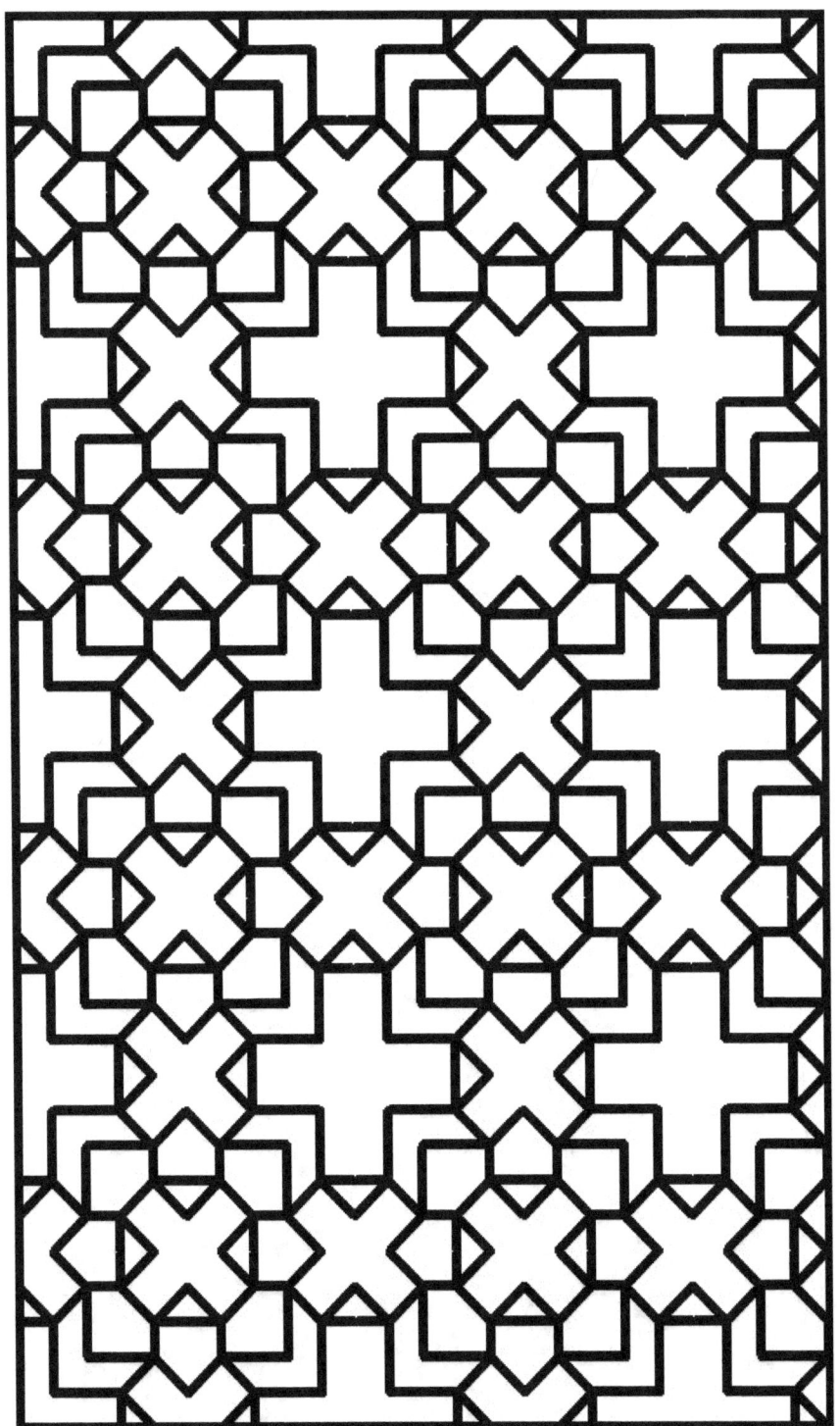

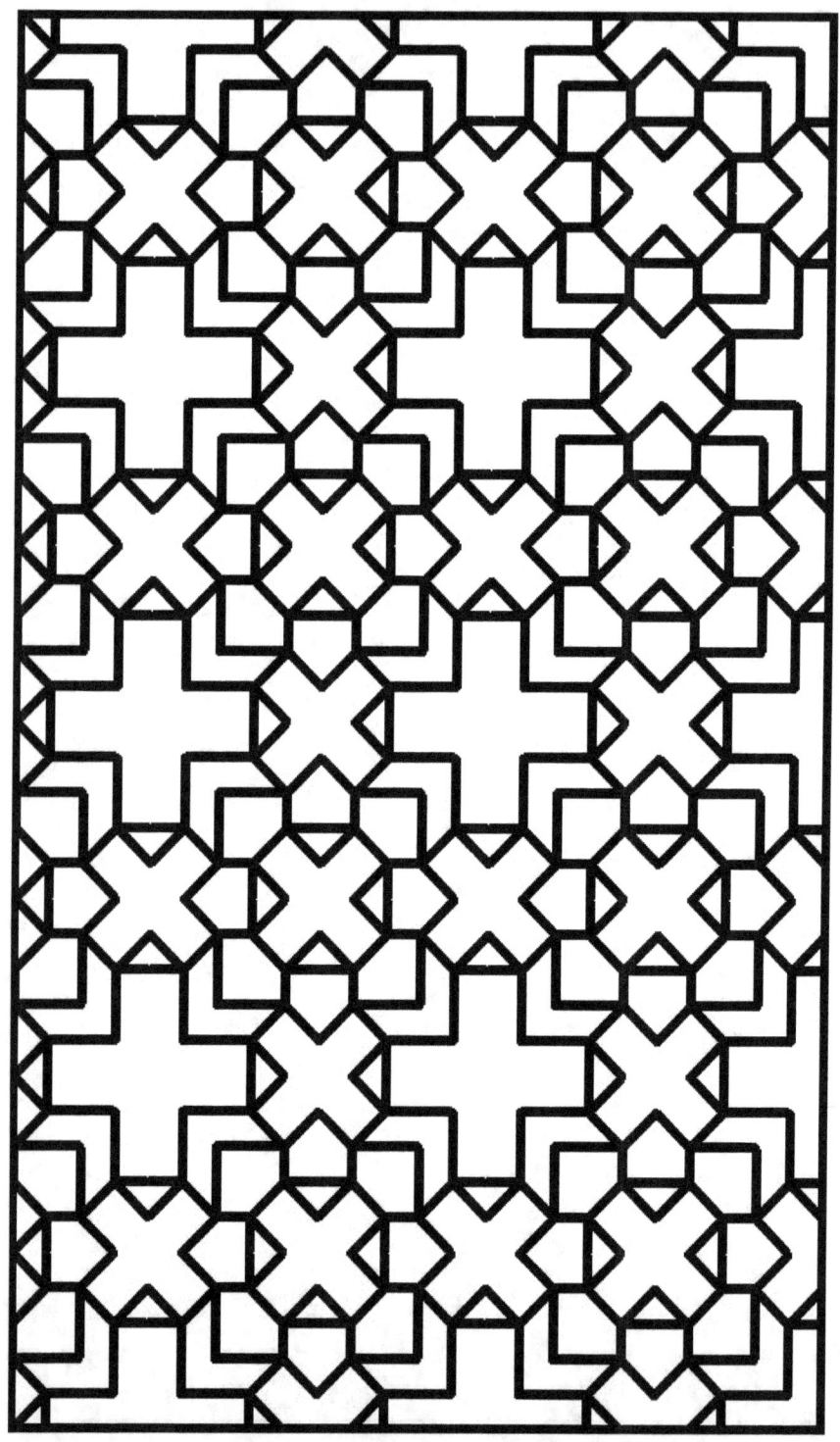

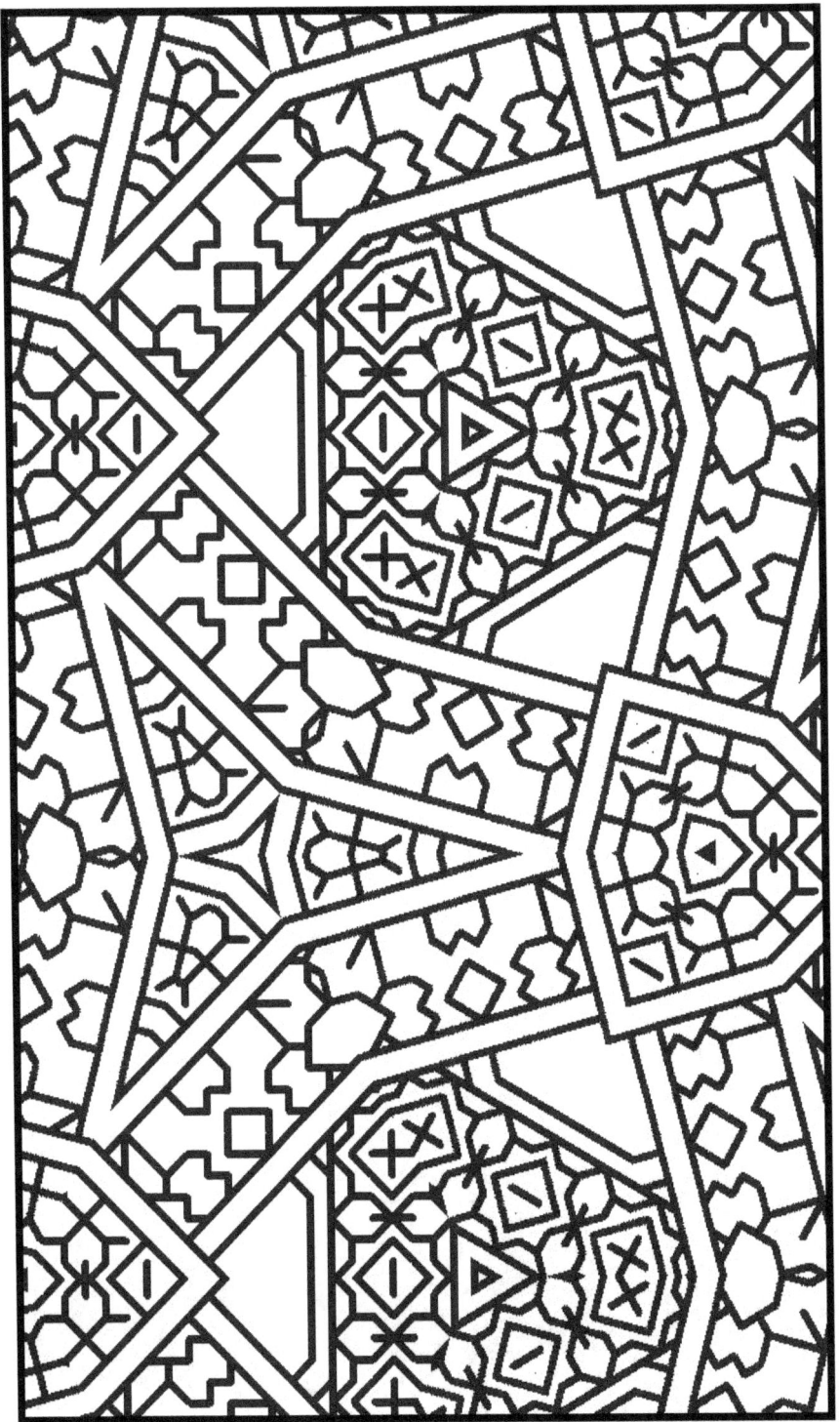

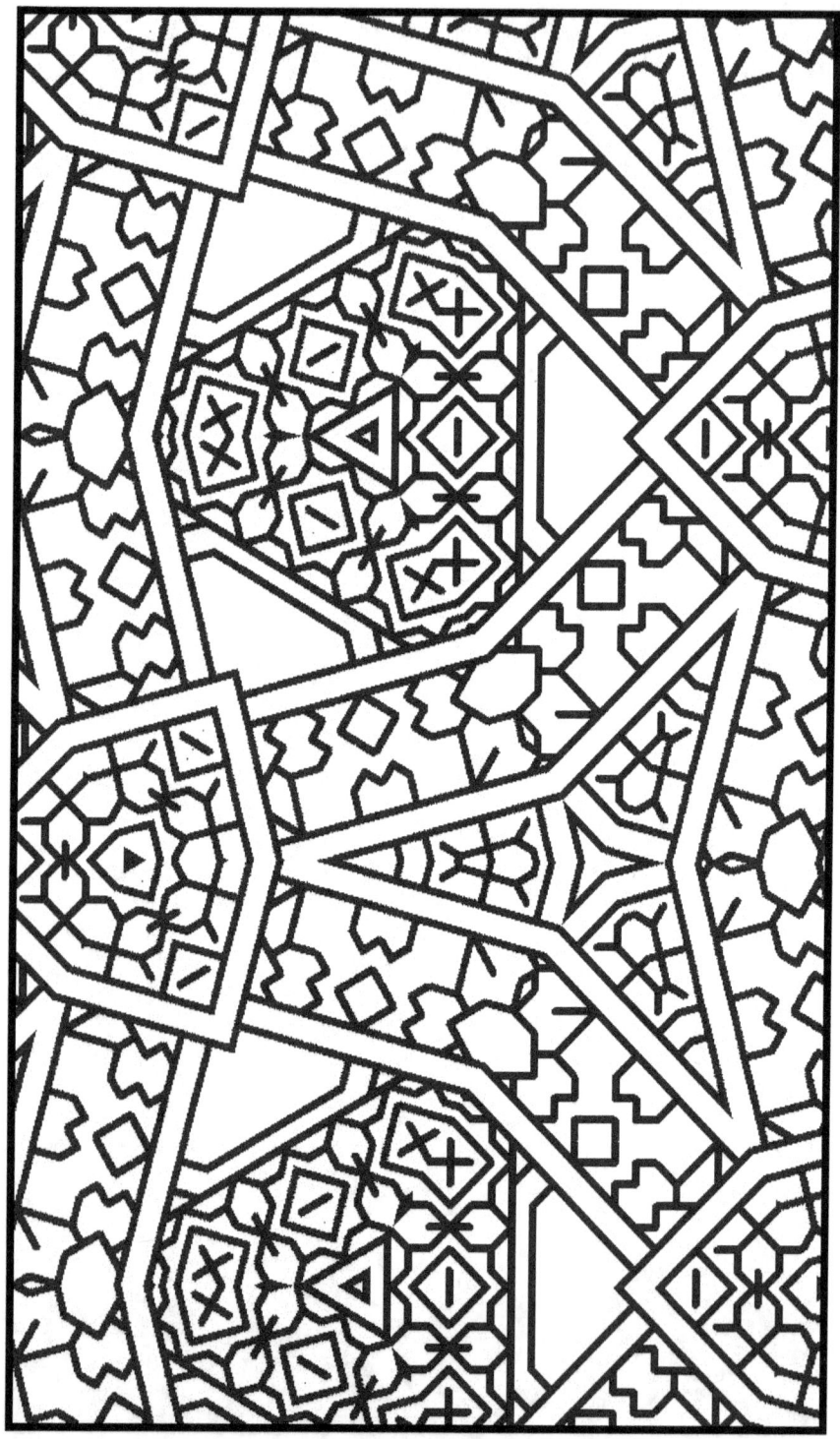

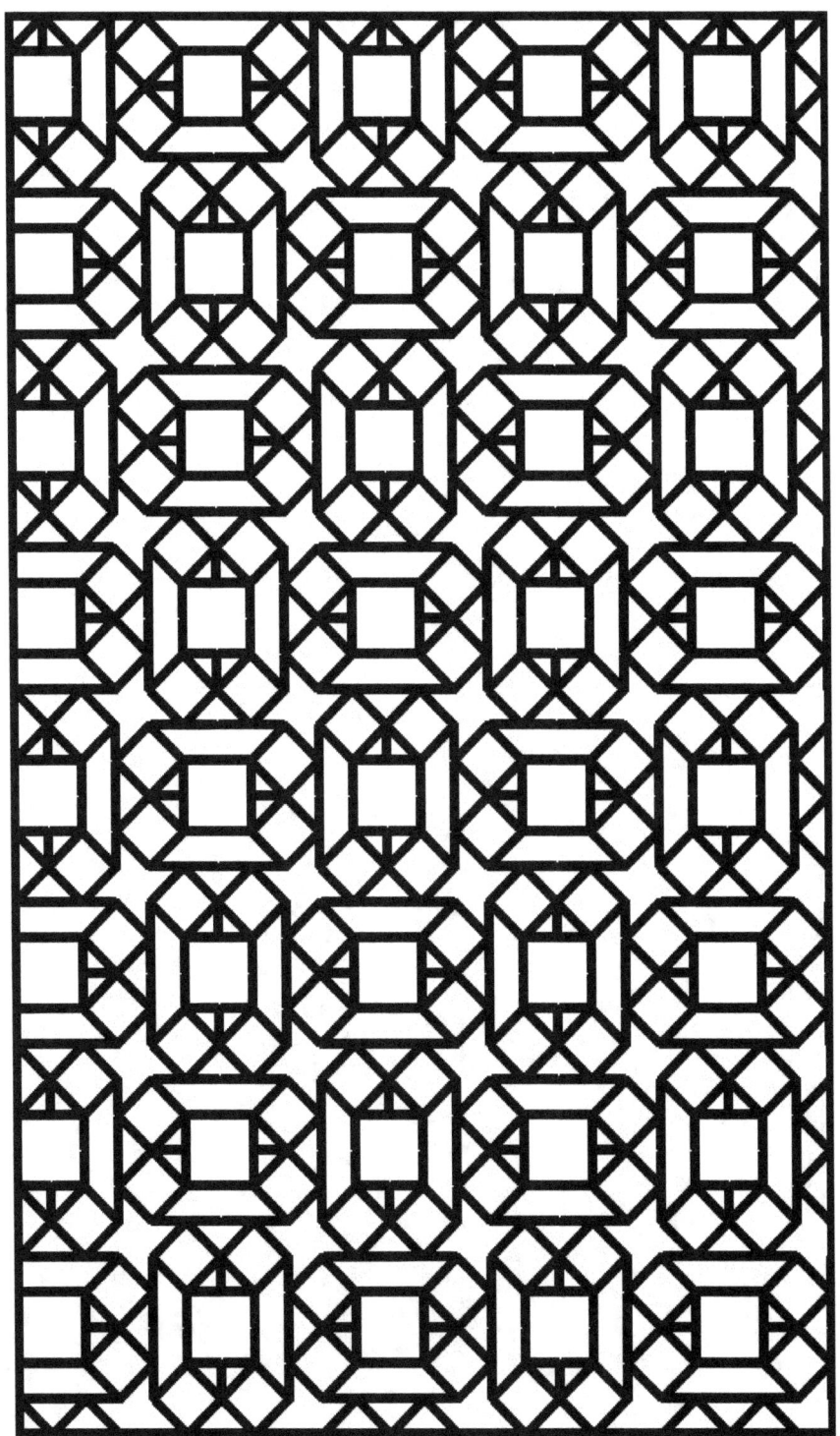

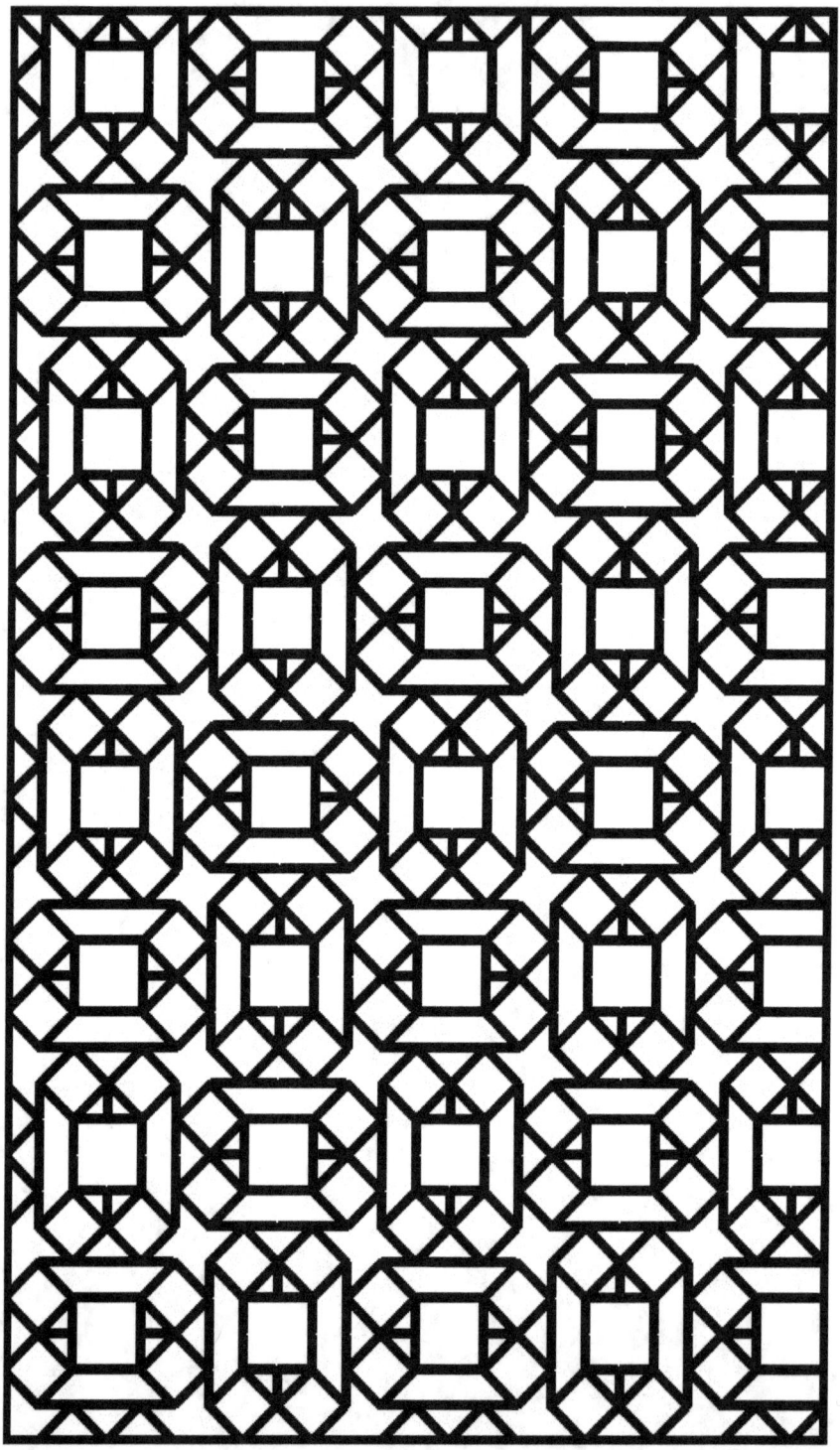

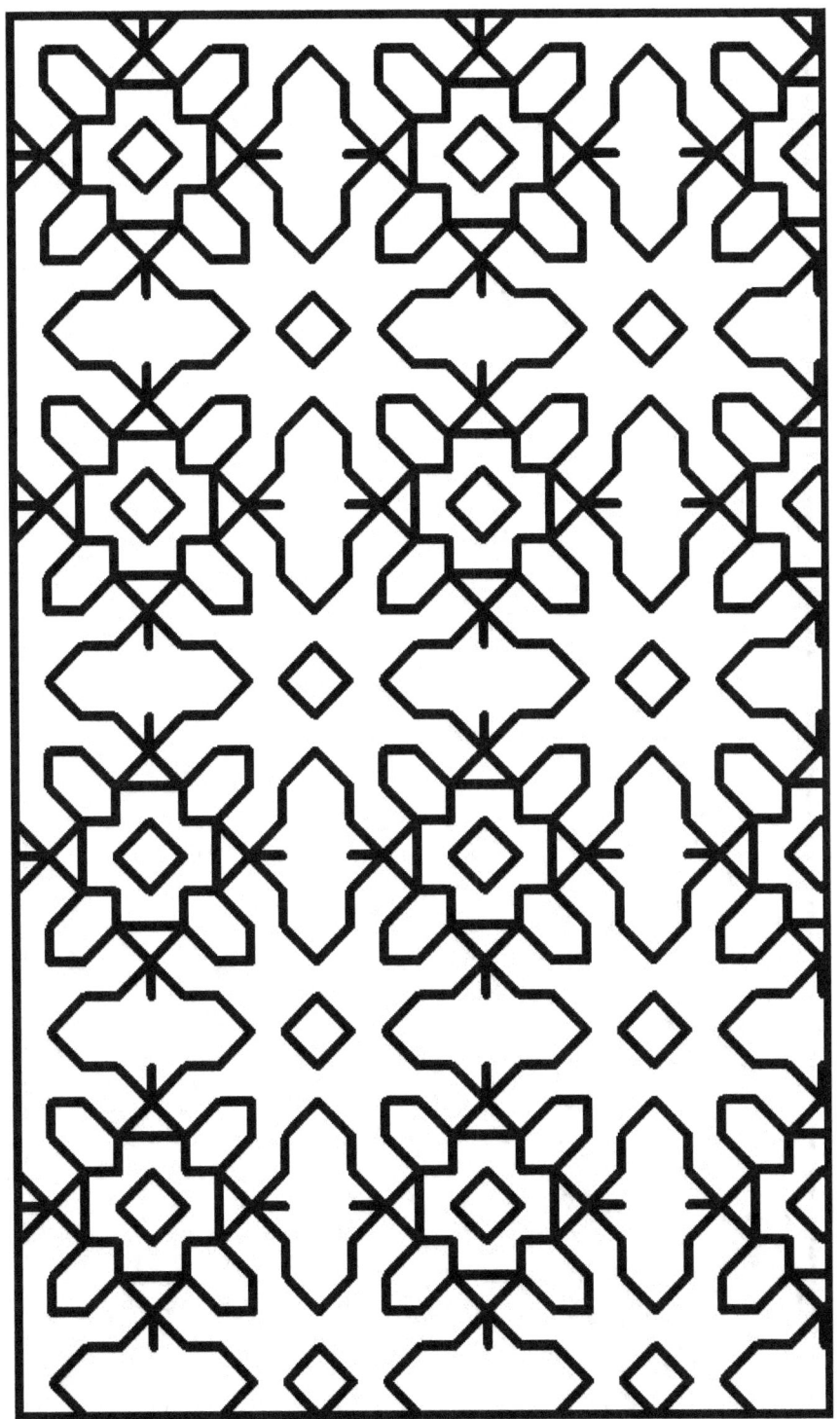

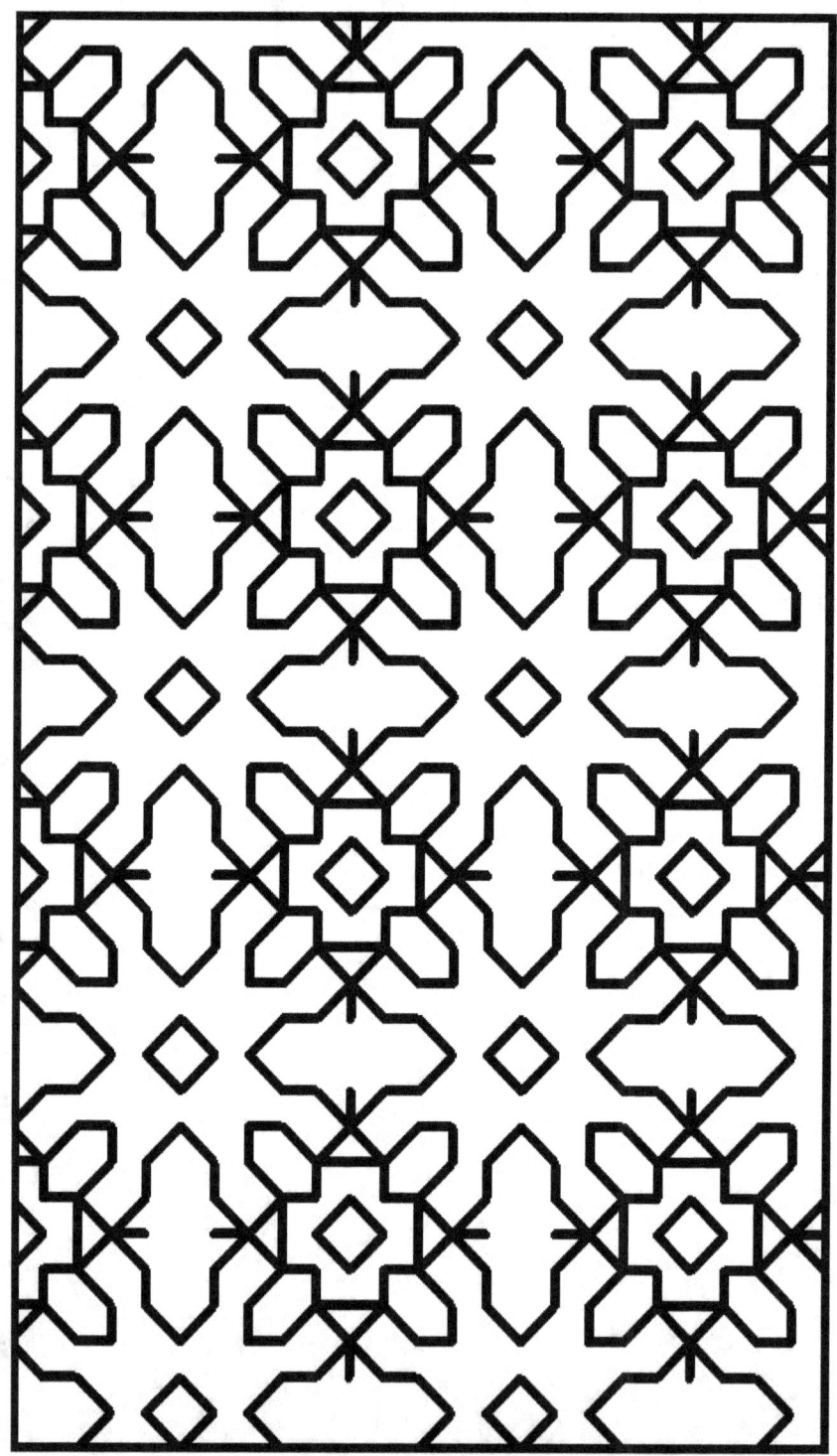

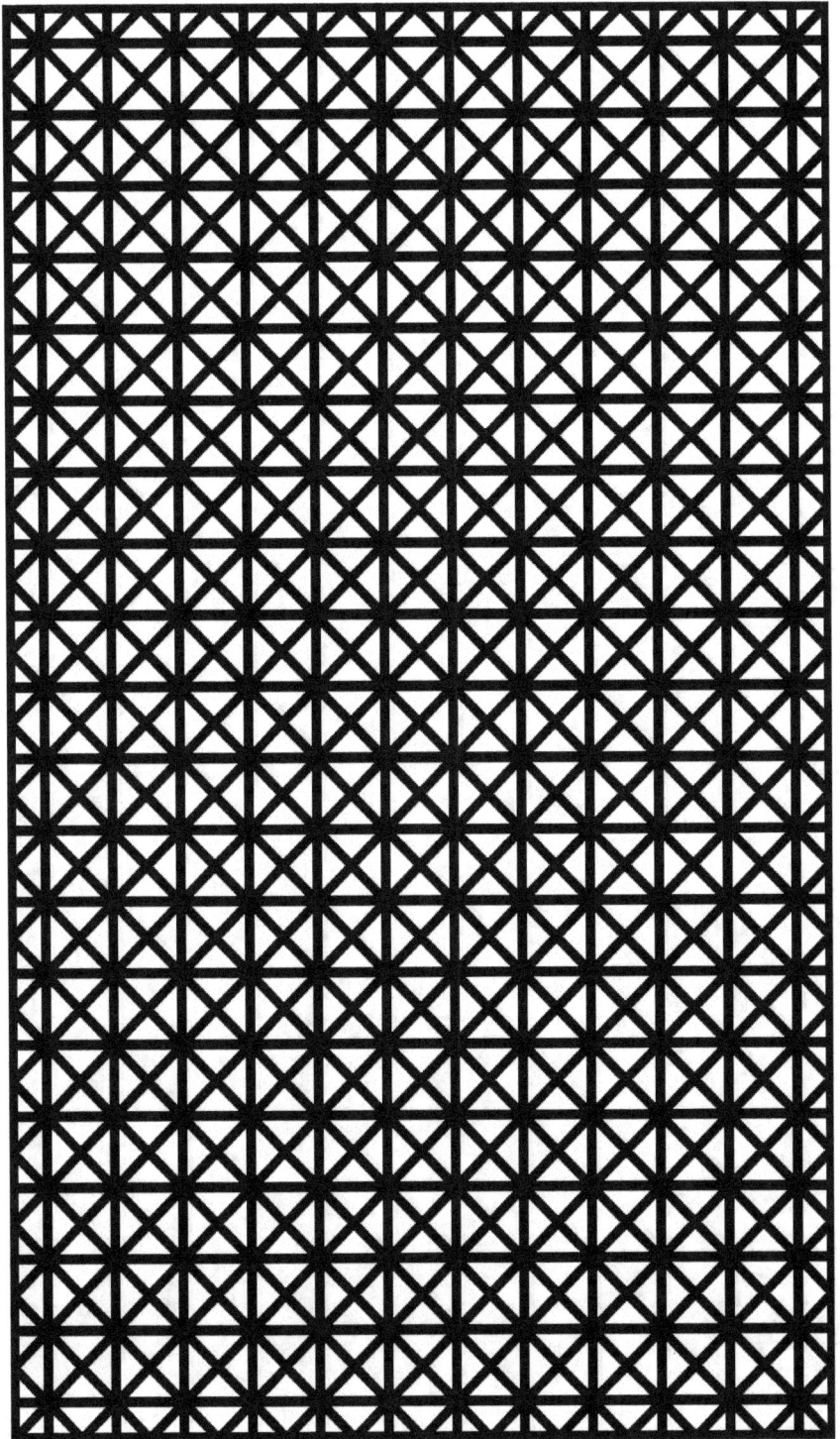

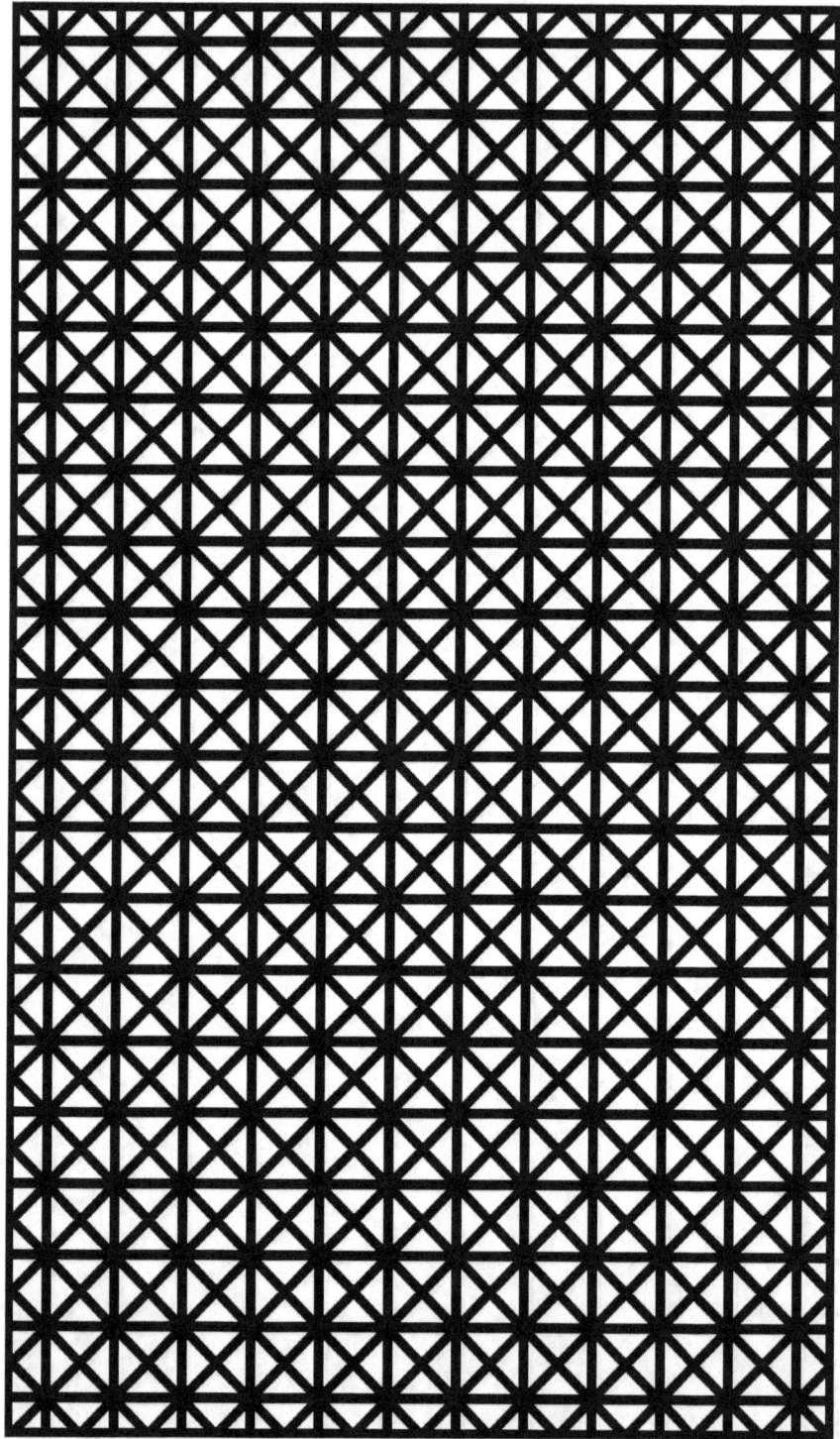

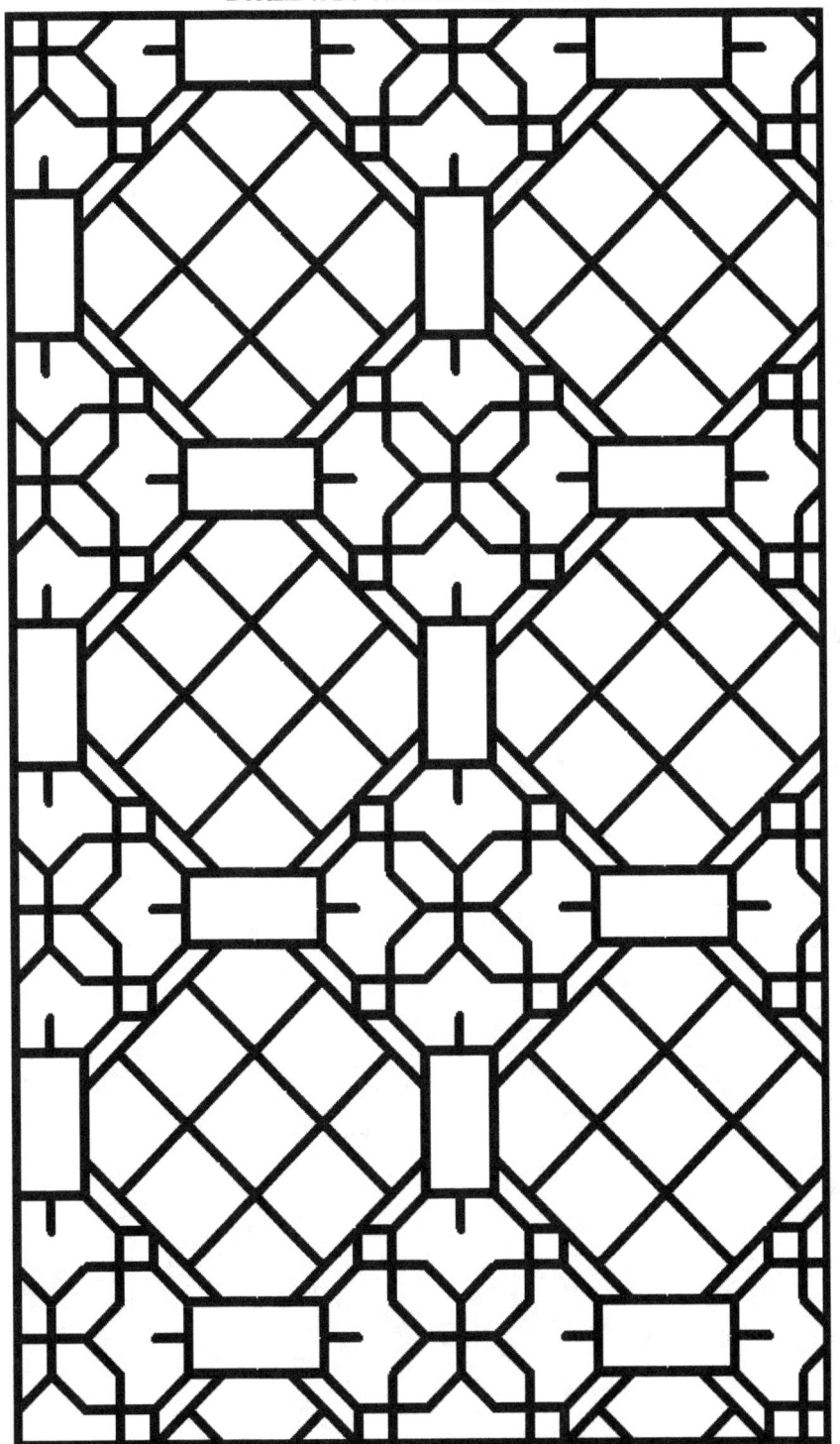

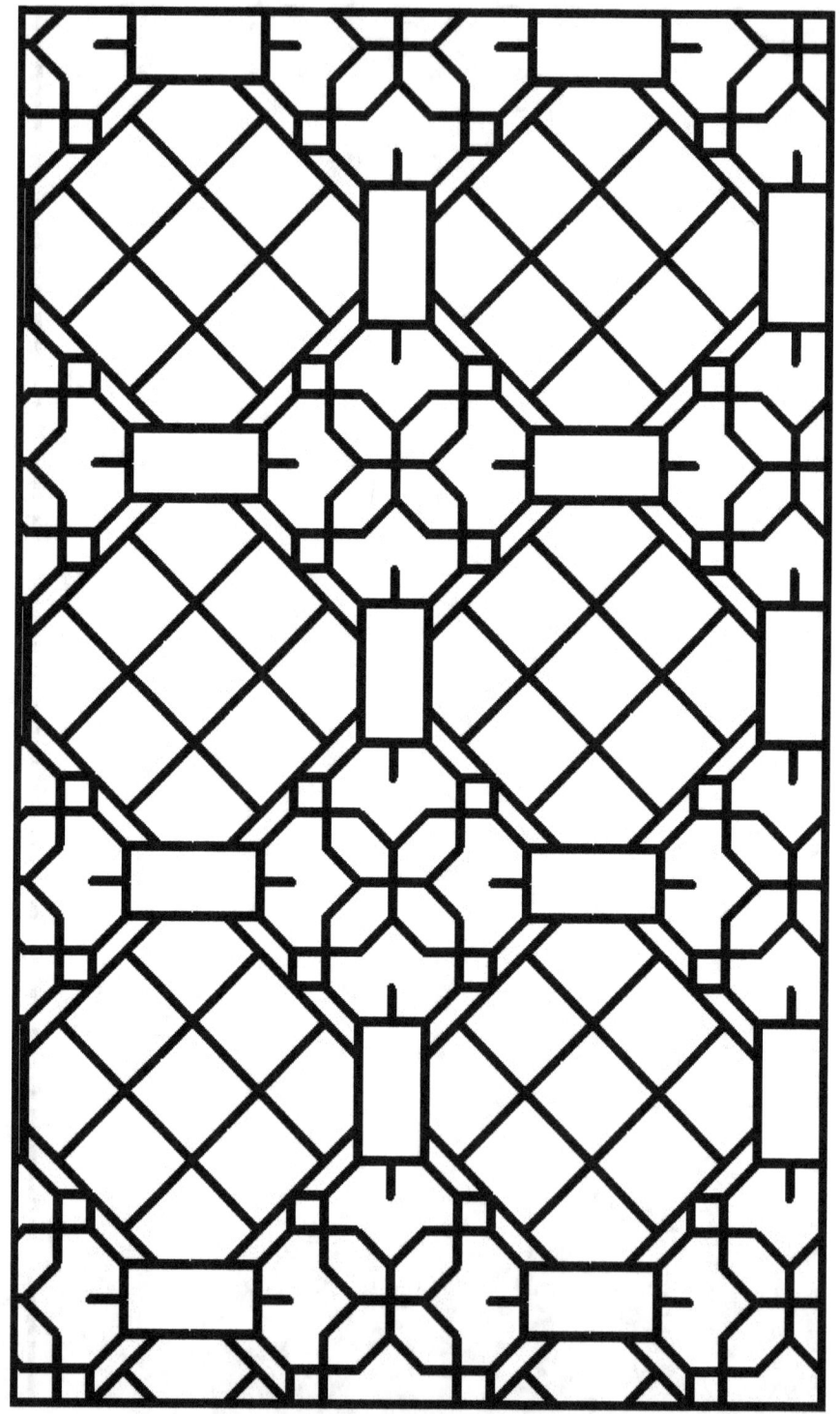

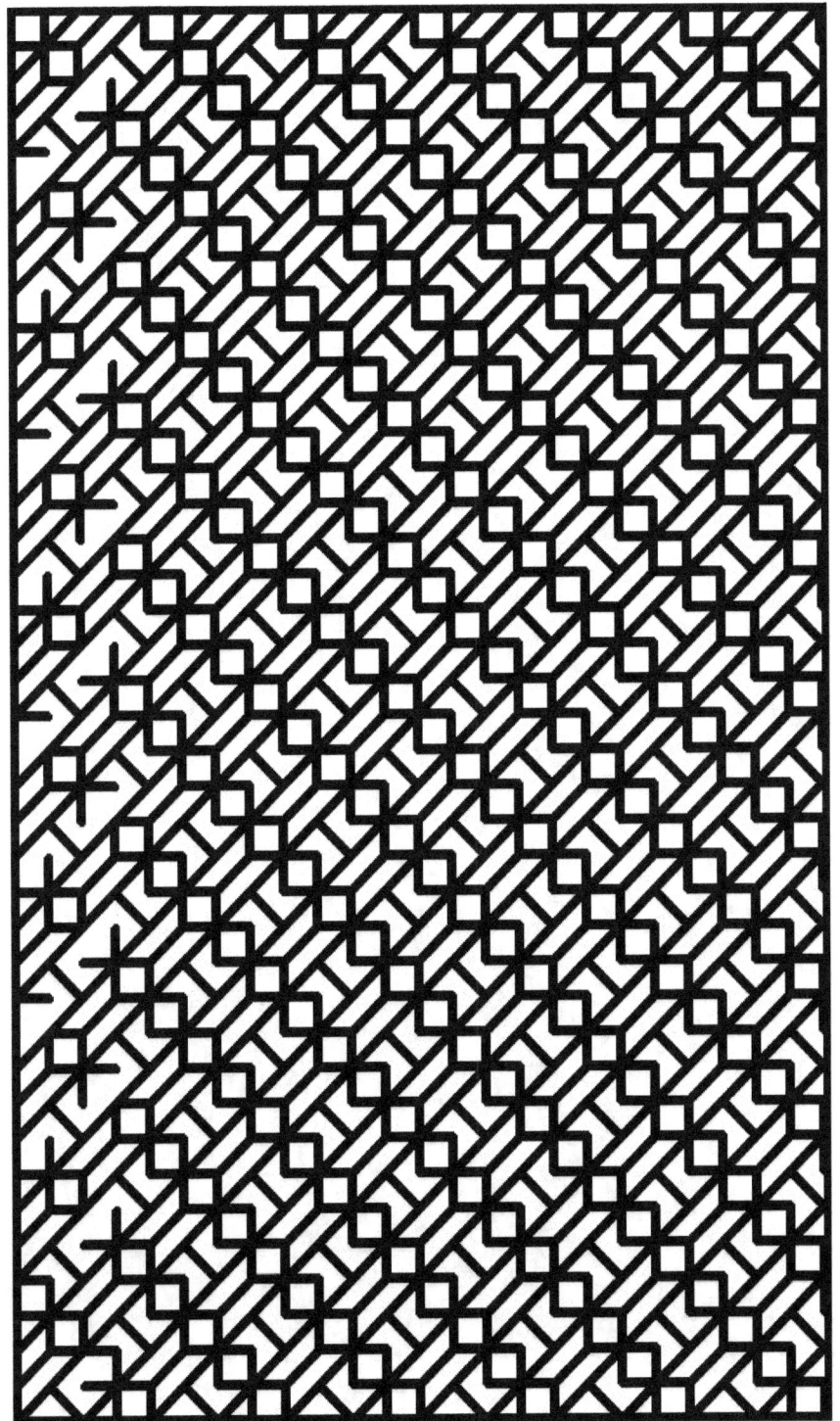

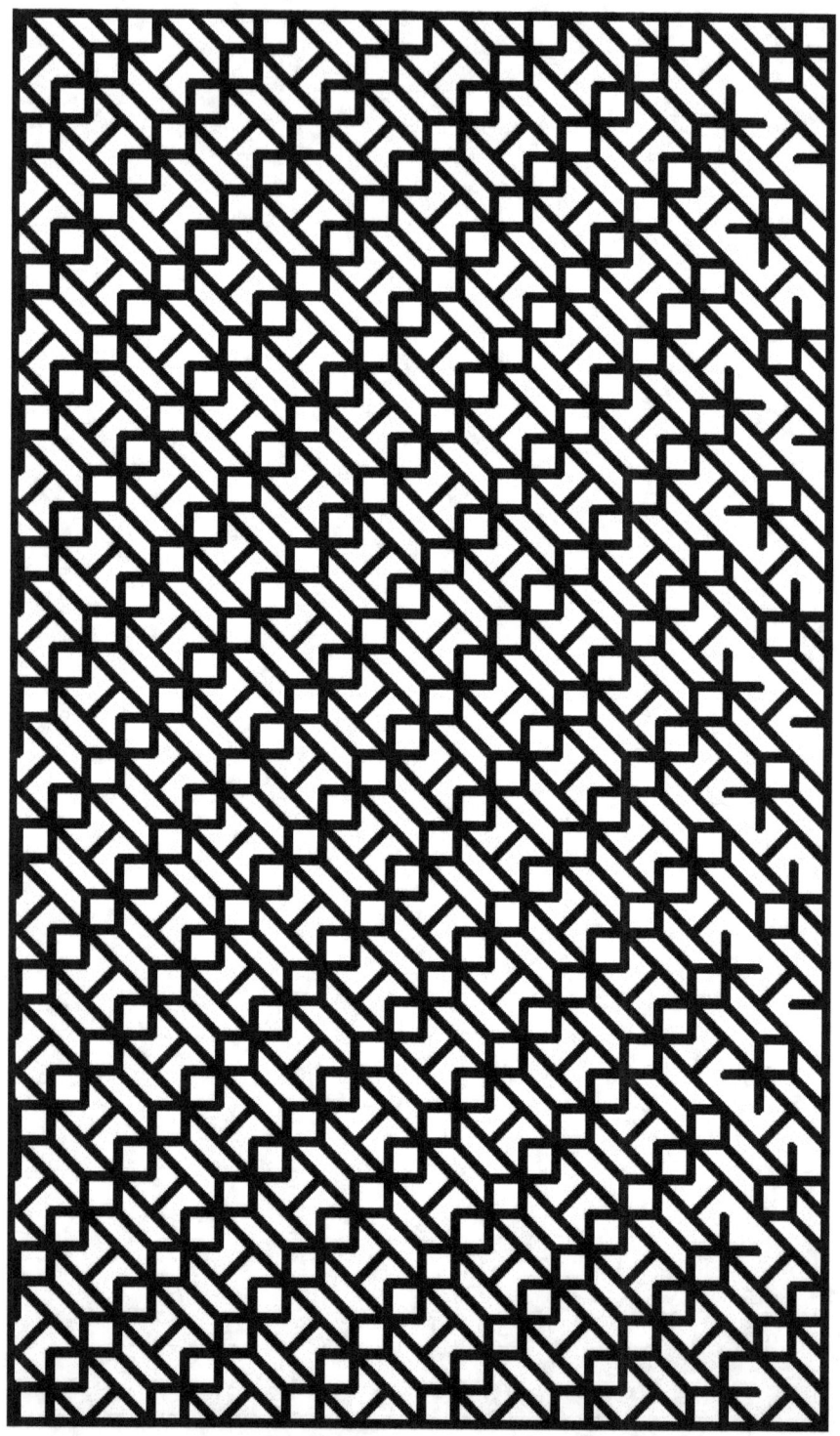

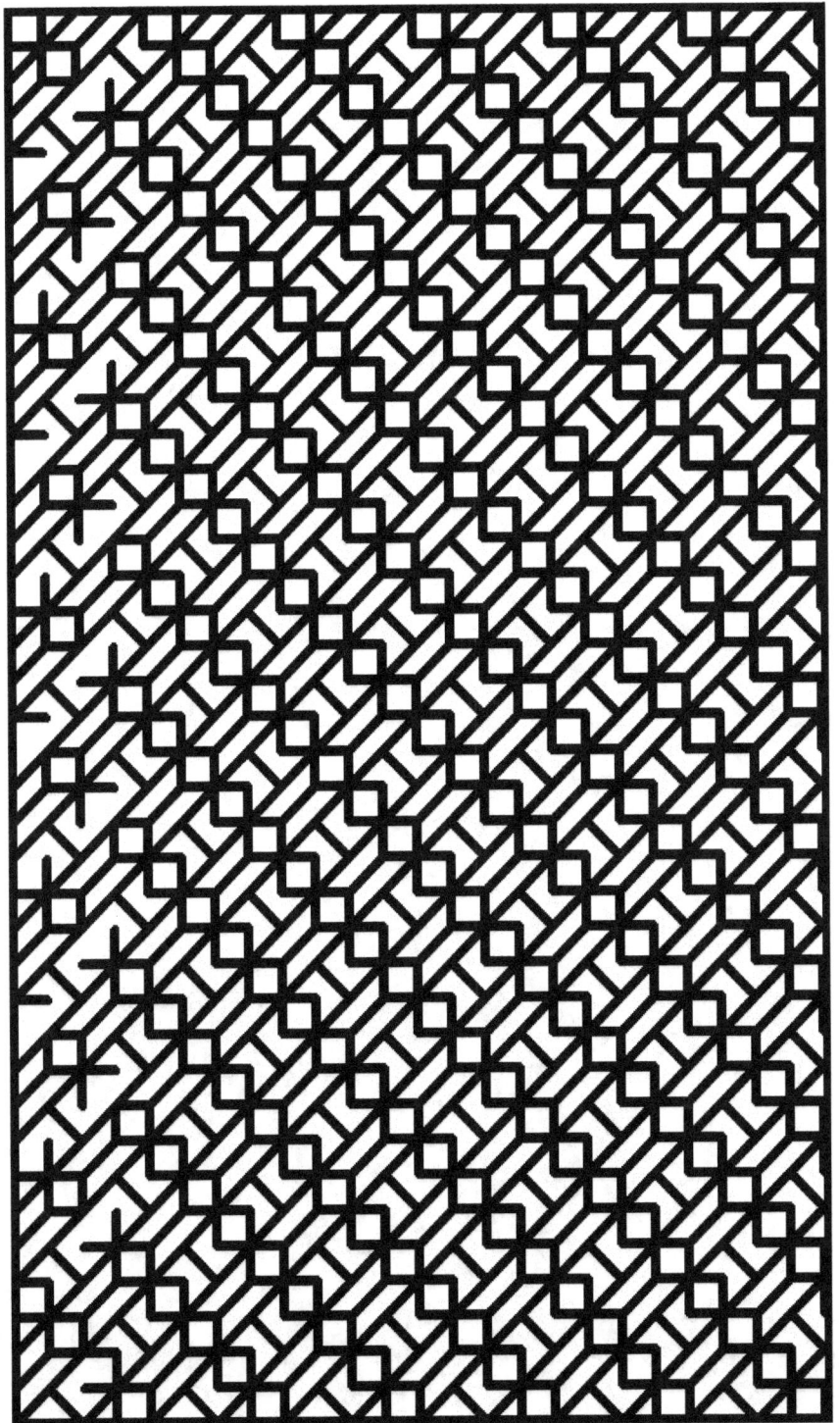

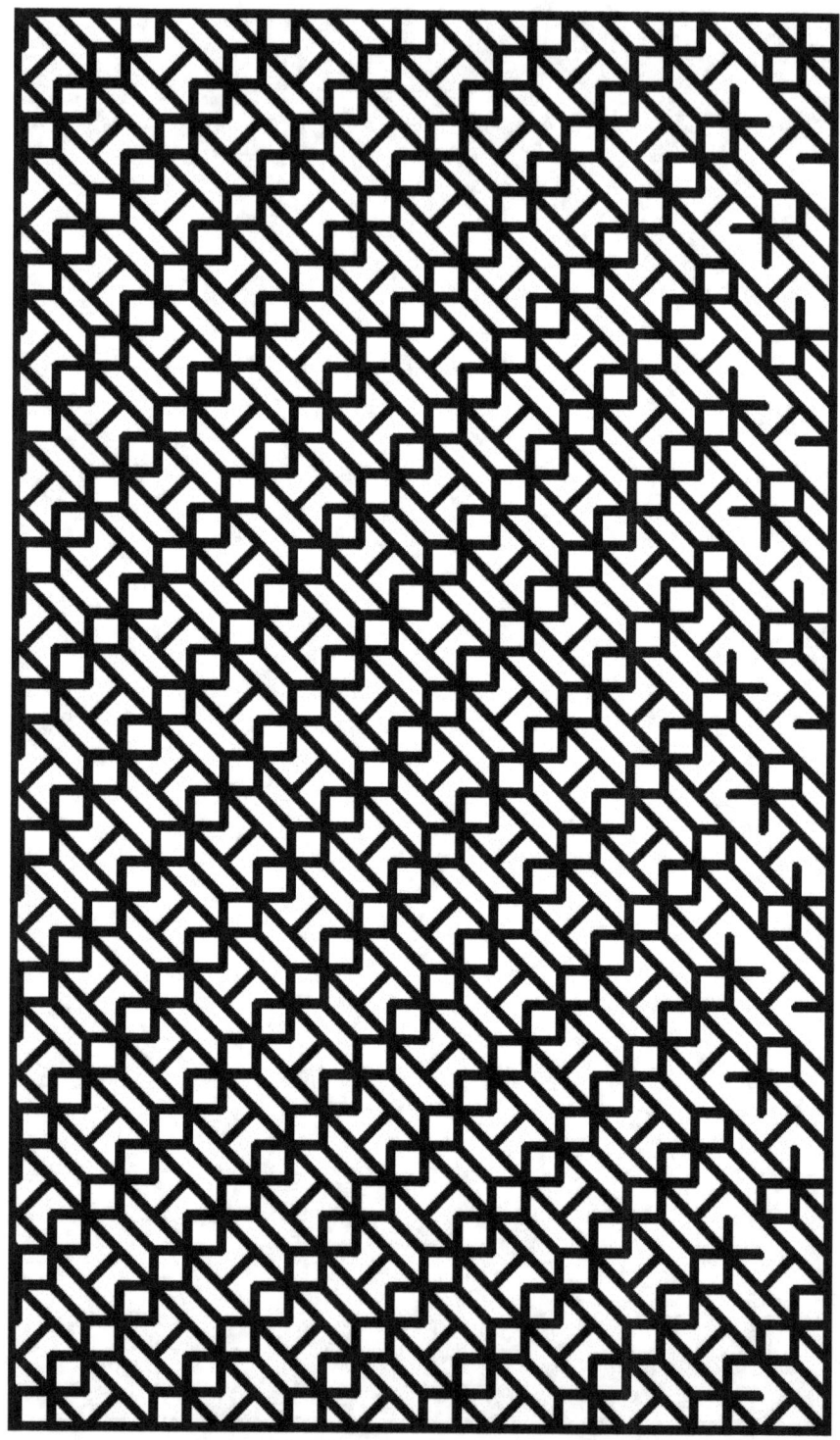

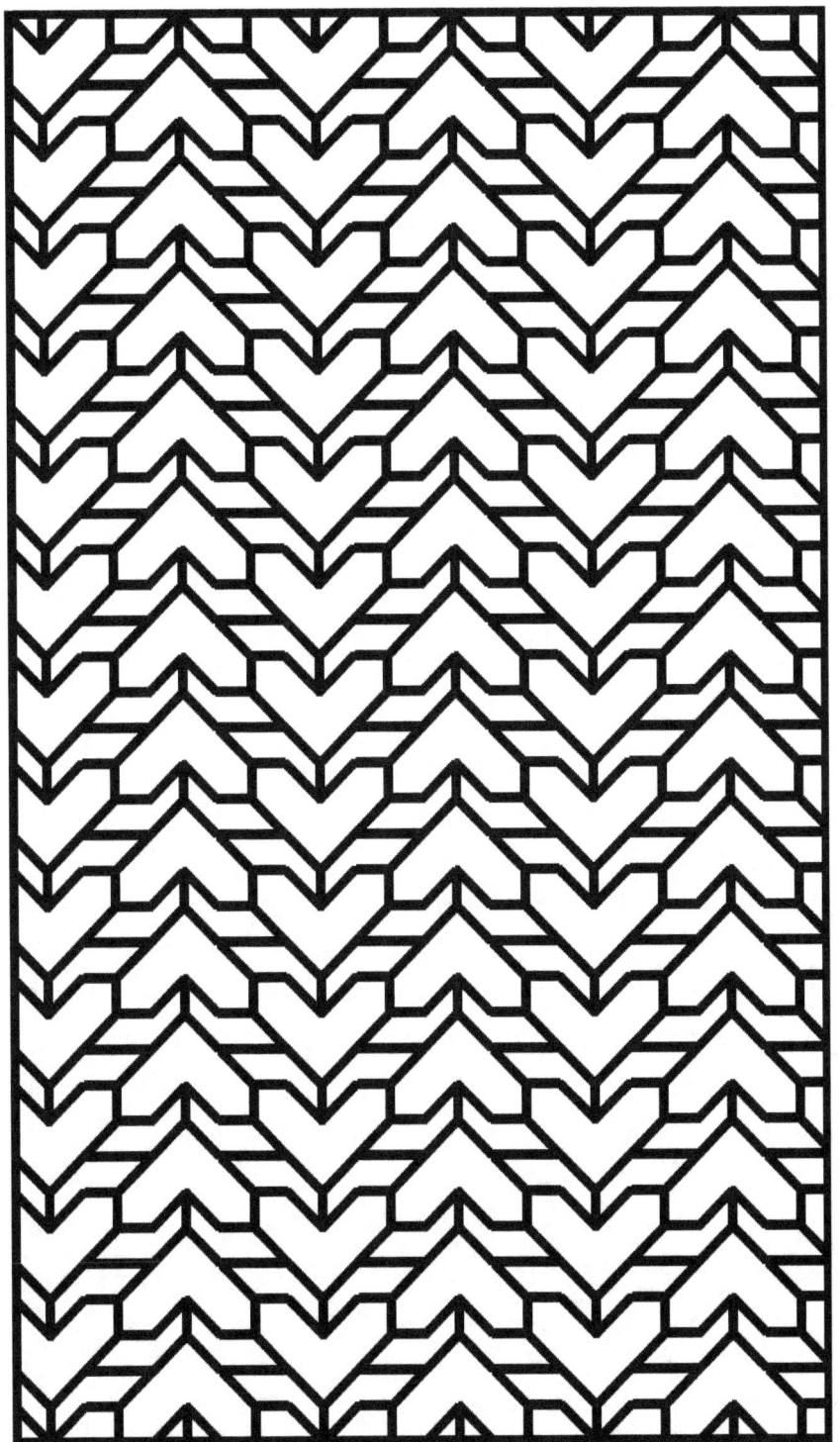

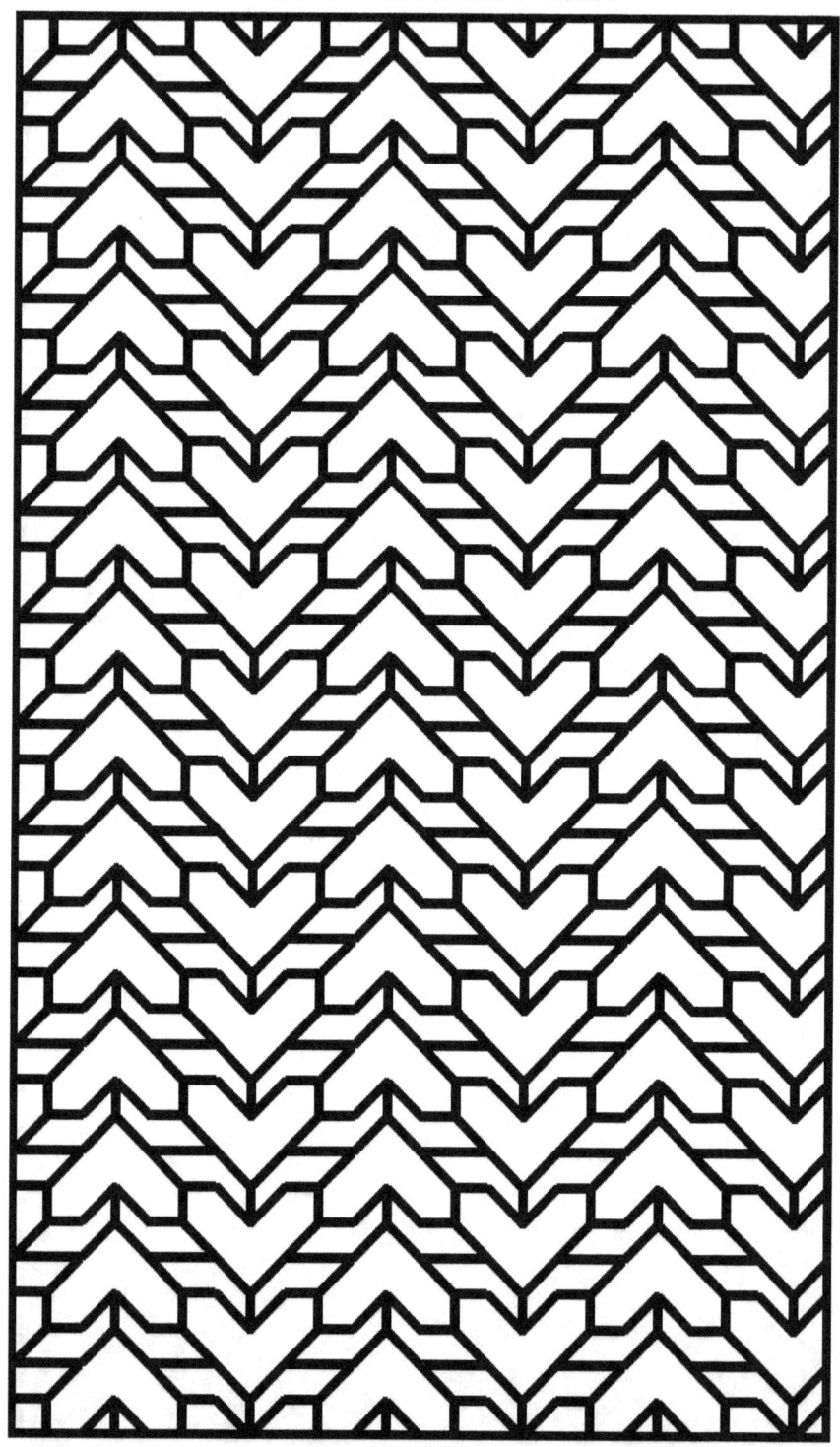

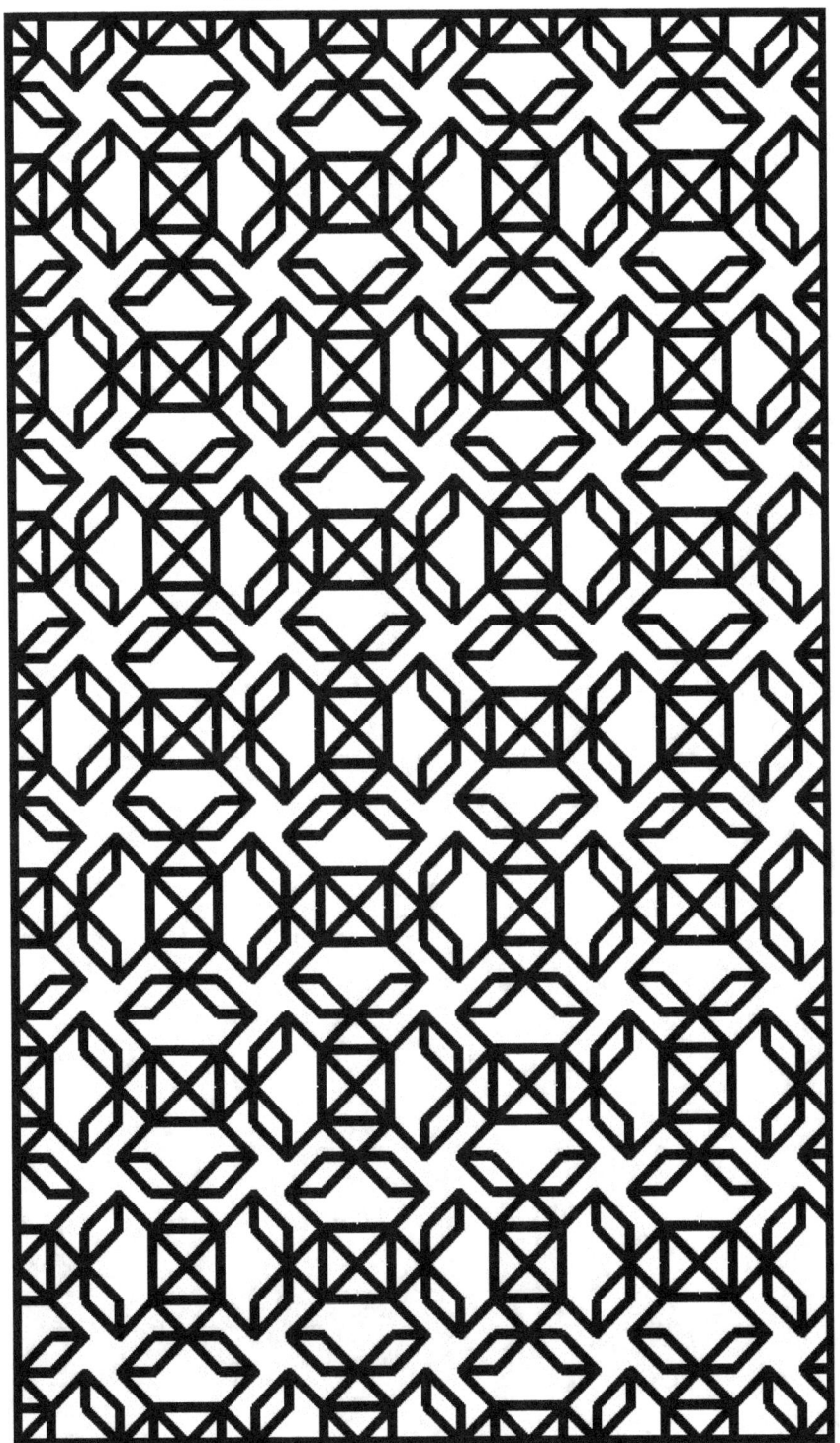

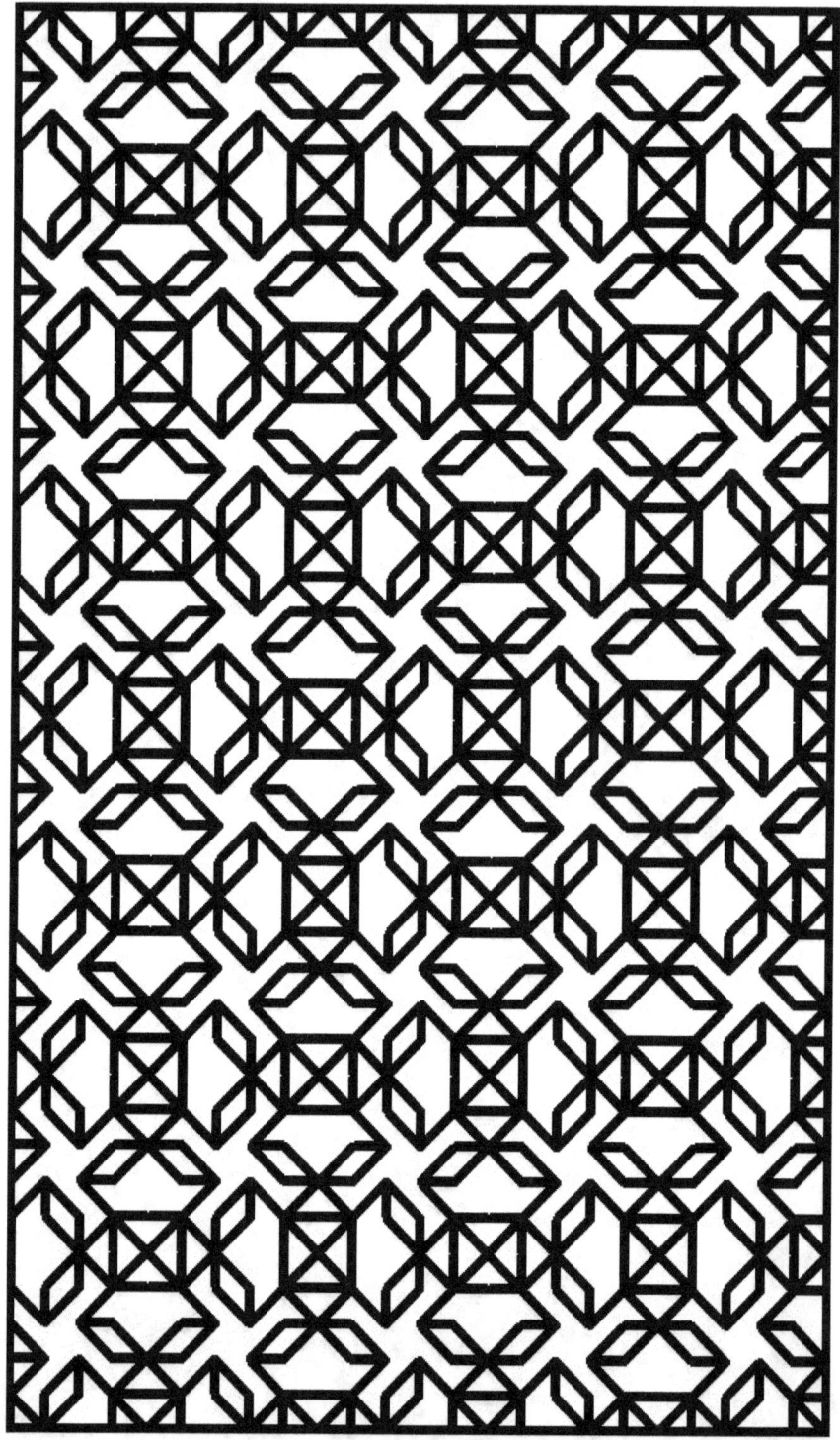

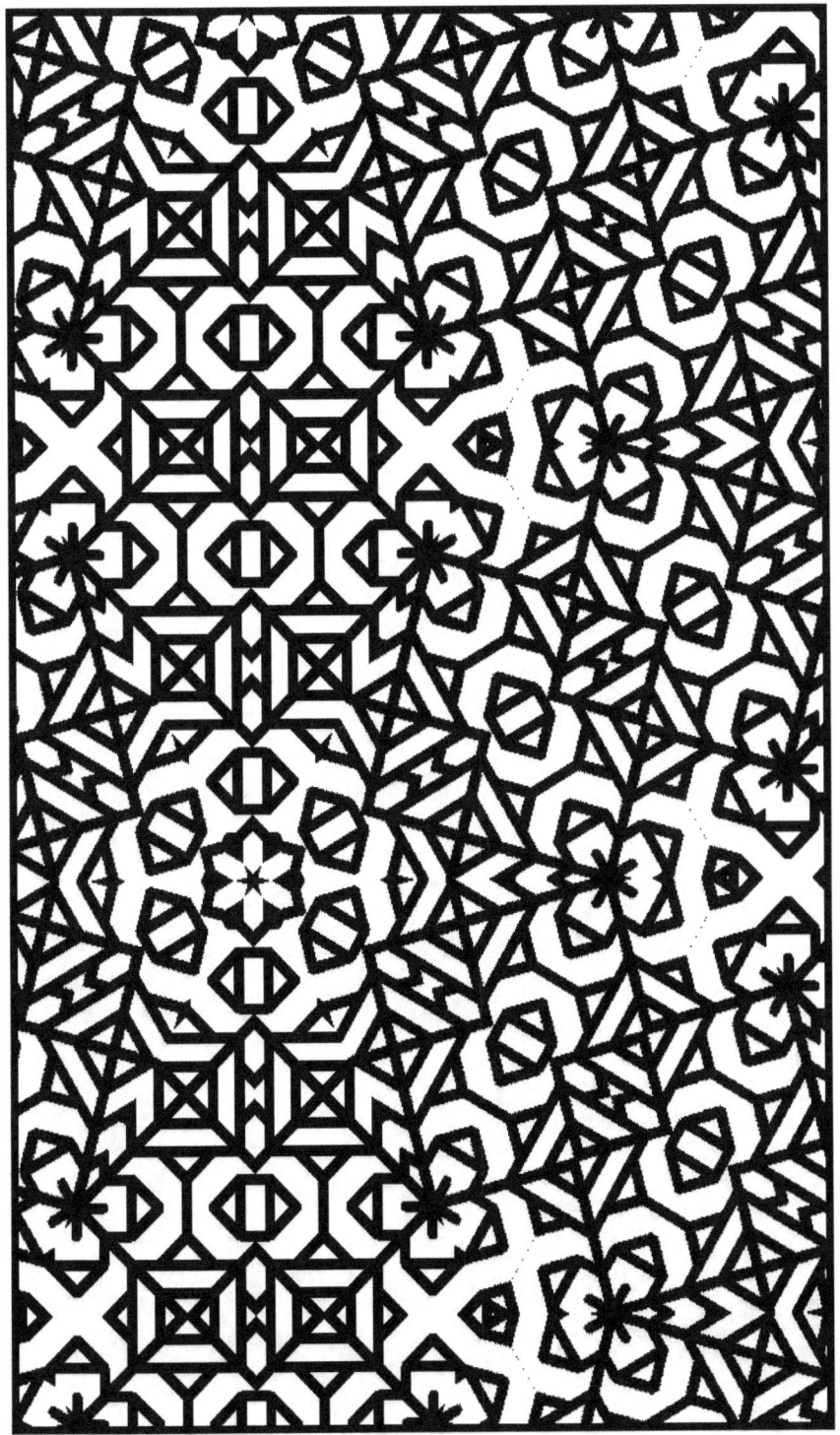

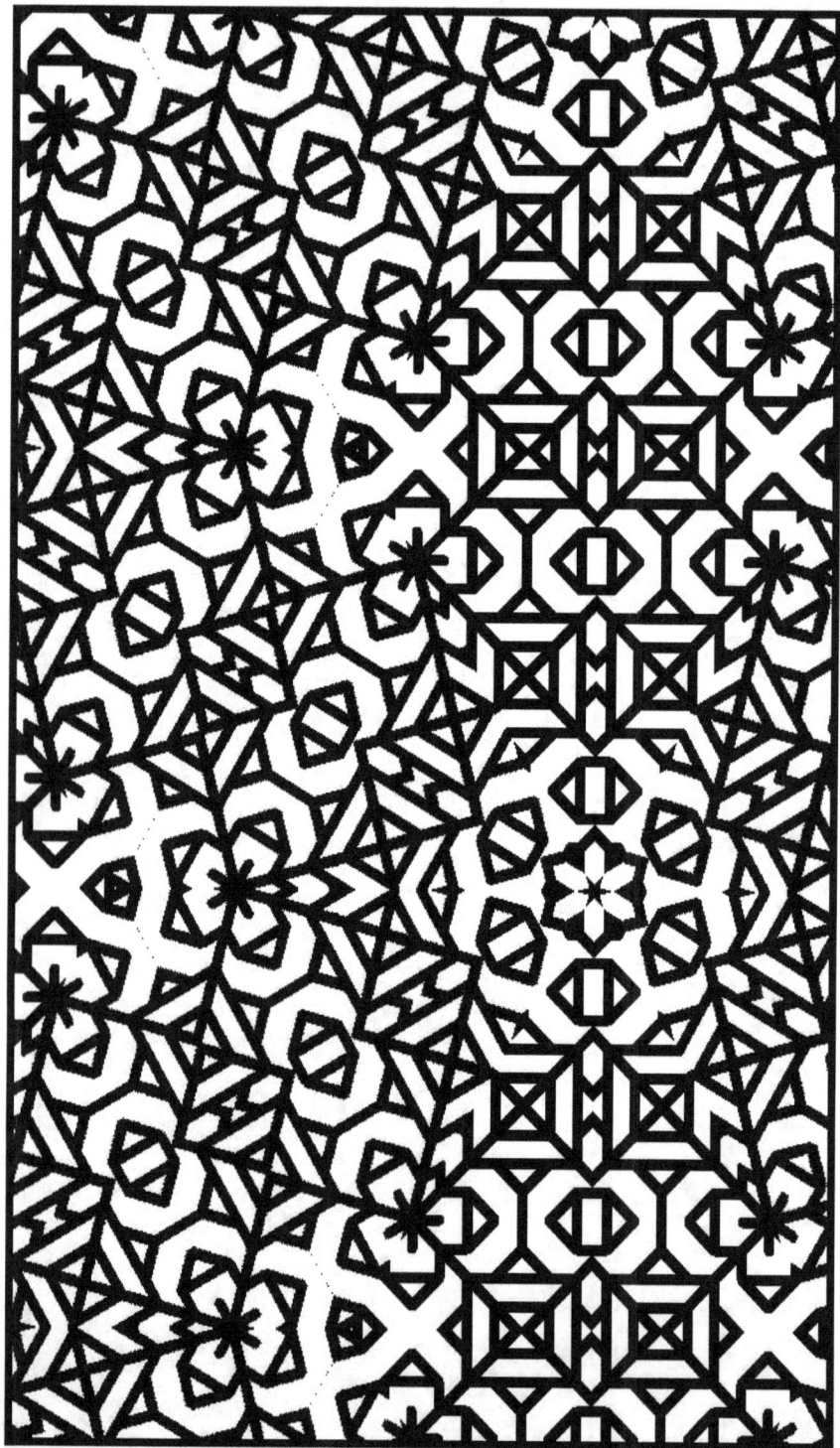

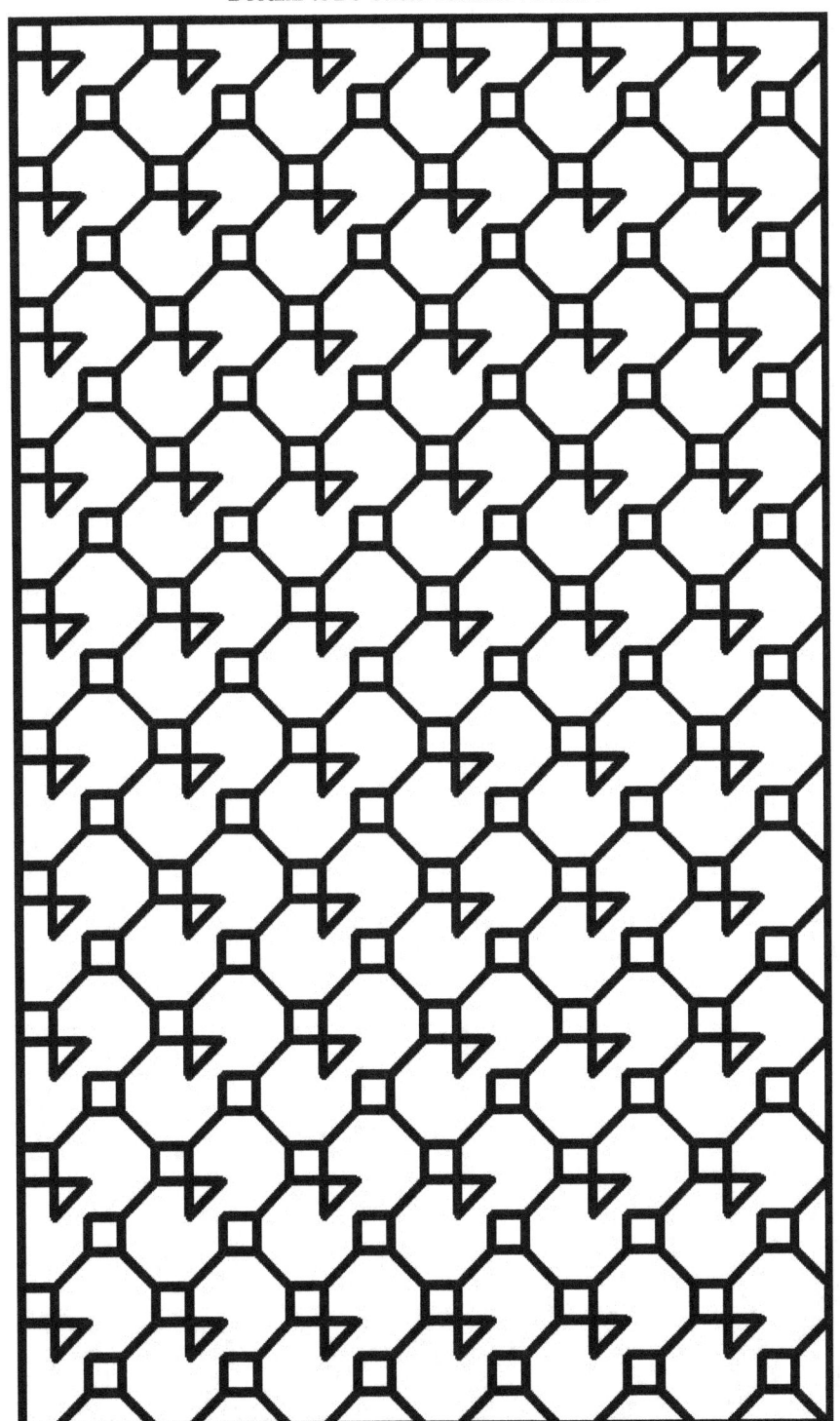

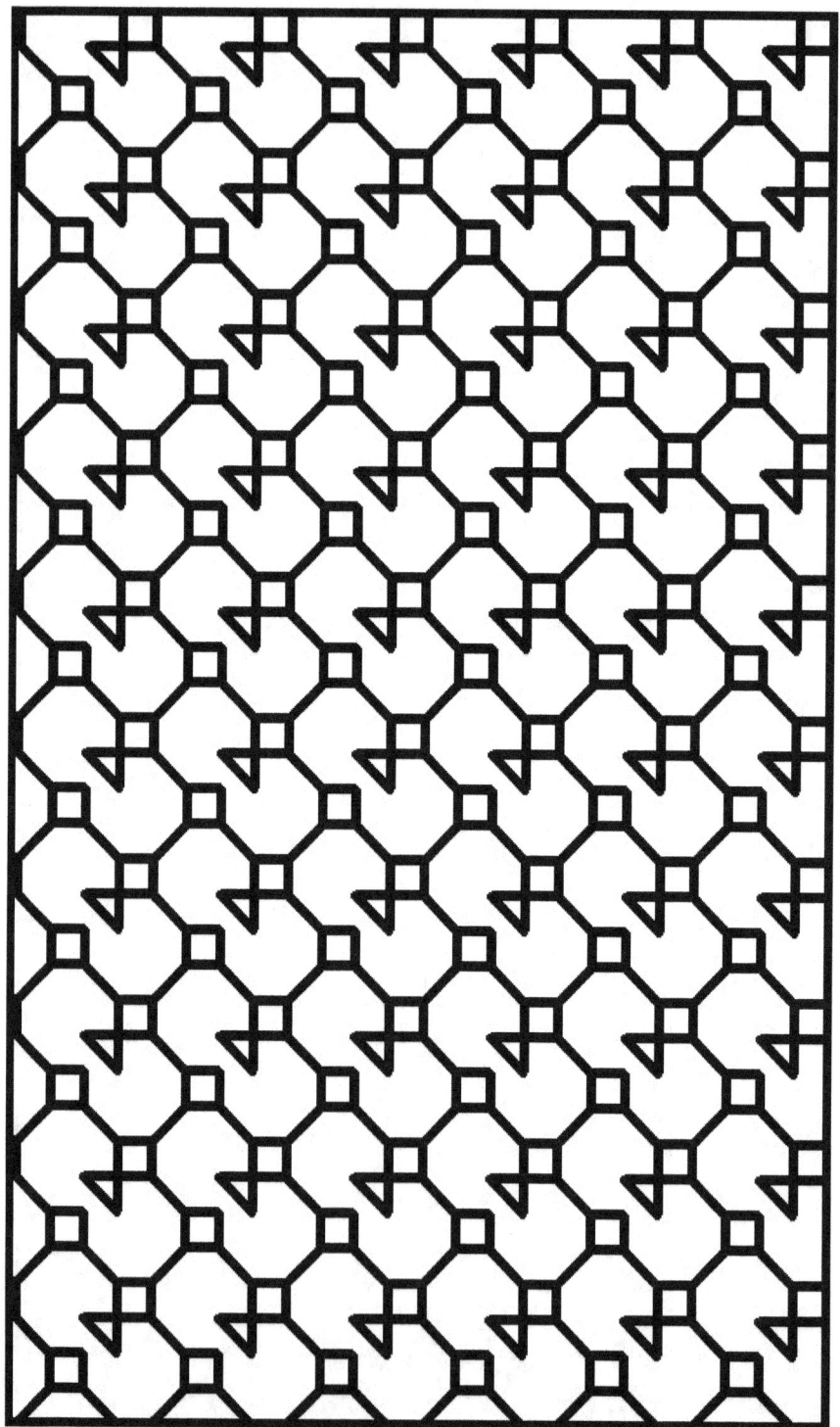

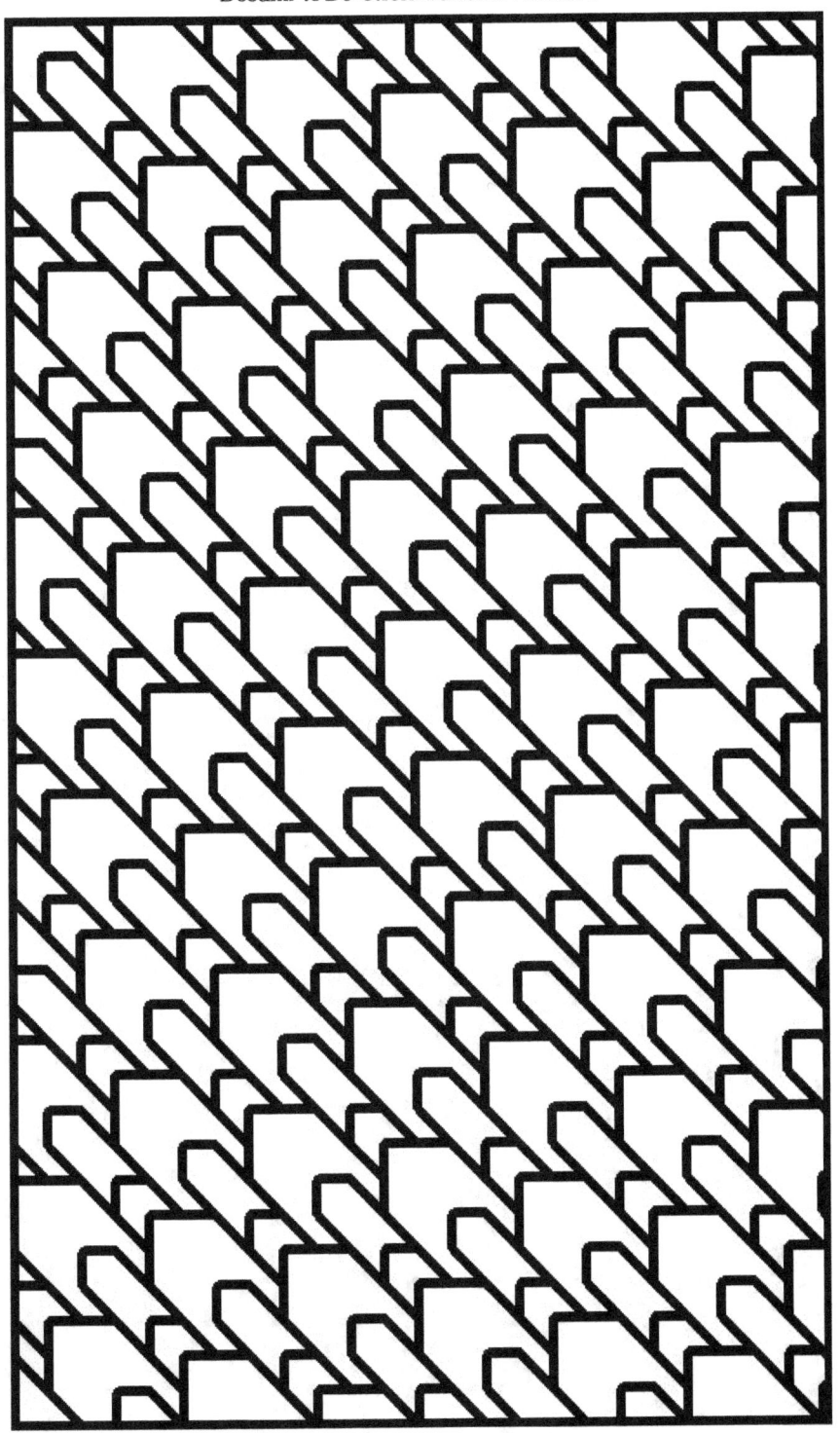

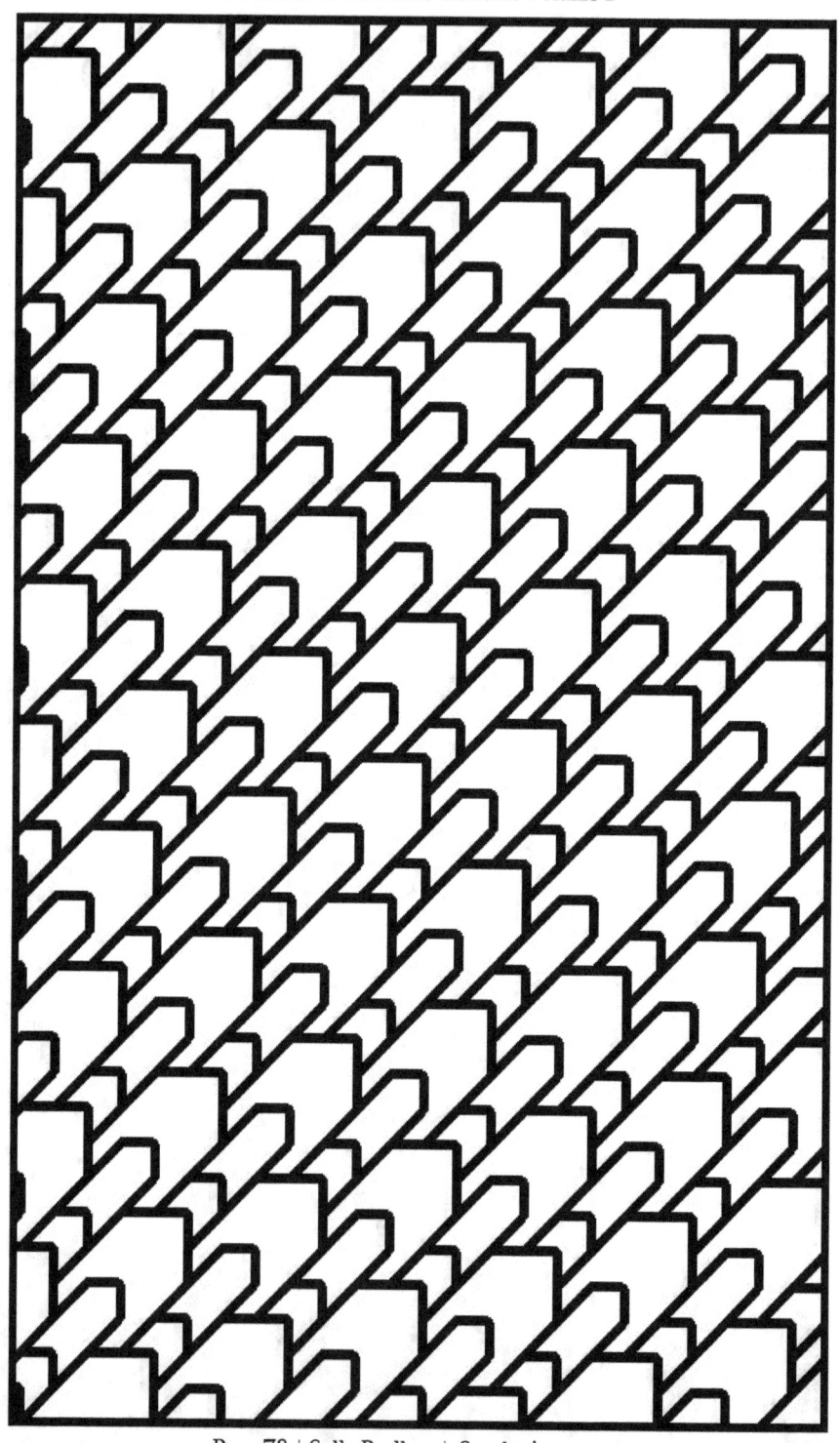

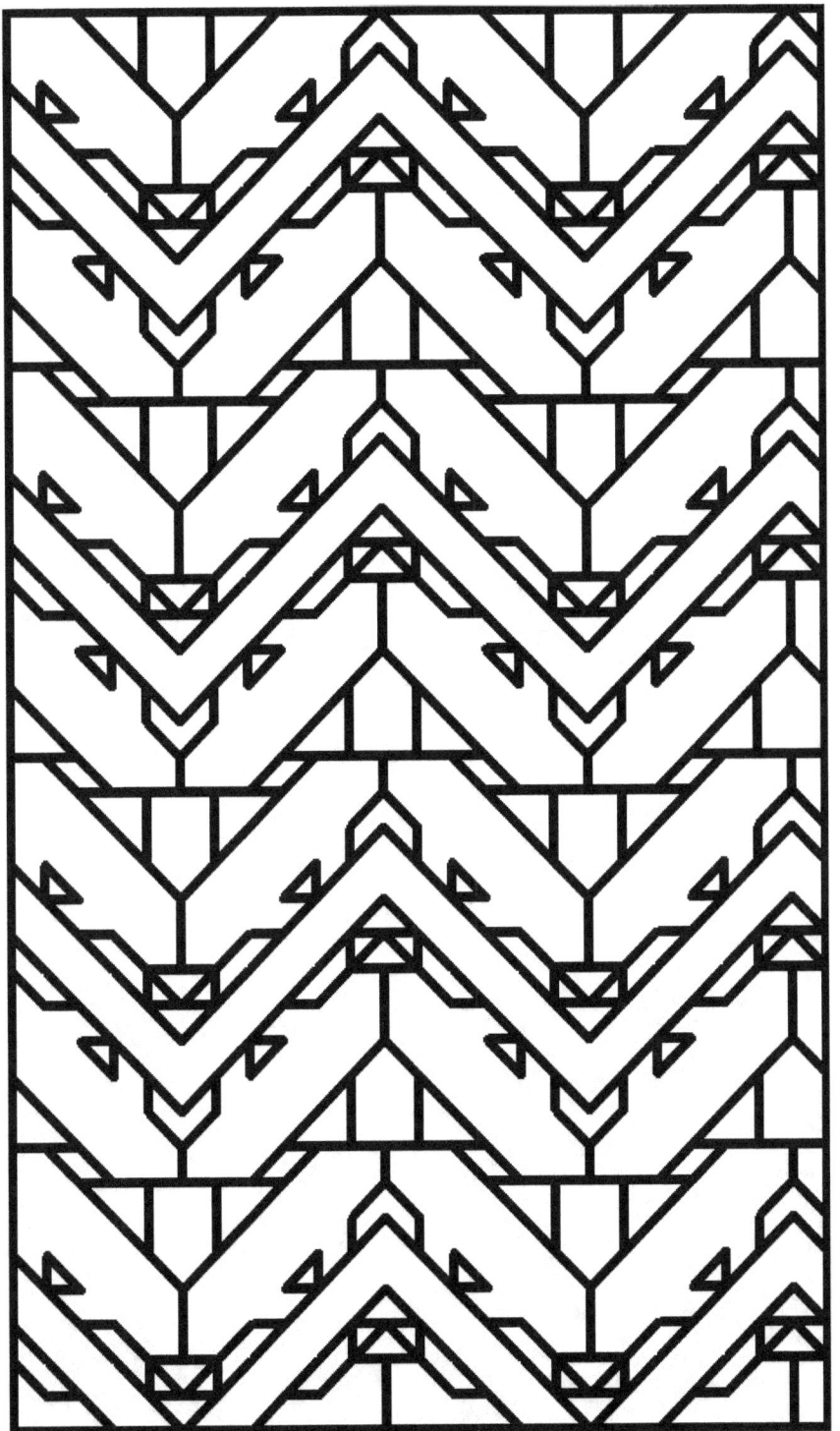

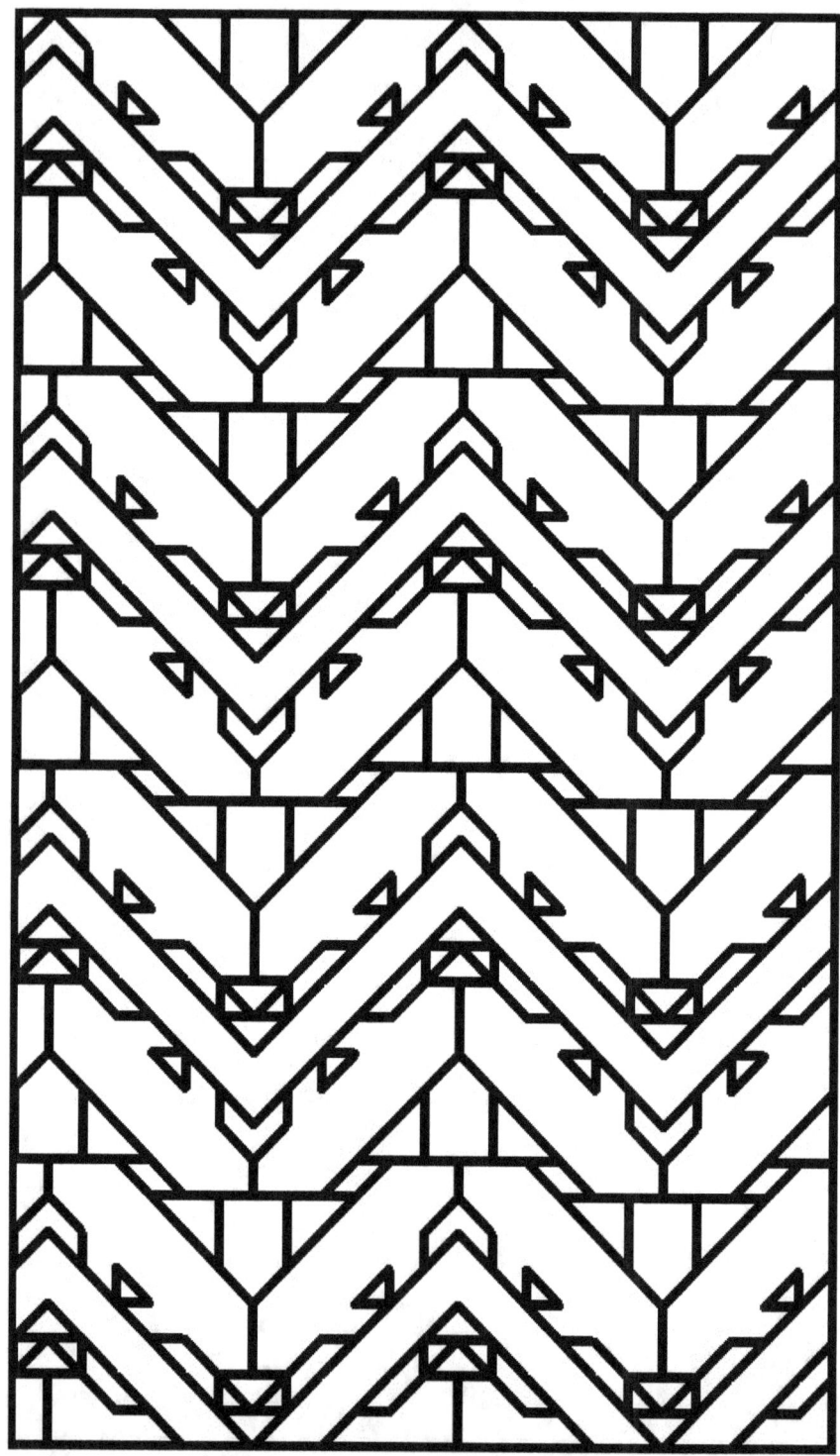

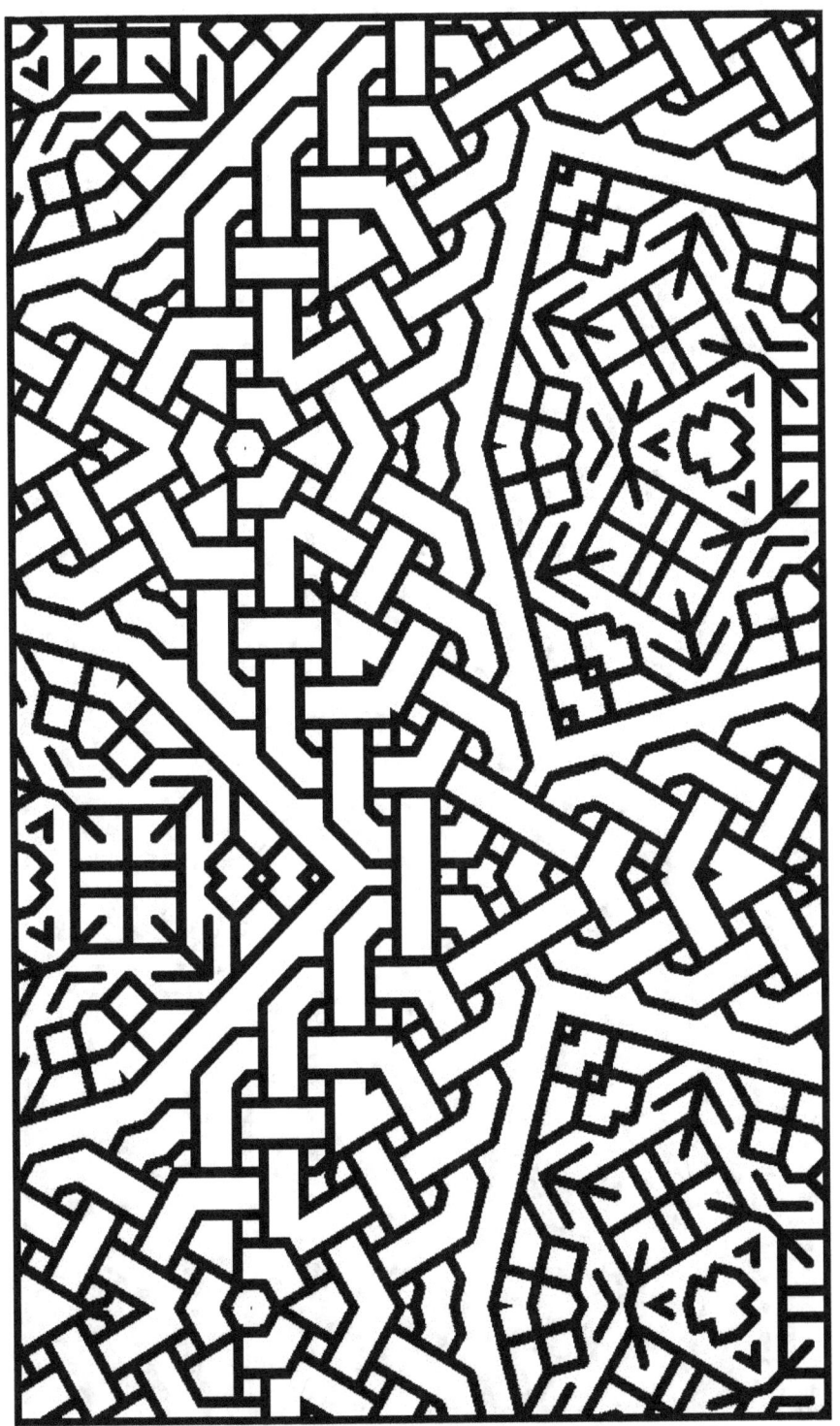

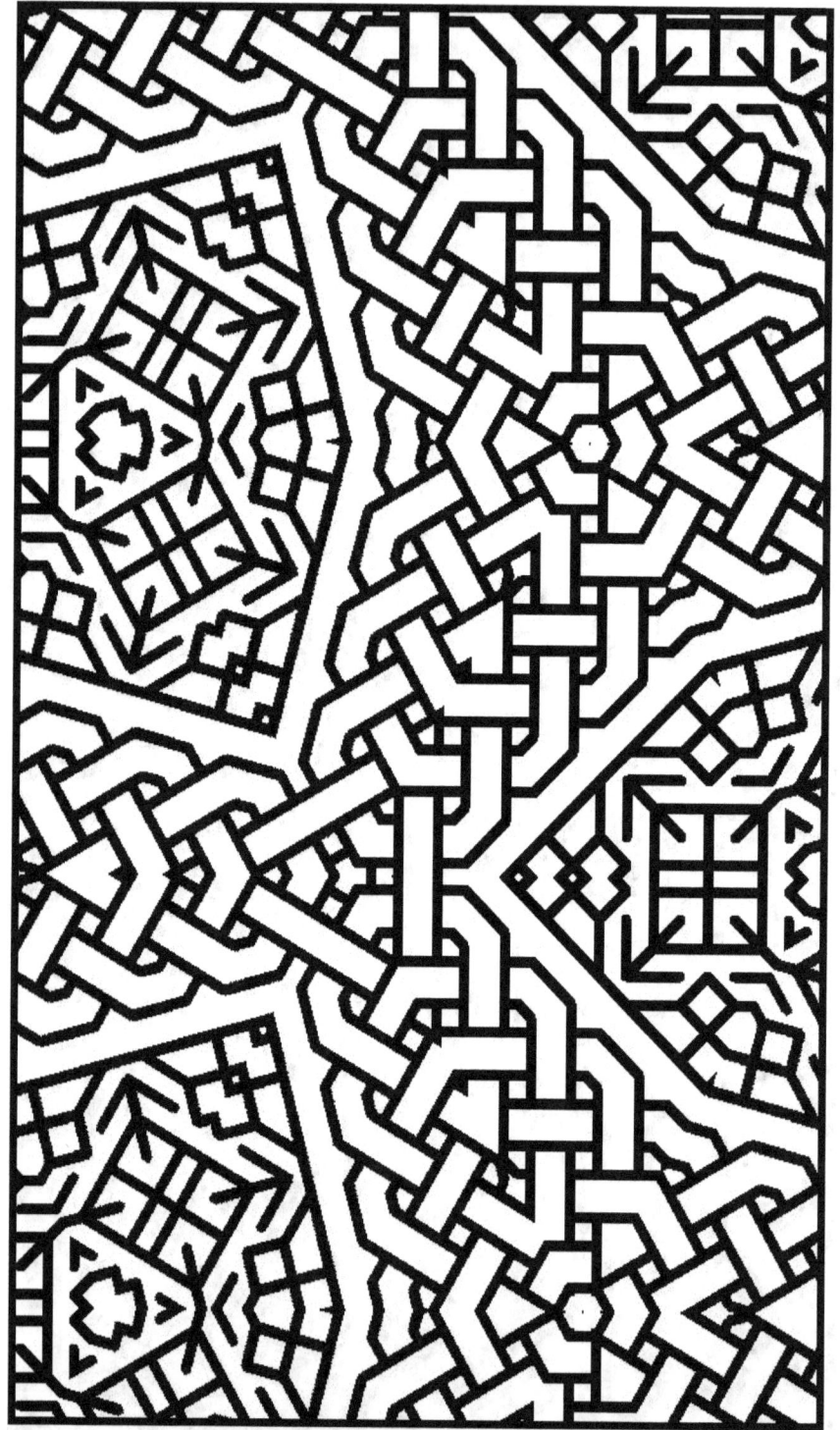

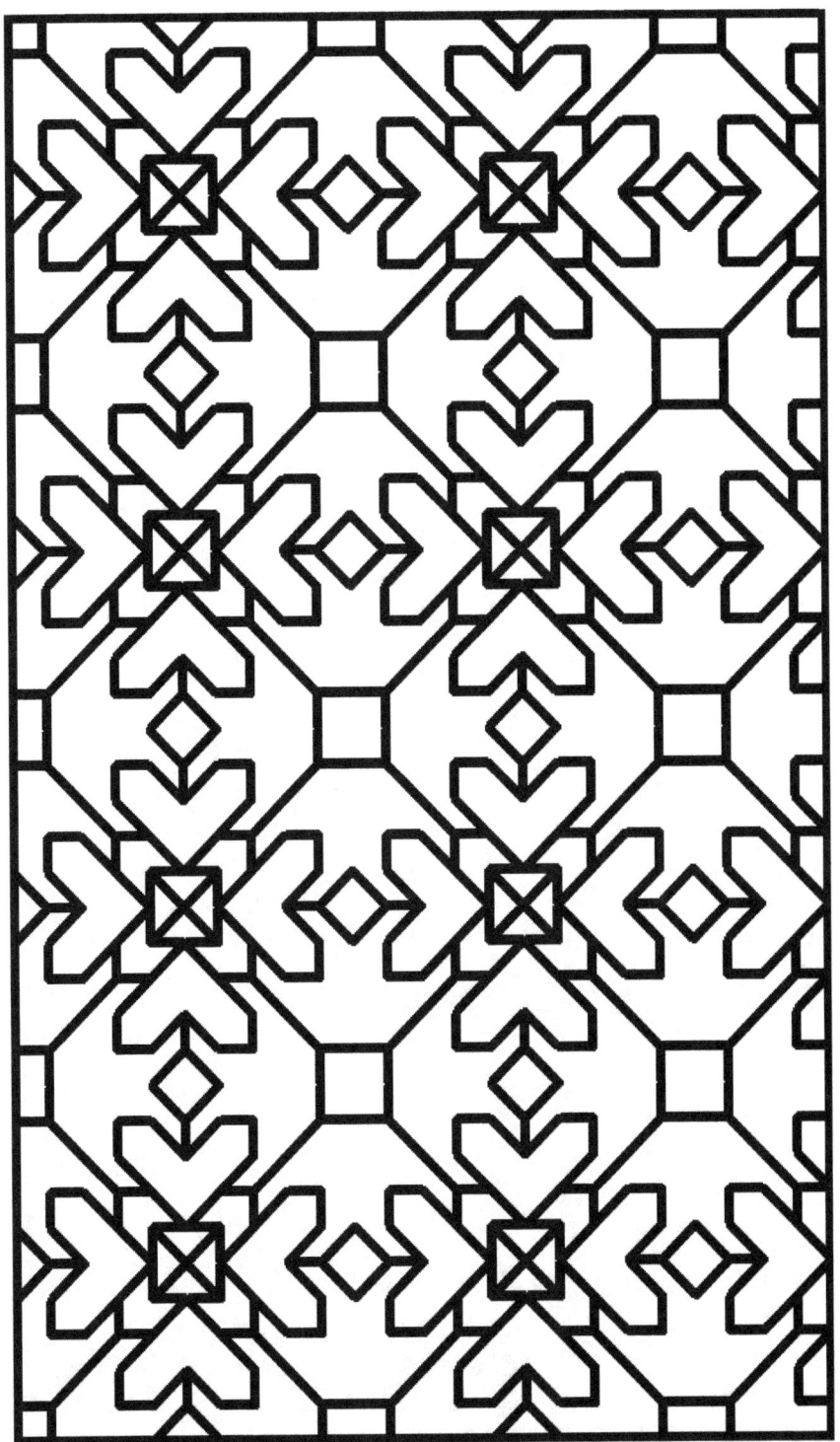

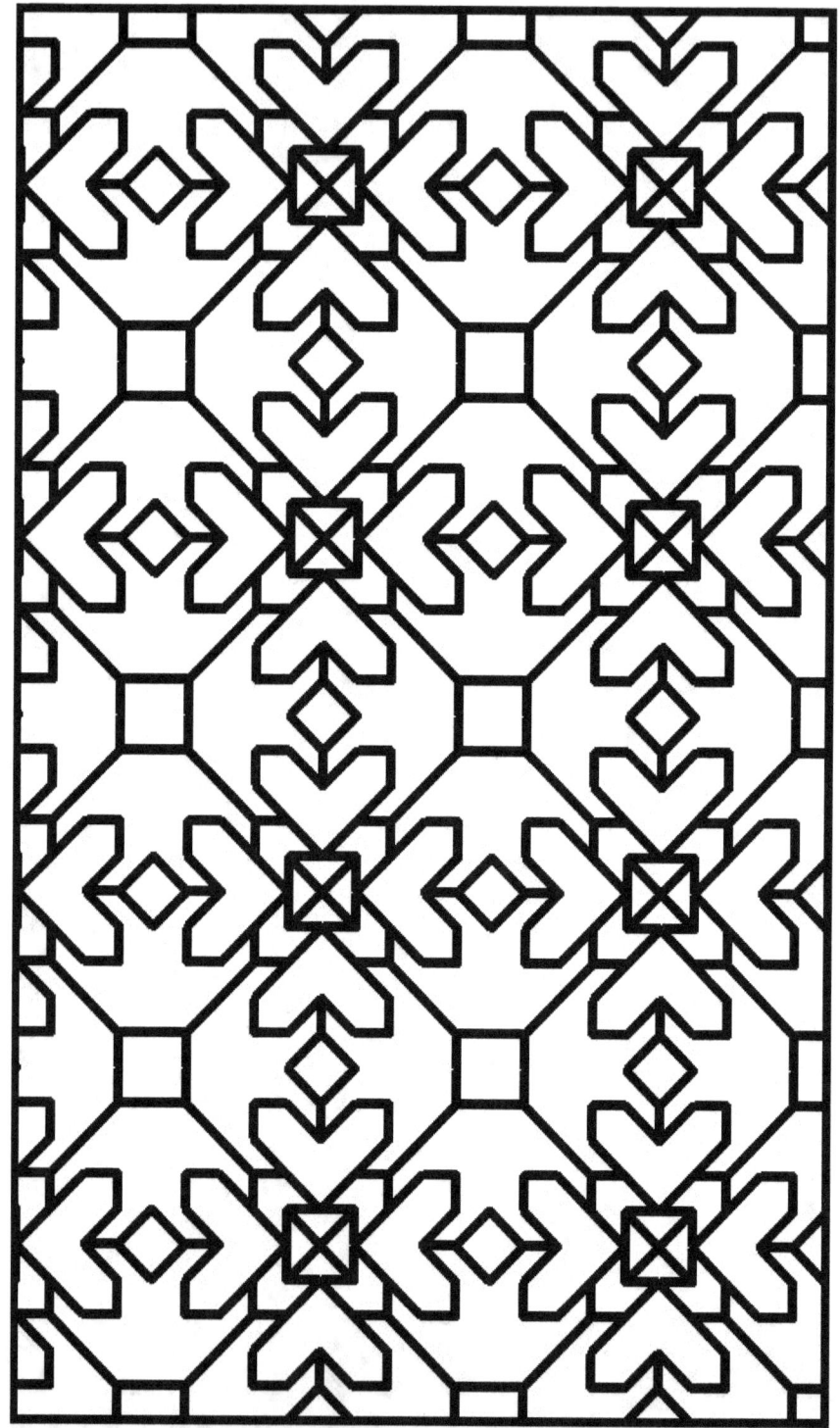

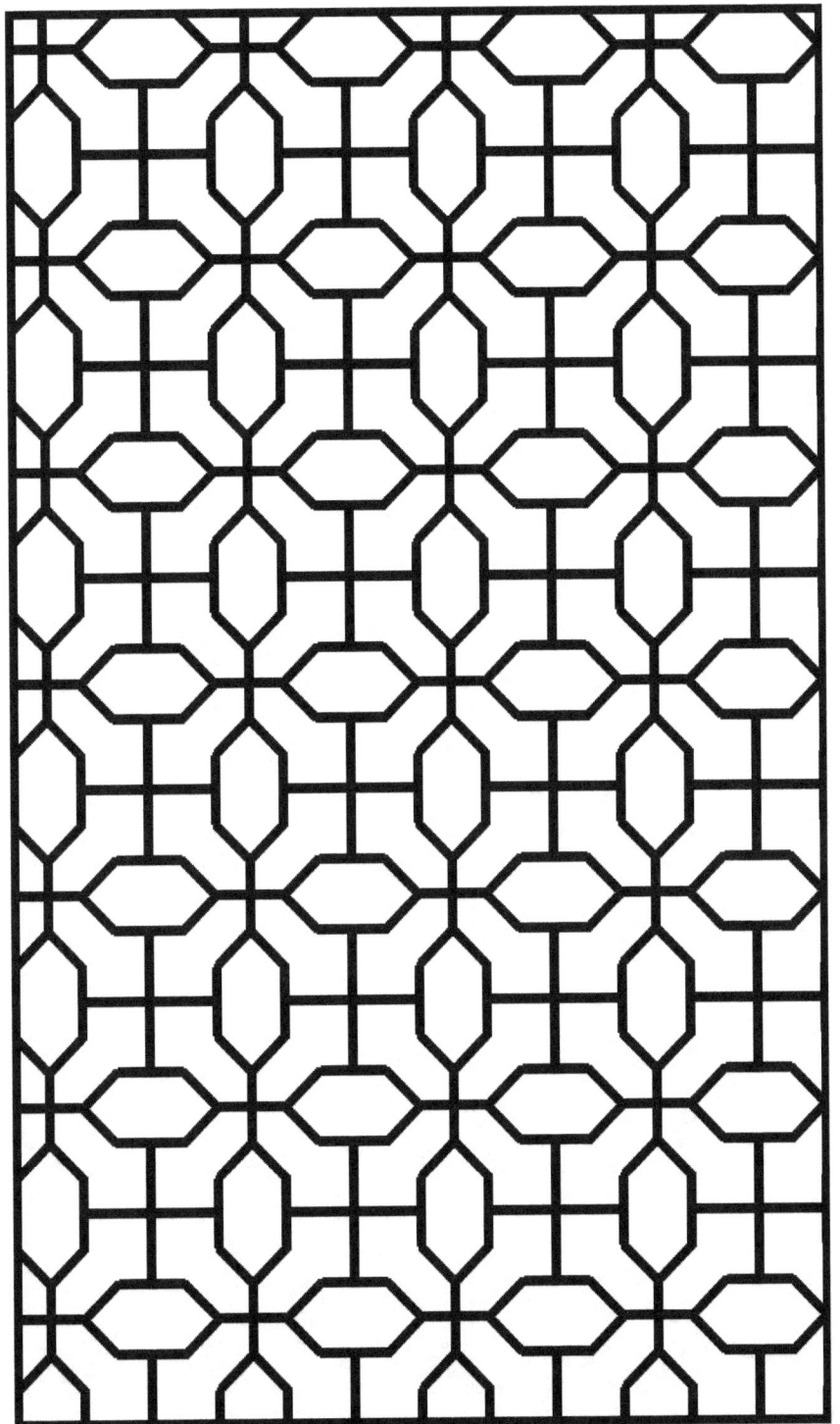

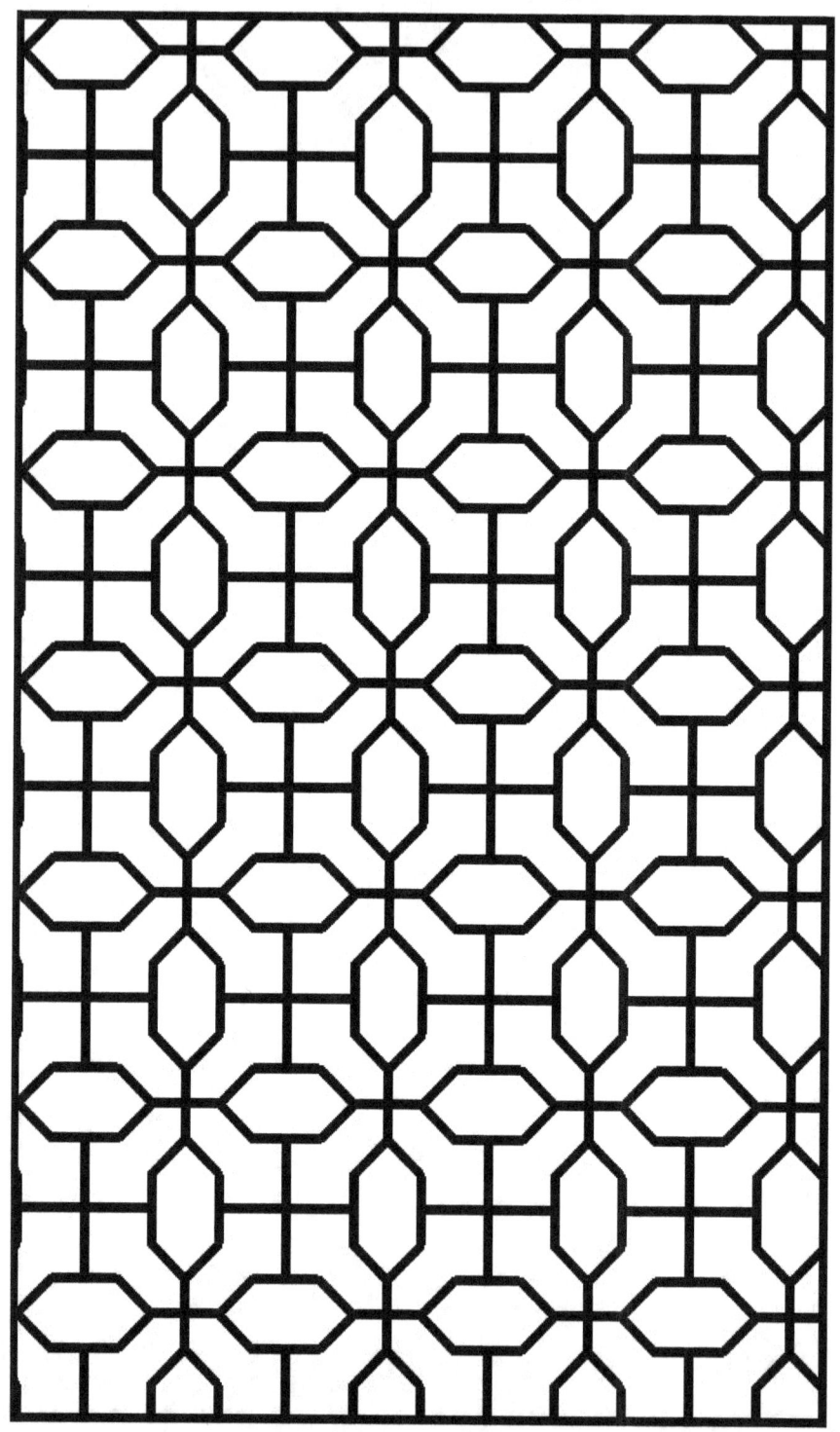

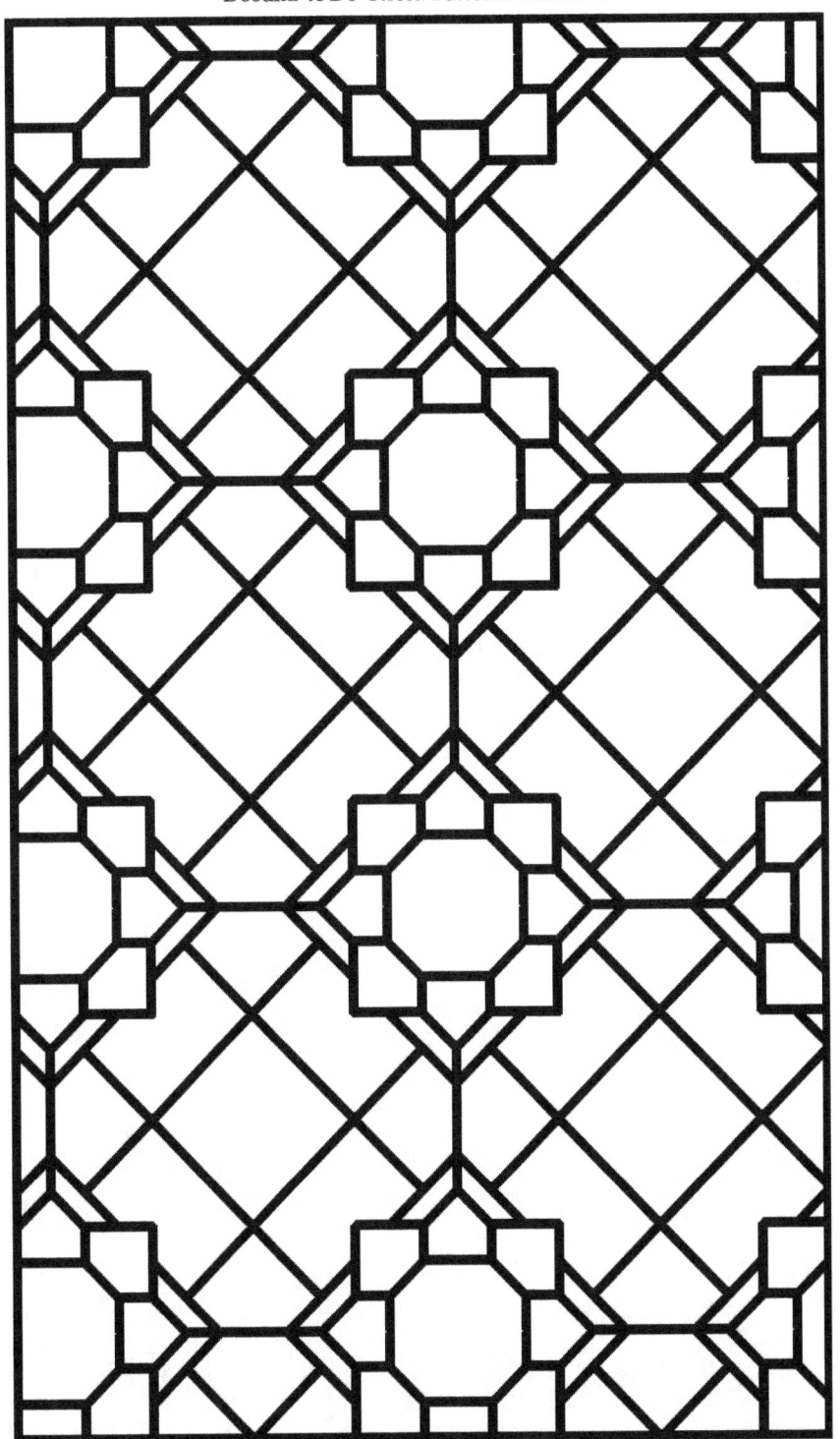

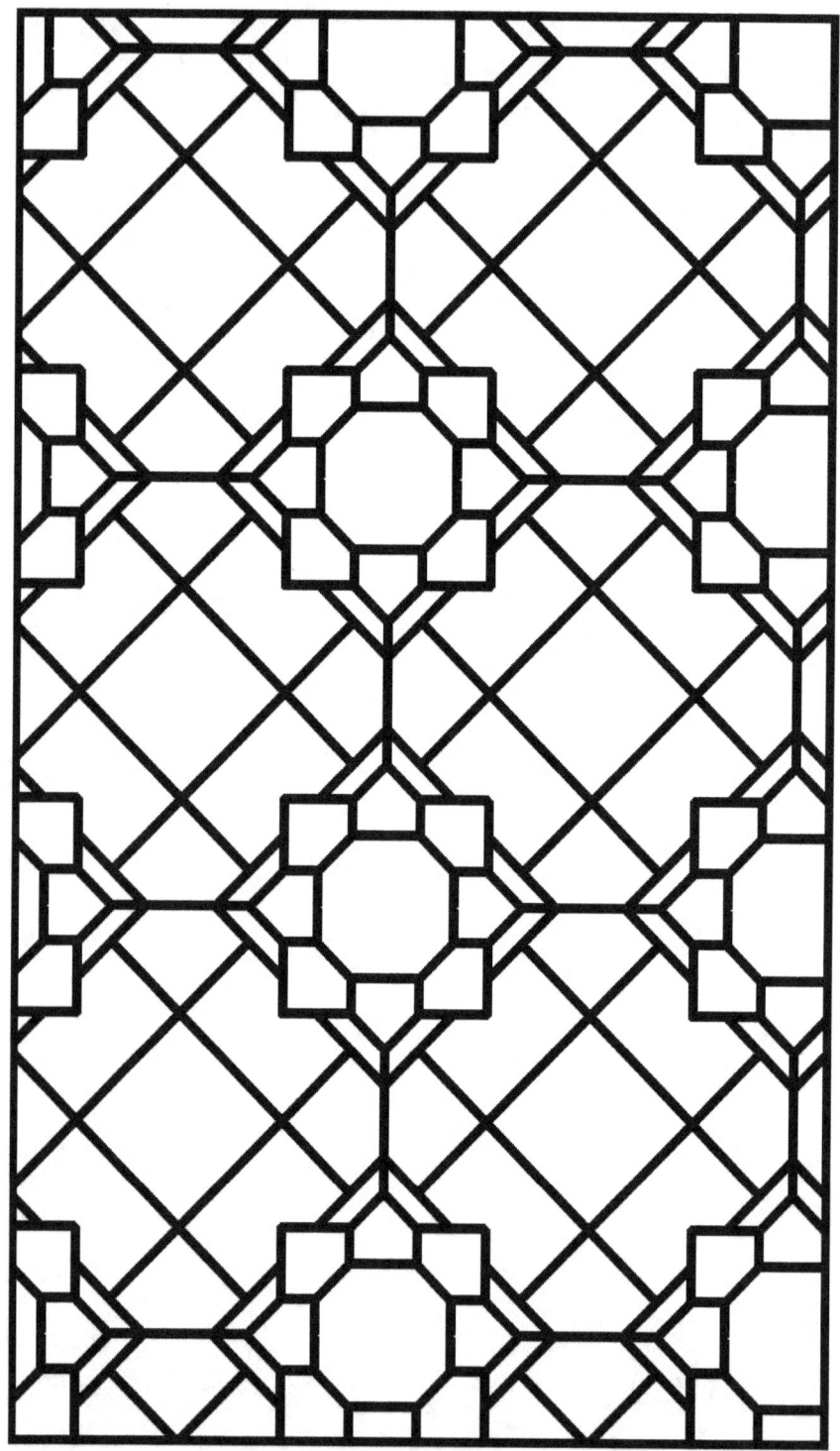

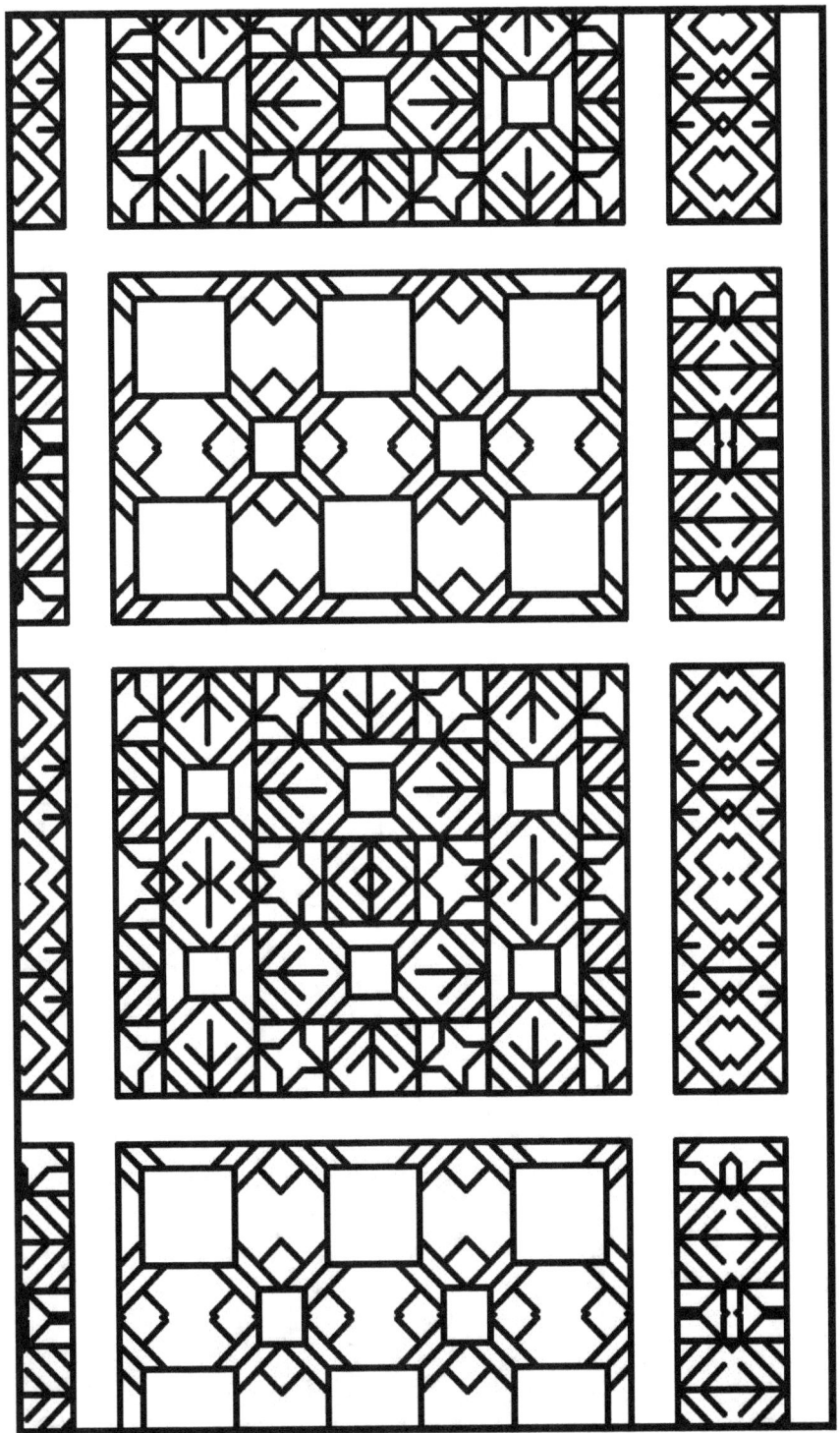

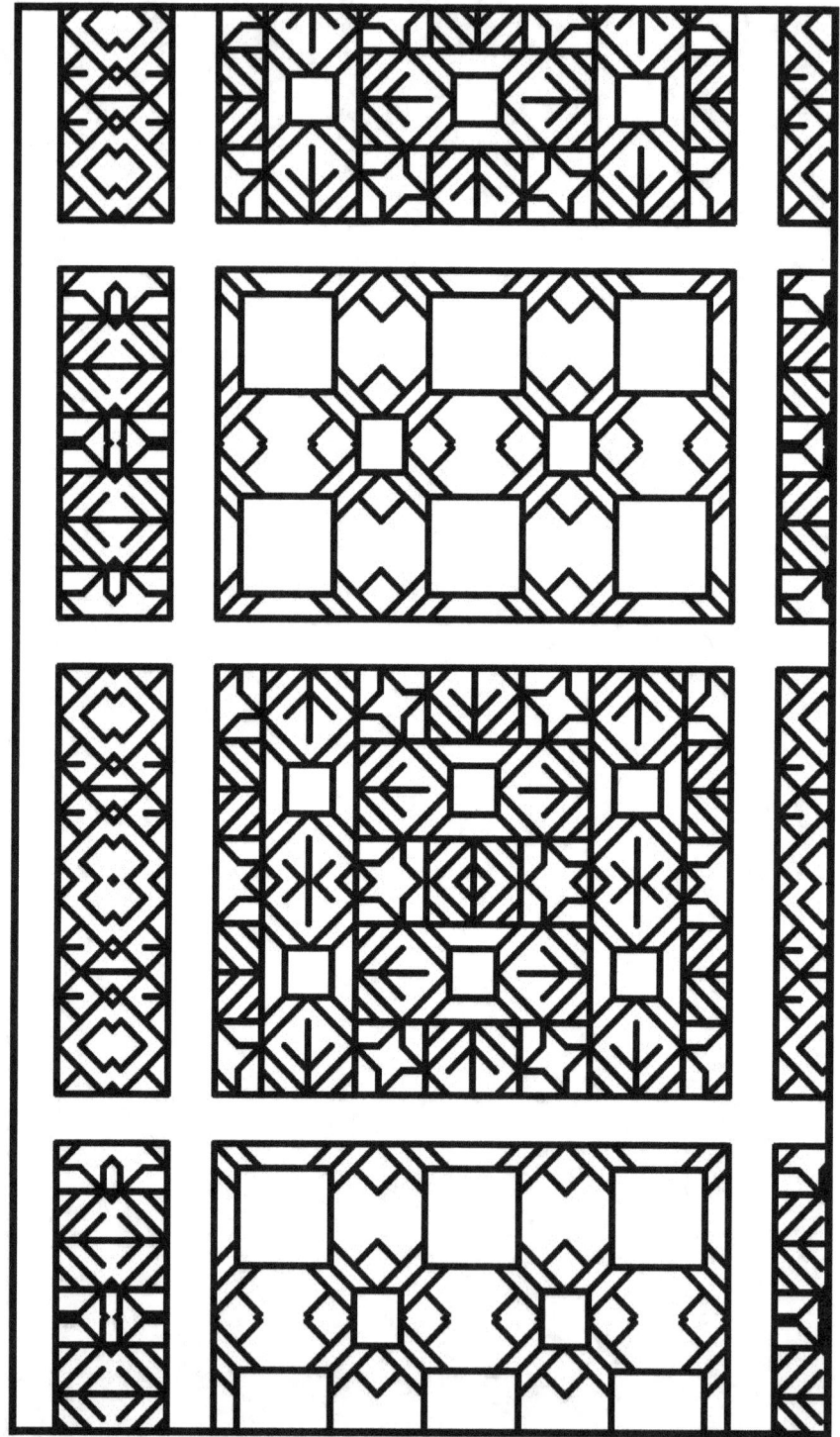

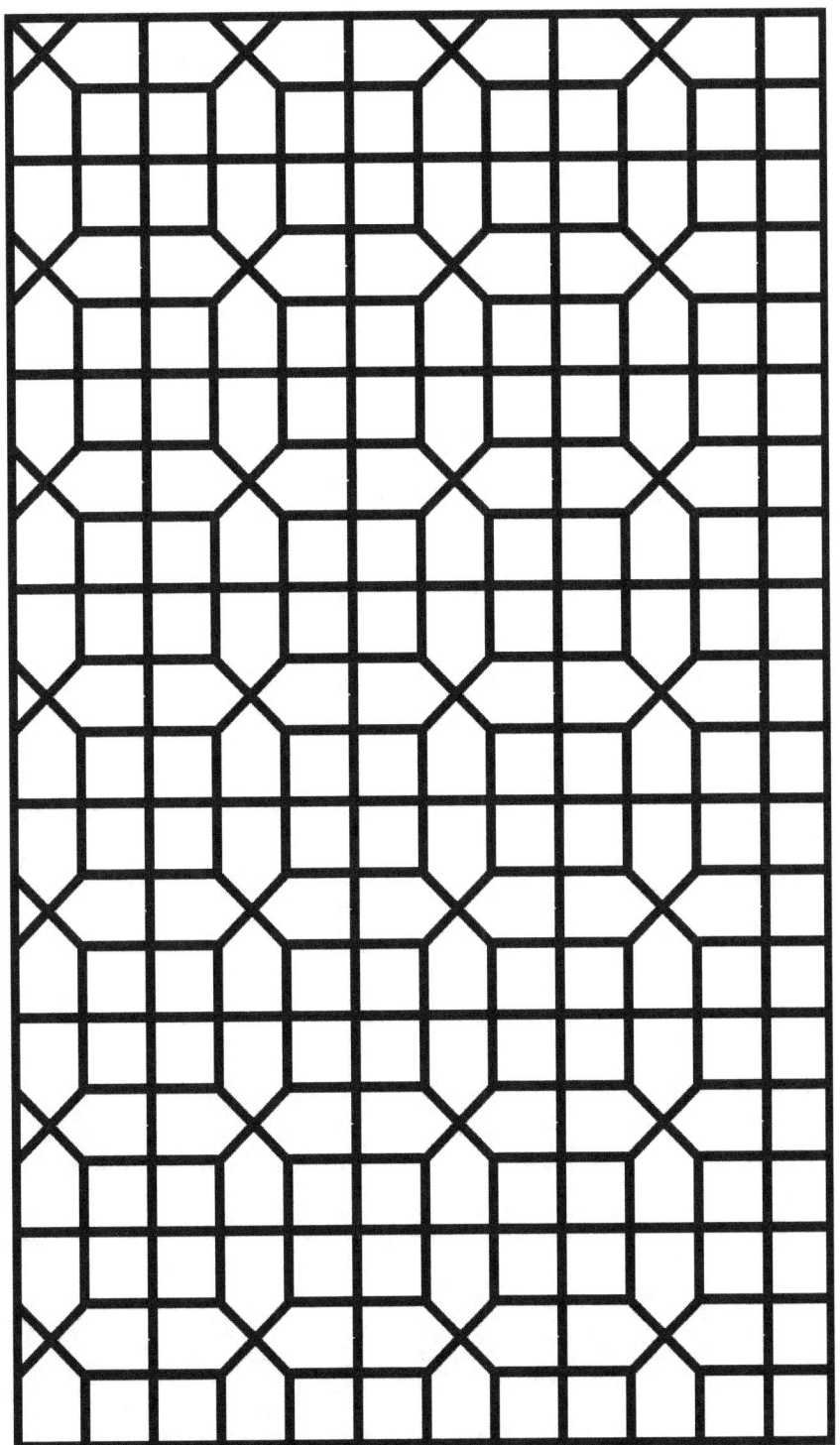

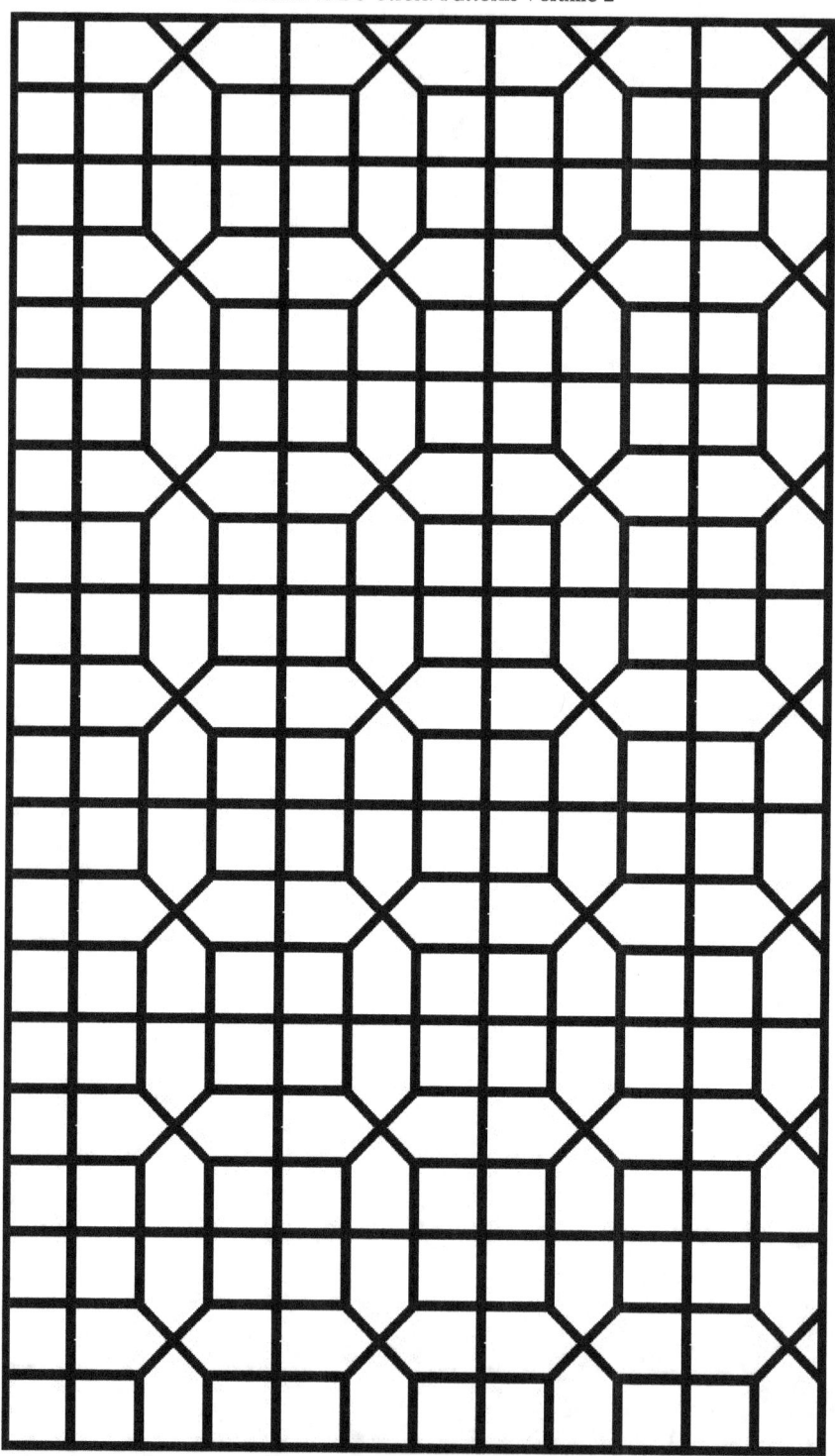

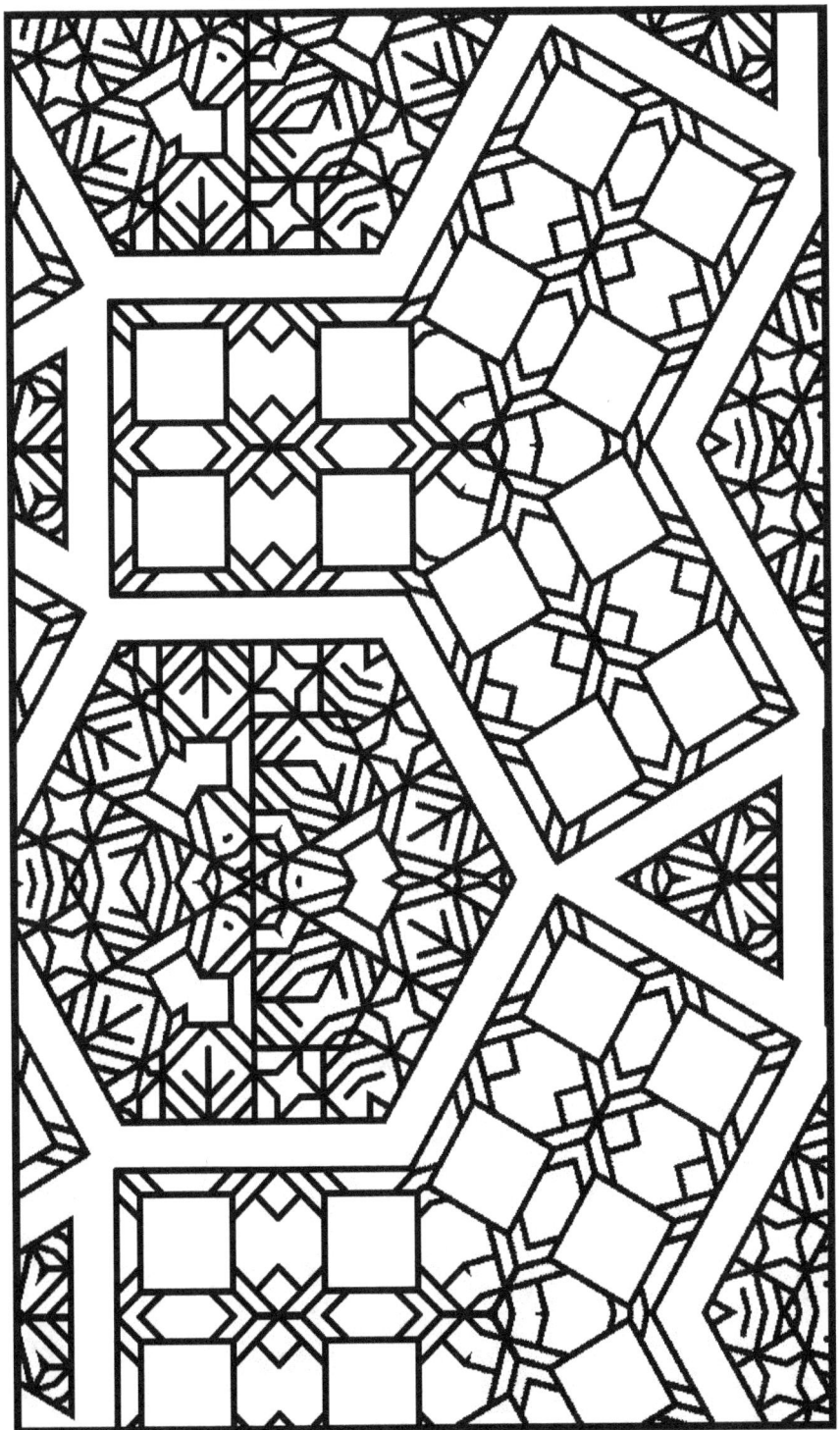

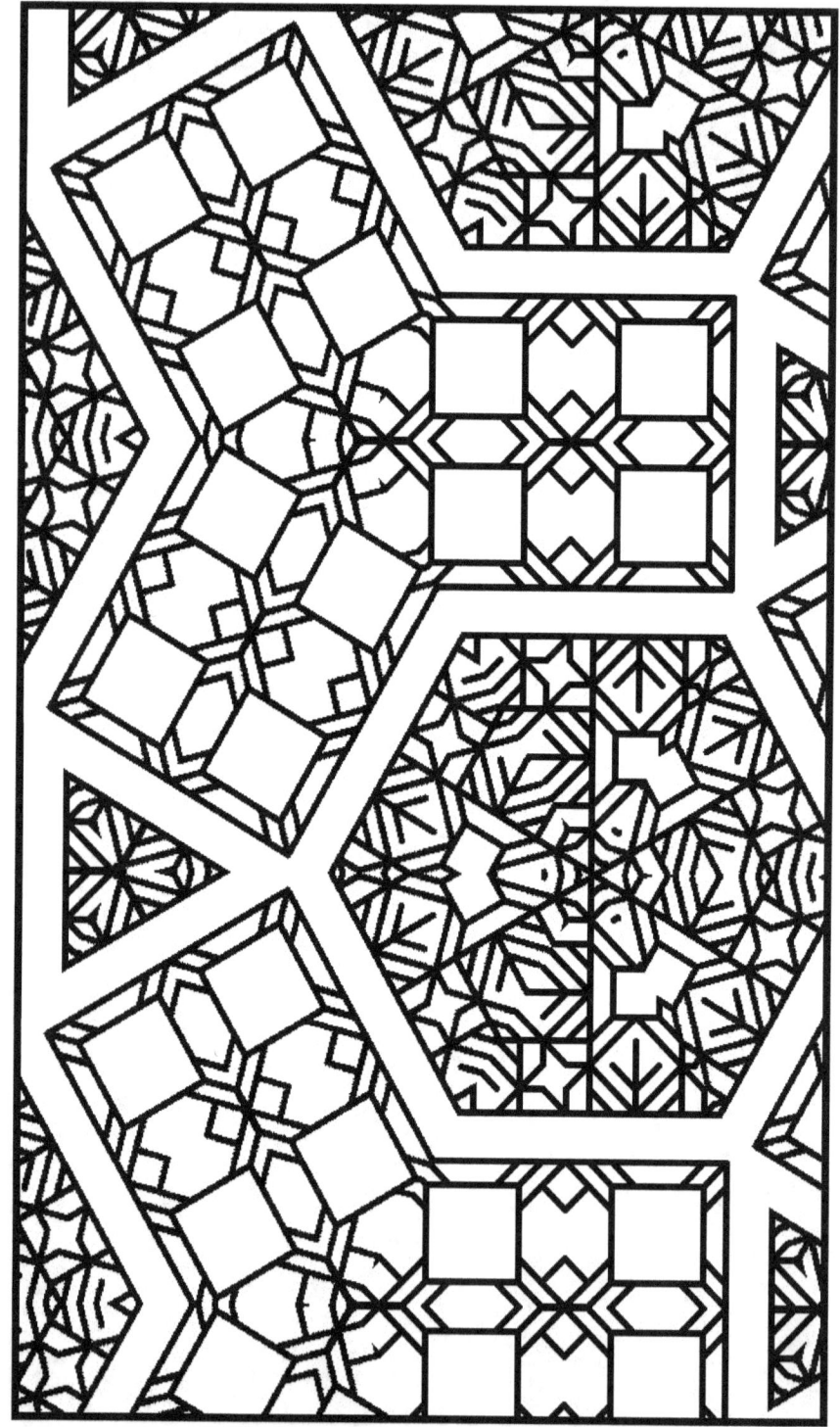

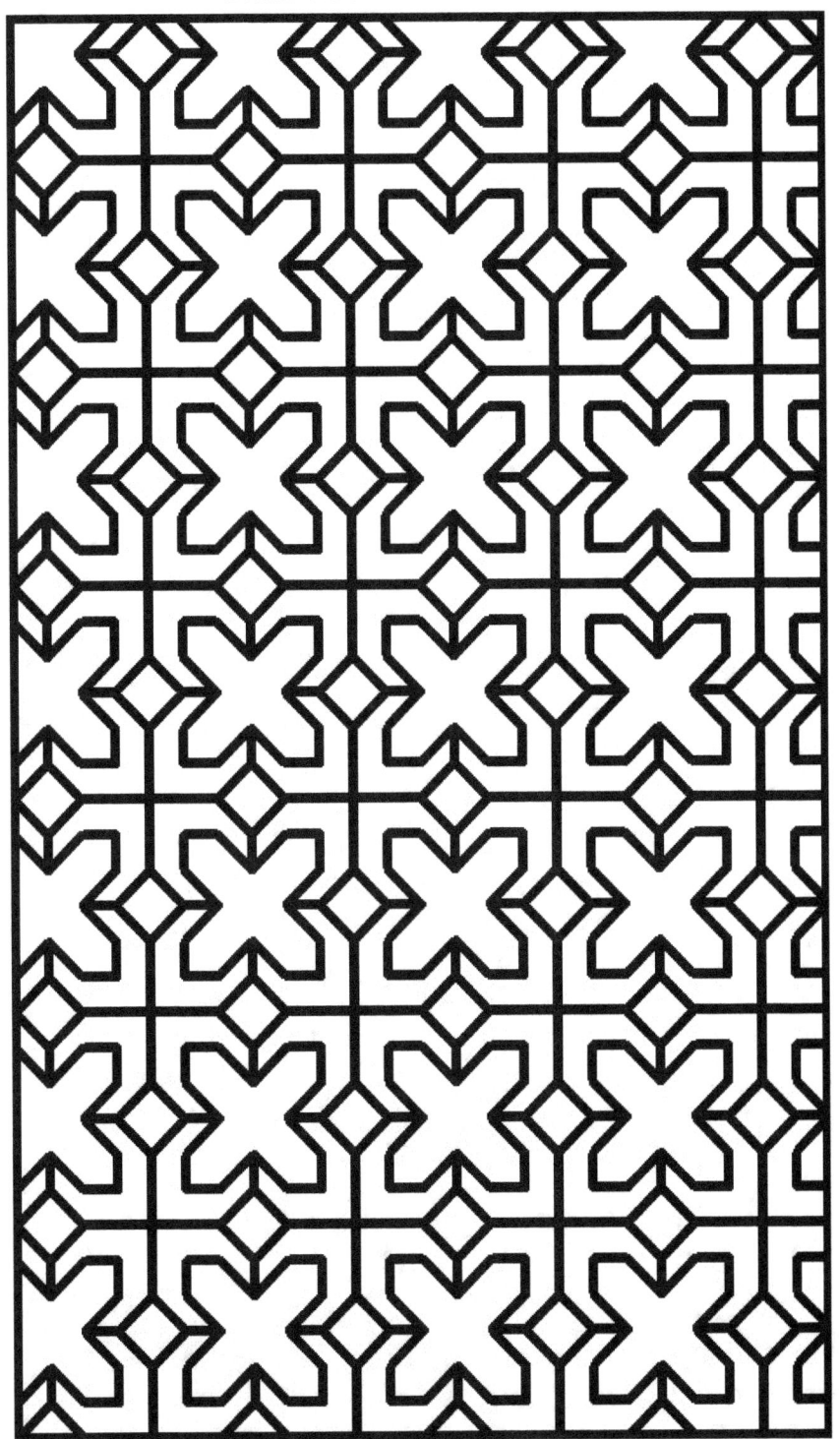

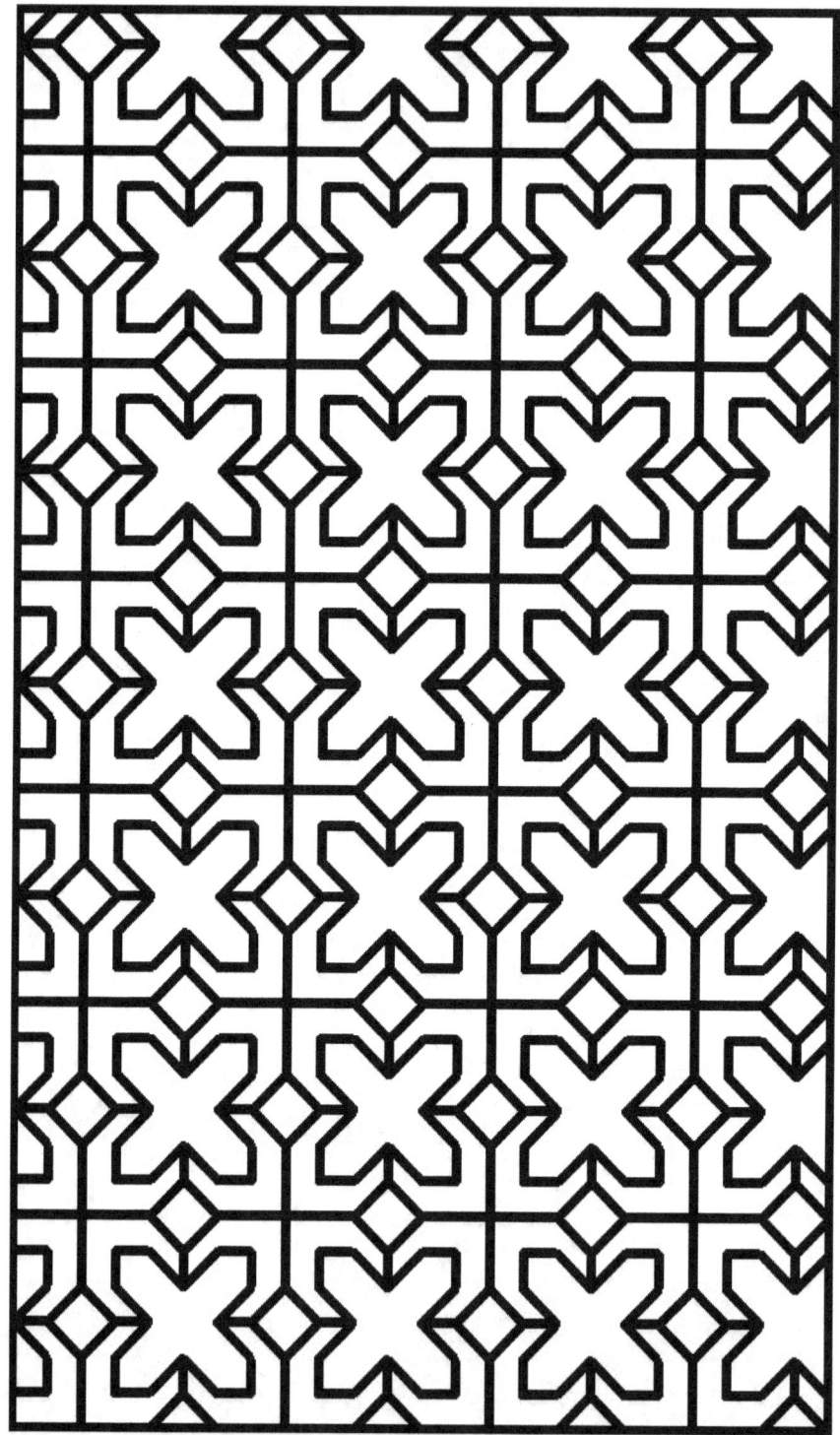

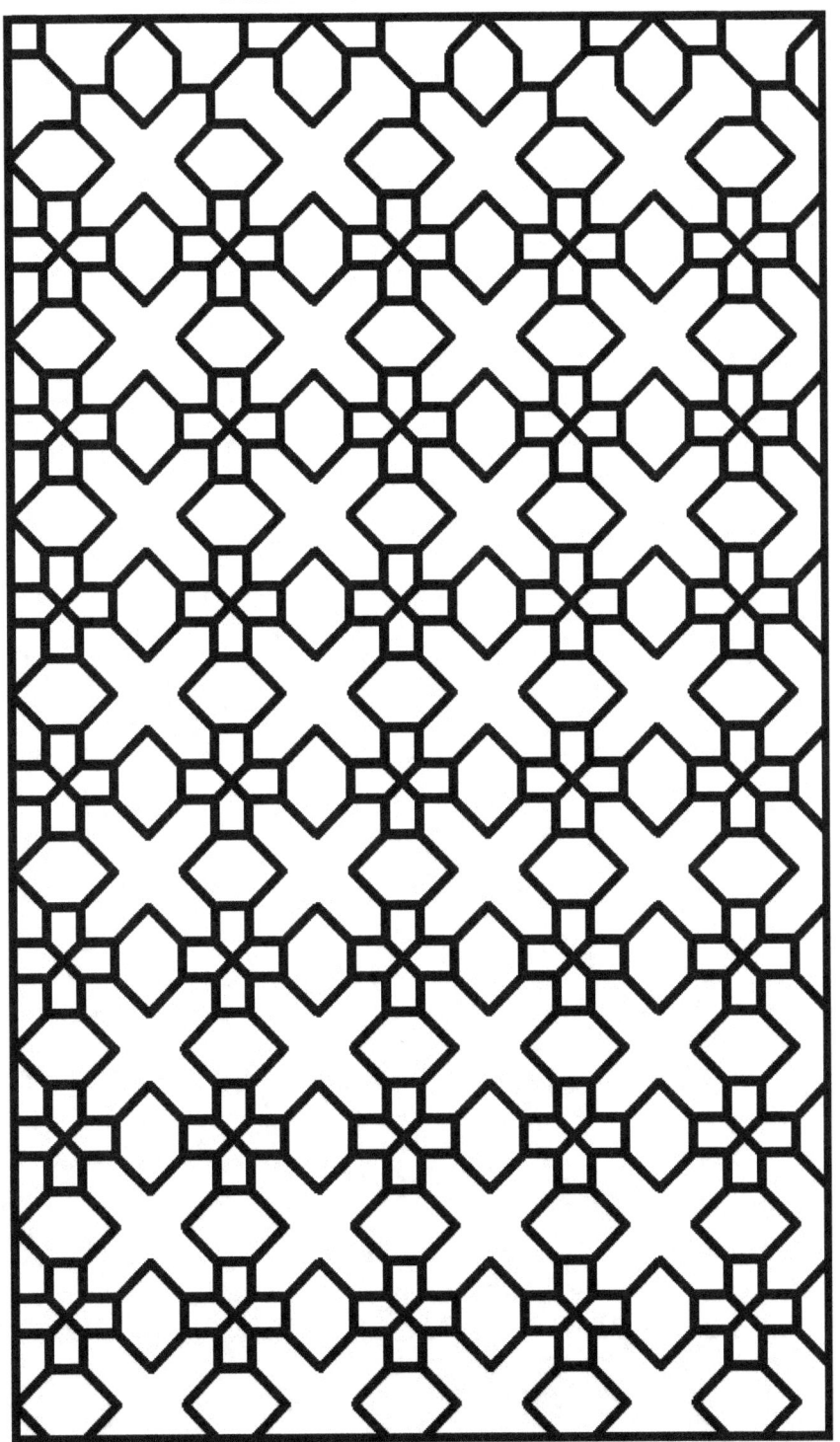

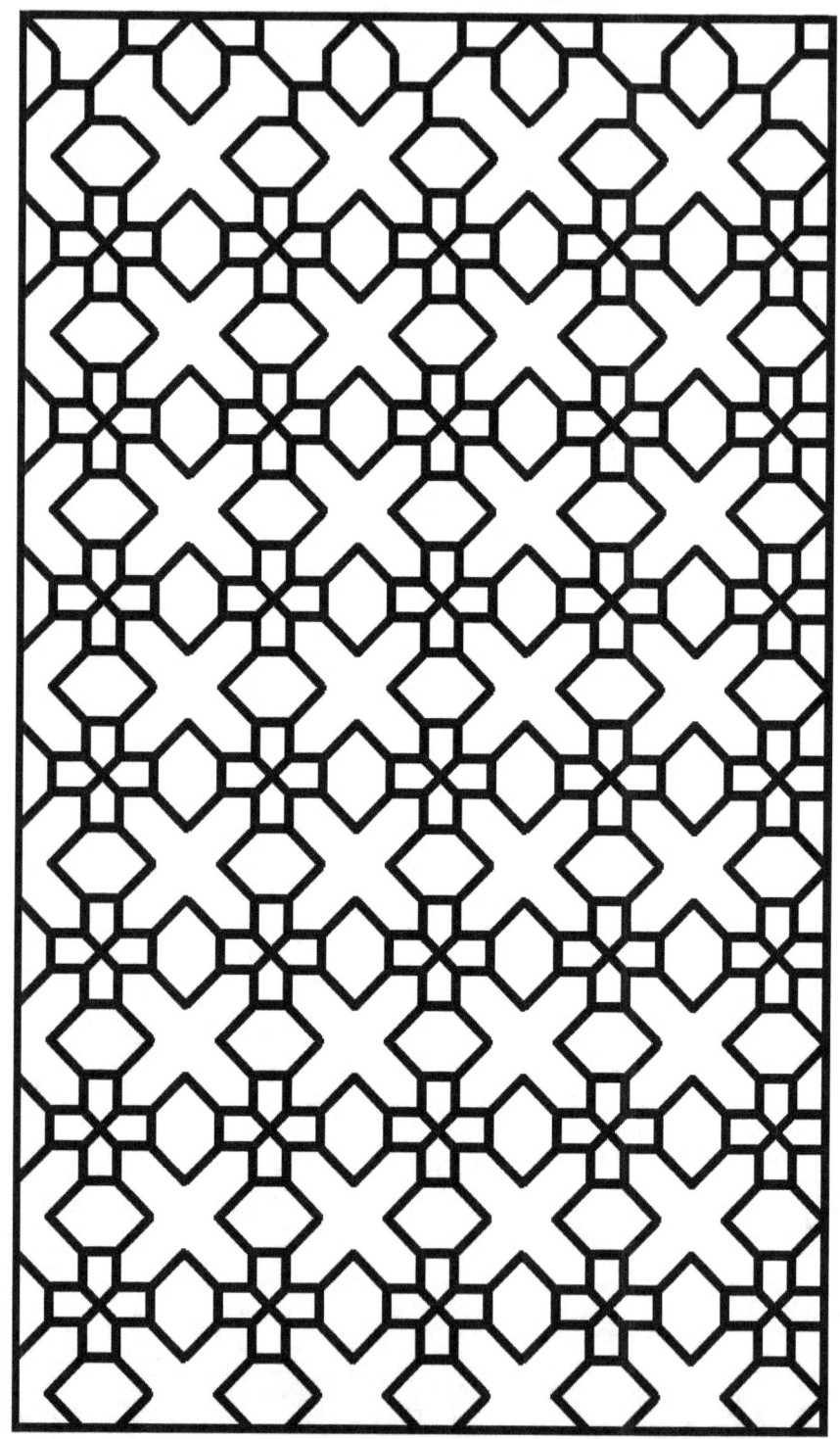

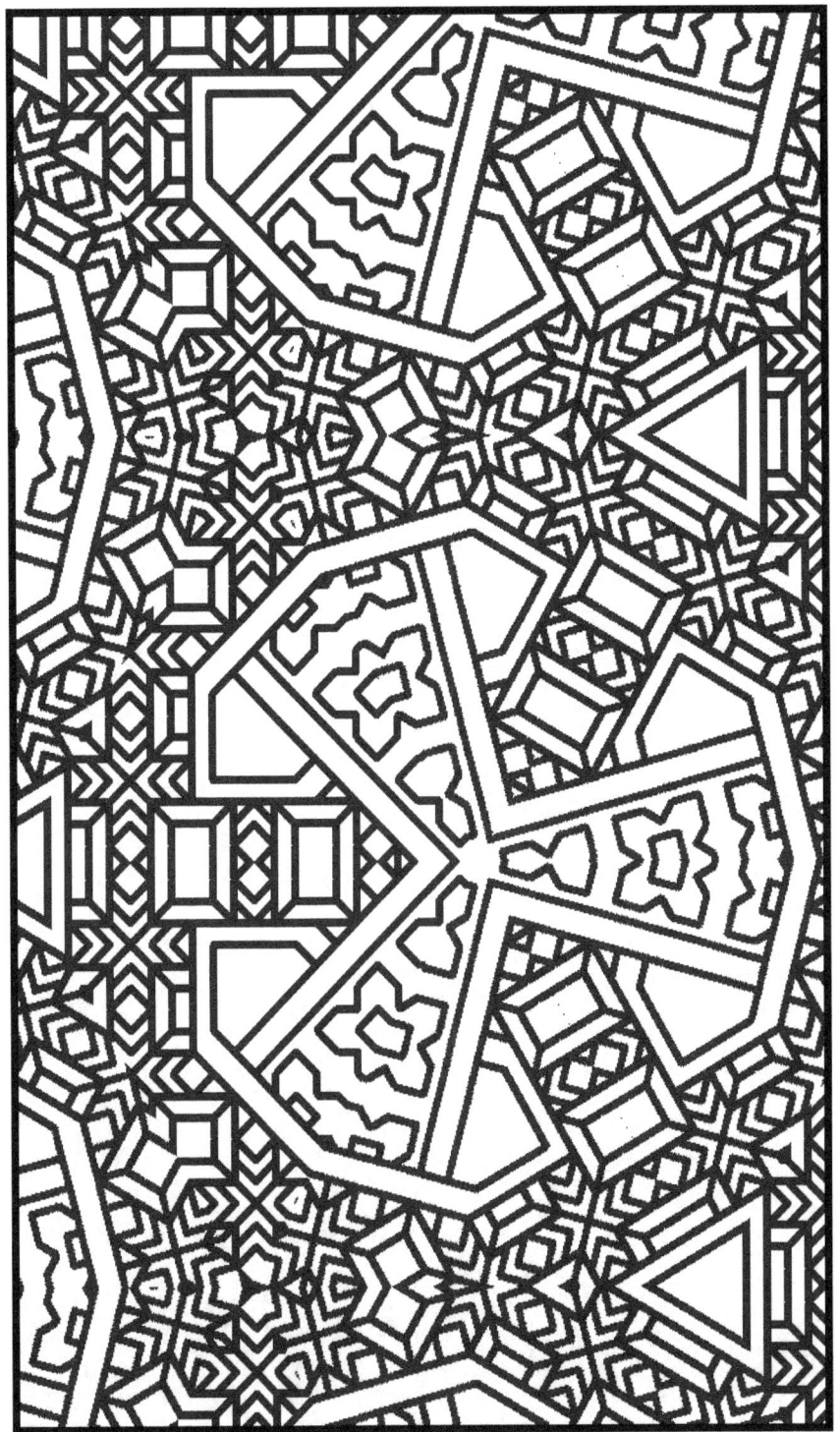

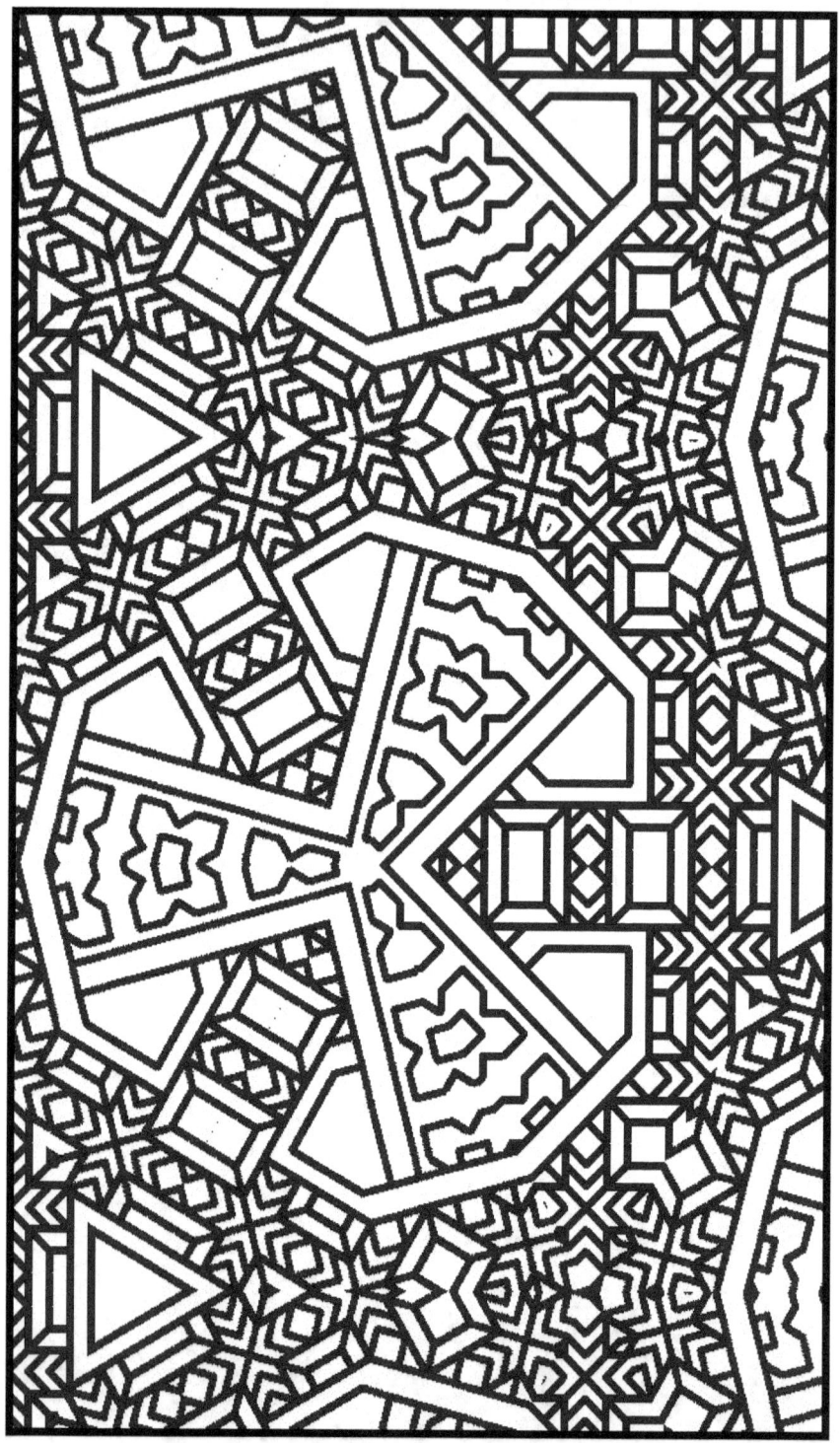

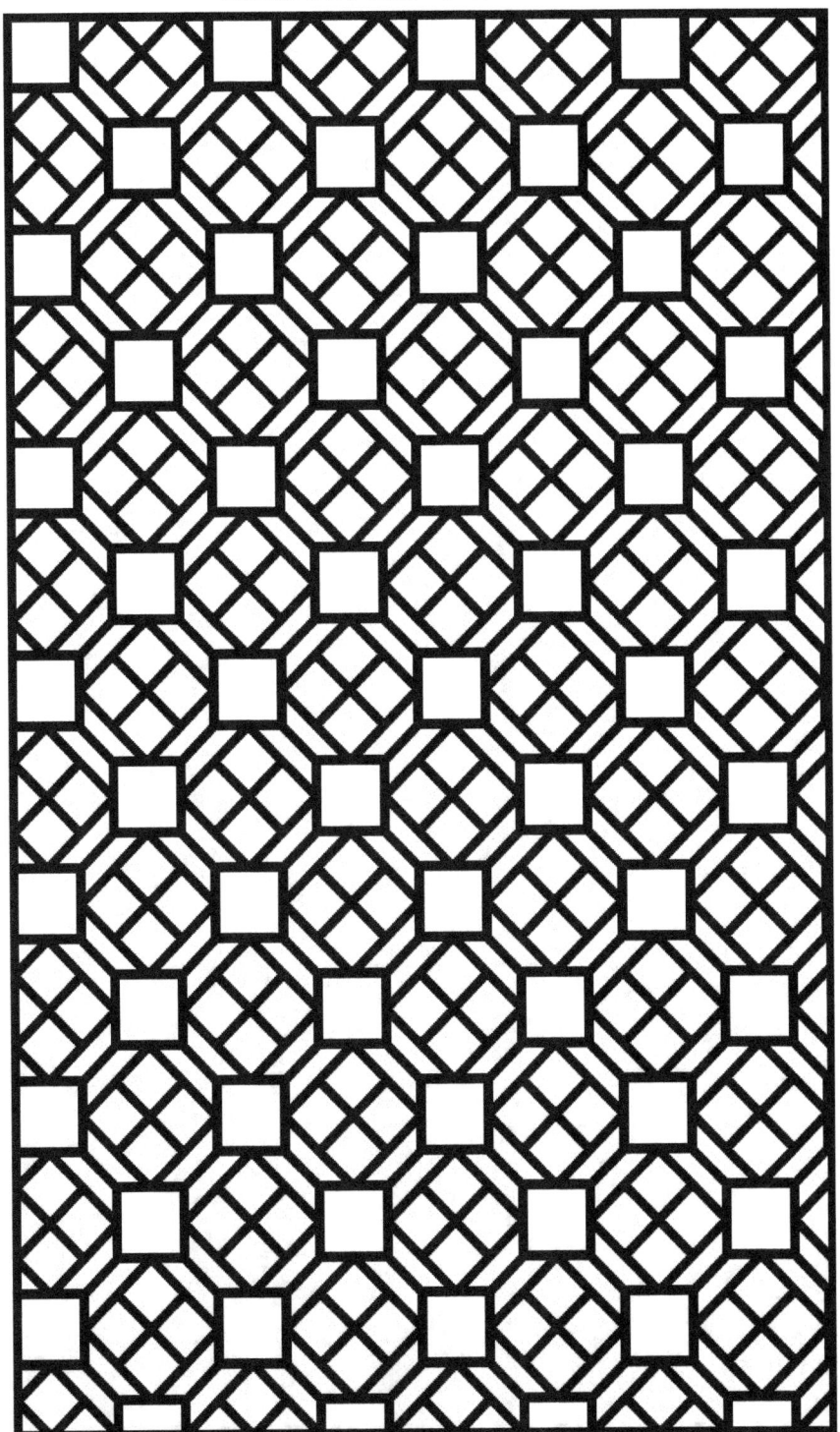

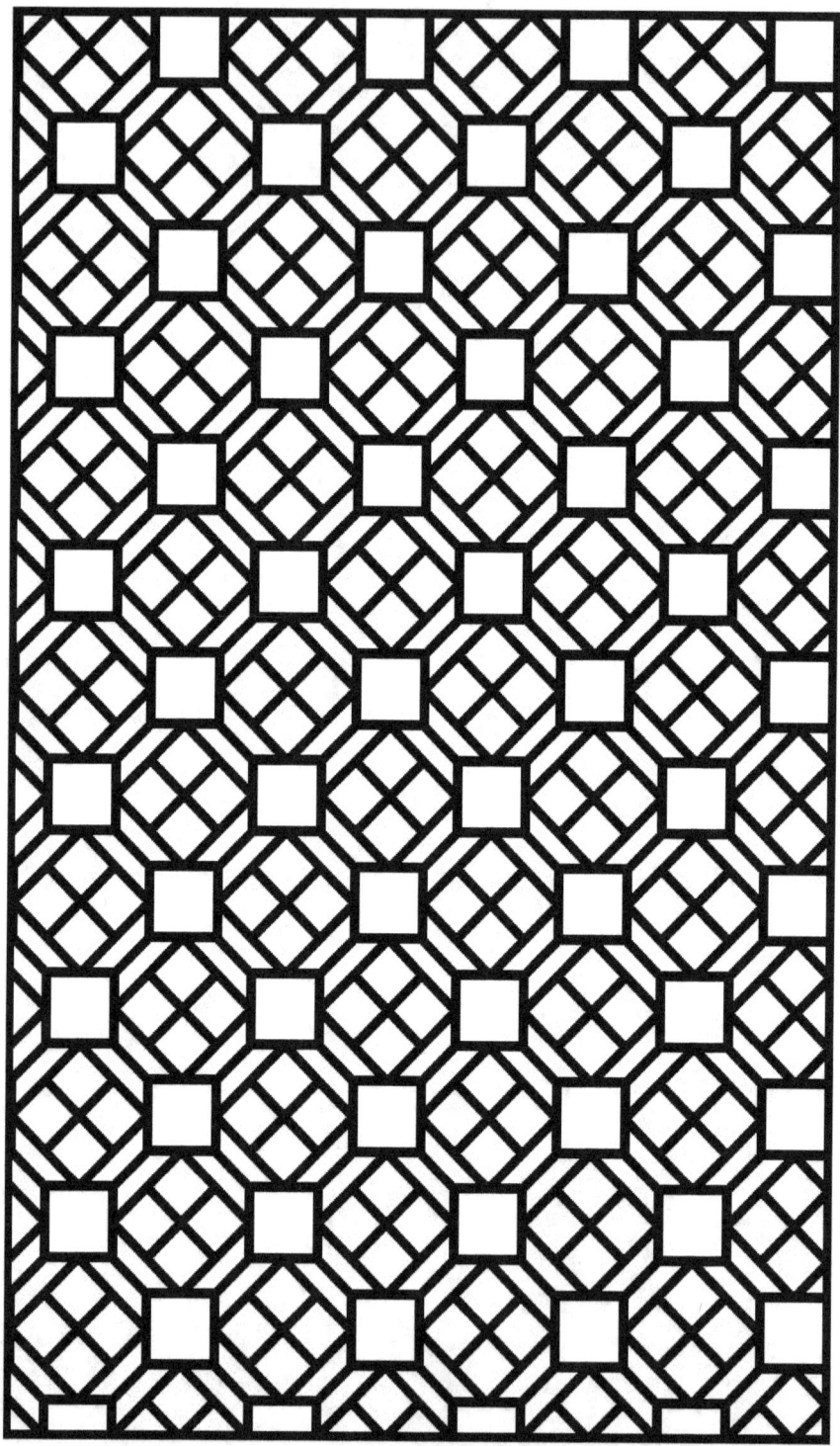

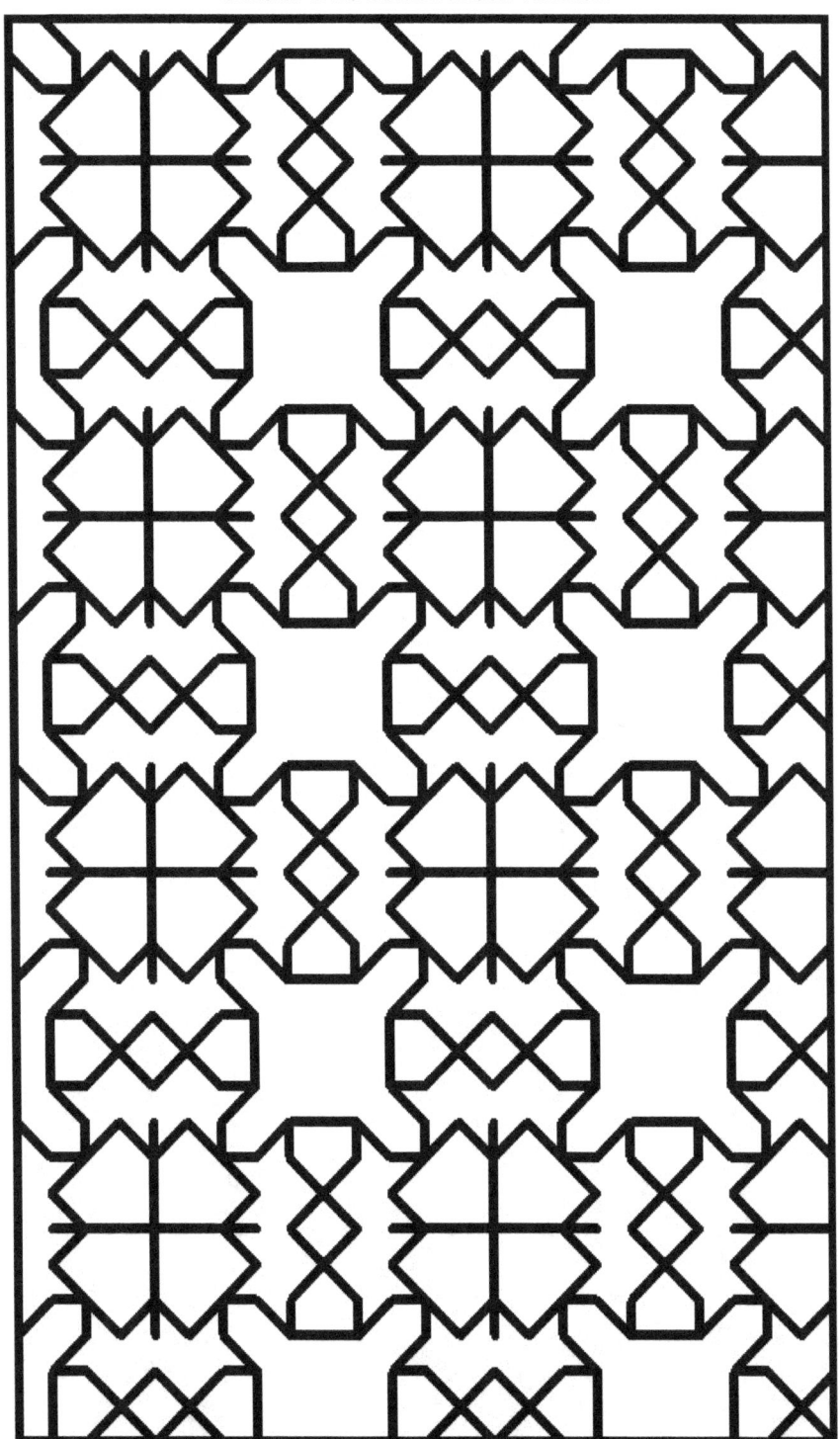

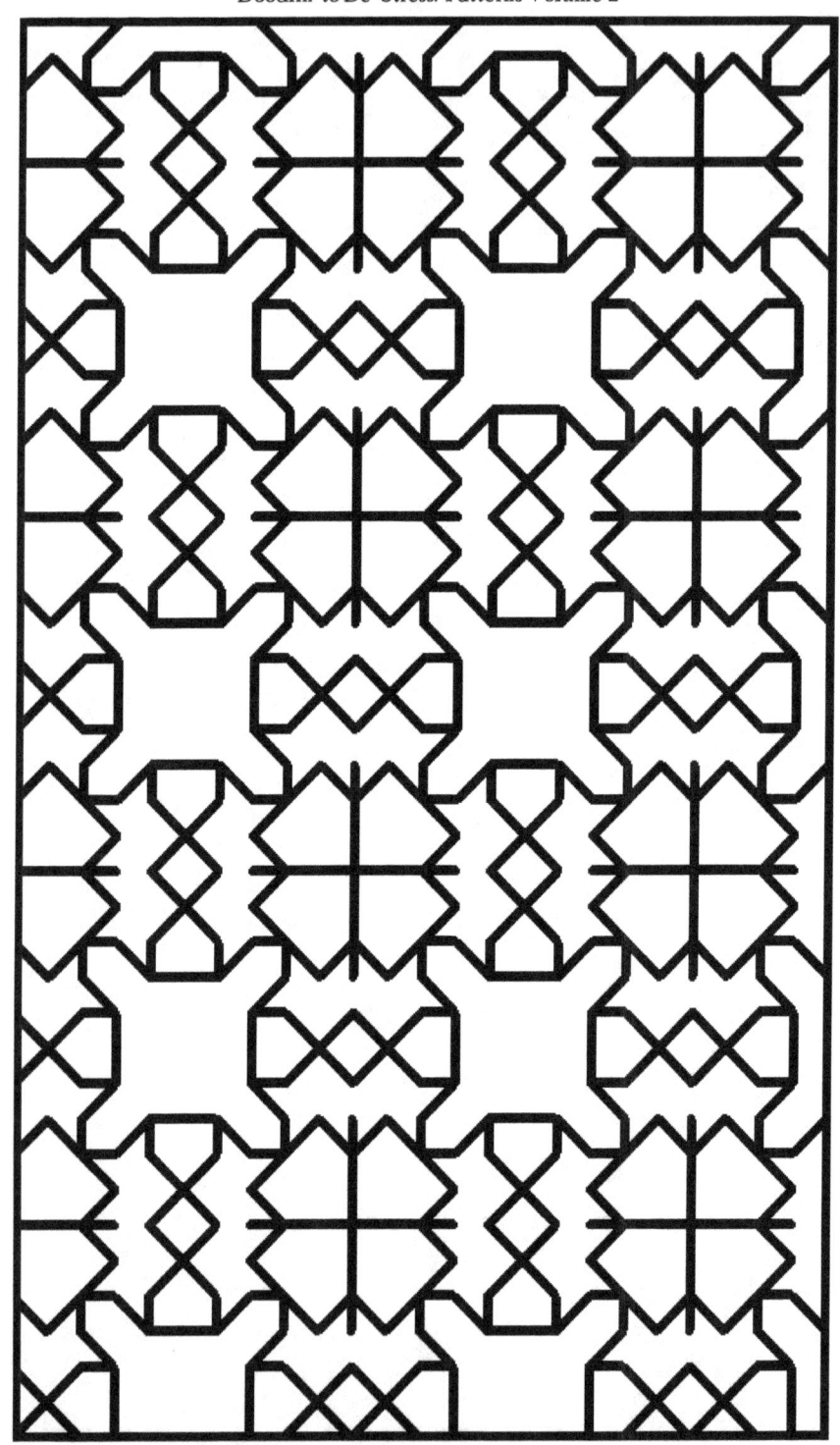